TRAVELS WITH ERNEST

Around the North of Ireland on a Vespa

by
RYAN KEITH

"I found in Ulster, from hill to glen,
Hardy warriors, resolute men;
Beauty that bloomed when youth was gone,
And strength transmitted from sire to son."

from 'Prince Alfrid's Itinerary'
transcribed by James Clarence Mangan

TRAVELS WITH ERNEST

Around the North of Ireland on a Vespa

by
RYAN KEITH

Cover design by Lindley Smith
Cover photograph by R.G.S.Woodburn

All rights reserved. No part of this publication may be reproduced, stored in a retrieval system, or transmitted, in any form, or by any means, electronic, mechanical, photocopying, recording or otherwise, without the prior permission in writing of the publishers.

© Ryan Keith 2011

The right of Ryan Keith to be identified as author of this work has been asserted by him in accordance with the Copyright, Designs & Patent Act 1988.

first published in 2011 by TwigBooks
Paperback ISBN **978 09560618 74**
EBook **978 1 907953 12 5**

this book is respectfully dedicated to the memory of
the designer of the Piaggio Vespa motor scooter,
Corradino D'Ascanio,
the fruit of whose talents and imagination
has brought so much pleasure to so many.

FOREWORD

My links with Ireland go back almost as far as I can remember. My mother's mother, my own grandmother, was the daughter of one Sarah Ann Cavanagh, from Cork, Ireland. Sarah joined the post-famine flood of Irish souls into exile in London, married a farm-worker from St. Albans, and together they ran a small market garden in Clerkenwell, not far from St. Paul's Cathedral.

I know she kept up her Irishness, because she passed it on to her daughter, my Gran. When my Gran married, she set up home just down the road in a block of working class flats built by the philanthropic Peabody Trust, in the heart of the busy street market of Whitecross Street. With shared washing and toilet facilities on each floor, these flats were luxurious by the standards of the time, and created a lasting sense of community.

My Gran was known locally as "the Irish lady" because every St. Patrick's Day she would change her ordinary pinafore for a brilliant green apron which she kept for the occasion. Then she would go and fetch her own Mum, and arm in arm they celebrated the Irish patron saint's day by walking around Peabody Buildings, singing Irish songs to anyone who would listen, and rounding off the day with a session in the Two Brewers, where they drank long glasses of Guinness, mulled with a red-hot poker. My Granddad kept out of her way on St. Patrick's Day, recognising that it was her special day.

In 1929 my Gran lost both her Mum and her husband, and she was left with six children to bring up as best she could. I knew her as an old lady with a twinkle in her eye and an enormous collection of Irish popular songs that she delighted in entertaining me with whenever I visited.

By the time I finally got to Ireland for the first time, my Gran was long gone. On arrival, I felt immediately comfortable and at home in my great-grandmother's homeland, and have been back again many times, whenever I can. Soon I discovered the West Coast, and this was even better. In a short time, I calculated I had visited every part of Ireland except the counties of Donegal and Sligo in the Republic, and

Northern Ireland, which I considered 'occupied territory'. I suppose that with only a romantic appreciation of the politics of Ireland, it was inevitable that my sympathies should be Republican.

As I grew up, I began to feel uncomfortable about my English nationality. A dream began to take shape after a friend told me he had successfully applied for Irish nationality on the basis of having an Irish grandparent. The relationship between Ireland and the United Kingdom is much closer than either country cares to make public.

There were no immigration controls between the two countries long before the European Community came along. Irish workers who were driven into exile in Britain by economic necessity were surprised to discover they were allowed to vote in British elections. Irish laws closely shadowed British laws, and tax provisions in the annual Westminster Budget were generally echoed across the Irish Sea, with only a few notable exceptions. Eventually, I put my dream to the test, and wrote to the Nationality Department of the Irish Embassy to apply to join their club, and become Irish.

There followed a correspondence with a lady called Maureen, who at first turned me down flat and enclosed a printed form explaining what were the only acceptable grounds for a successful application.

My Irish blood was roused by this curt, unfriendly reply, and I wrote back explaining that my Grandmother was known in Peabody Buildings as "the Irish lady". Her brother, my great-uncle Walter, felt sufficiently Irish to join the London Irish Regiment in the First World War, and was killed in 1918. When the Irish State came into being in 1922, my Gran was over 40 and the struggling mother of six children. She wasn't about to dash up to the new Nationality Department to proclaim her Irishness, as she had every right to do. My own Mum didn't realise she was in danger of losing her right to Irish nationality by not toddling up to the Irish Embassy to register during the school holidays. And then they both just forgot.

According to Maureen, my Mum could still apply because her Gran was born in Ireland, and then of course if my Mum were Irish, I too would have the right to lay my claim. Maureen doesn't know my Mum.

It would be very difficult to explain to her that the only way I could get the Nationality Department to agree to take me on would be for my Mum to become Irish first. She would do it though, if I asked. It's the Irish in her. But I am too bloody-minded to put her through it. It must be the Irish in me. And while I was dithering, with just a drop of shilly-shallying, the Irish government upped and changed the law, and this right disappeared also.

In the 19th Century, James Clarence Mangan was a pioneer in rediscovering and re-evaluating ancient Celtic culture, and he translated many works into the English language. His phrase describing Ulstermen as "Hardy warriors, resolute men" rings true today, but in the more extreme elements I have detected an air of desperation as they realise time is running out.

In a very short time, emigration and rising birth rates will bring about a shift in the balance of the population. Catholics will become the majority in the North, and in a democratic society both sides have to be ready to accept the changes that a numerical advantage brings. The Republic of Ireland and Northern Ireland both have to be prepared to make important constitutional changes to make a relatively peaceful accord possible.

At the time when I rode around the northern provinces of Ireland, I discovered there a community which is a member of the European Union, the EU, what used to be called the Common Market; these were the citizens of an Eire which was booming, – the Celtic Tiger – where investment by multinational computer companies was rapidly catching up with and overtaking traditional agriculture (which was also doing rather nicely). Young Irish school-leavers were proving themselves to be excellent workers in the prevailing hi-tech environment, and the government's tax schemes were attractive to investors.

Northern Ireland too has benefited from grants and investment from Westminster, and from Brussels. The traditional pattern of long queues of weekend traffic taking shoppers from the South across the border to the North was reversed, and the traffic now flowed in the other direction. One result of the strong, over-valued UK pound against the EEC-linked Irish pund, was initially to make all shopping cheaper in the South, but with the weakening pound and the euro, the traffic has once again changed direction.

But the changes are more than just the anomalies of artificially drawn frontiers. Membership of the EU has blurred the edges, and prosperity and the ongoing, systematic dismantling of discrimination has obliterated the sympathy of the man in the street for what may be called terrorists, or on the other hand – freedom-fighters. The men and women of violence are now recognised as a tiny, tiny group, and their supporters are thin on the ground. They have often become identified with protection rackets, gangsterism and drug-dealing.

When the IRA killed an American tourist with the Harrods's bomb, they started a process of isolation from their most important source of funding and support. American politicians have seized the opportunity to take part in the process of bringing peace to Ireland, and we should all be very grateful to them. Almost without exception, I met people in Northern Ireland who were as committed to peace as their southern neighbours have been for many years. The 1998 Good Friday Agreement would not have been possible unless this were true.

A final paradox: in the historic first meeting between the two representatives of Sinn Féin and the Unionists, although their spellings were different, their names were the same: Maguiness of Sinn Féin met with Maginnis of the Unionists.

"TRAVELS WITH ERNEST"

CHAPTER 1
PLANS

The writer contemplates the serious nature of the venture which he is about to undertake, and compares notes with Ernest.

Travel broadens the mind, and riding broadens the backside, just as Guinness broadens the belly, and conversation should broaden the way we look at the world. It seemed quite logical, therefore, for me to ride a Vespa motor scooter around the northern part of Ireland to visit a few pubs, and get some answers to important questions. But it didn't start that way.

I have seen most parts of Southern Ireland, the Republic, Eire, the 26 Counties, but the two most remote counties had escaped me. Donegal and Sligo are the most northerly part of the island of Ireland, and together with the 6 Counties of Northern Ireland, form the ancient Province of Ulster.

At one time, I was contemplating visiting the Battlefields of the Peninsular War in Spain and Portugal, and I thought it might be original to do it in the same way as had the Duke of Wellington, on horseback. Not being a lover of horses myself, in my mind I have changed Wellington's mount "Copenhagen" for my own trusty motor scooter, "Ernest", a Piaggio Vespa T5 Classic.

I named him Ernest after a line by a character in Oscar Wilde's *The Importance of Being Ernest*. Cecily explains her obsession with the name by saying of Ernest: *"There is something in that name that seems to inspire absolute confidence"*. It is a name for heroes! And a fitting name for my companion on such a journey as I now contemplated.

A view of the landscape is very unsatisfactory from inside a car. A car travels too fast, and visibility is very limited. It is difficult to stop wherever the fancy takes you, without the risk of causing a traffic jam or an accident. A car must almost invariably keep to the asphalted highways. A horse – or a scooter, I reasoned – is less restricted.

A few years back, I was taking a short cut in a hired car across country in County Clare by a series of twisting lanes, or boreens as they are called over there. Unsure of the way, I saw a local standing outside his house as I drove by. I reversed to ask directions, and since he didn't make a move towards the car, I drove onto the grass verge to draw within speaking distance. I leaned out the window and asked if I was on the right road for Killaloe. He looked oddly at me, and it occurred to me he might not "have the English", but eventually he spoke. "Go straight on down, and you'll see it come up in front of you. But keep to the tarred road." The last bit sounded a bit strange. I looked down at the grass where I had stopped. Behind the man was a lawn mower. I suddenly realised that I had driven off the road onto his lawn. He was politely asking me to get off his grass, and out of his garden. I drove off carefully, trying not to leave any tyre marks on his lawn.

My personal view of the politics of the Irish situation was conventional, un-informed and prejudiced. With a blinkered black-or-white simplicity, it seemed clear to me that the division of Ireland into British North and Republican South was an aberration, brought about by the intransigence of the British politicians negotiating the Treaty of 1922, and the self-sacrifice of some of the heroes of the

Irish Revolution in accepting half a loaf rather then no bread.

As far as I was concerned, the North was occupied territory, and I refused to set foot in it, in the same way as I still refuse to visit Gibraltar. This narrow view was supported by the fact that in the past the Protestants had treated the Catholics in the North as second-class citizens, and constructed a society which kept them repressed, and under-privileged. It seems hard to believe that until very recent times, in this part of the United Kingdom, most Catholics had no vote. Even when they won the vote, gerrymandering ensured that the number of representatives they were allowed to elect was in a smaller proportion to their numbers than in Protestant areas. They were kept out of certain employments by the most tightly closed of closed shops.

When the almost entirely Protestant Royal Ulster Constabulary allowed Protestant gangs of thugs to beat up, murder and put to the torch peace-loving Catholics, it seemed almost reasonable to me that the dormant Irish Republican Army should be revived as the Provisional IRA to defend Catholic citizens from the worst attacks. This was as recent as the late 1960's. And we're not talking ancient history here - the Beatles were already contemplating breaking up, mini-skirts were turning into hot-pants, and American B-52 high-altitude bombers were dropping high-explosives on North Vietnam.

I knew that a solution couldn't be simple, but as an outsider, I couldn't know just how complicated things really are. Whatever form it takes, I remain convinced that a solution is only a matter of time. Eventually, Ireland will be united again, in some way. In 100 years, or 50 or 10 the inevitability of re-unification will become a reality. Sadly, it will not have been a bloodless revolution.

Helped by the thought of the Peace Process which brought a cease-fire to Northern Ireland in the mid-1990s, I decided to face up to and explore my own prejudices and those of others, by riding my scooter through Northern Ireland on my way to realise my ambition of visiting Donegal and Sligo. The IRA ceasefire had been dramatically broken when the IRA set off a car bomb in London's Docklands in February 1996, claiming a lack of conviction in the British Government's approach to the Peace Process.

At the time, the Conservative Government relied on the support of the Unionists to maintain their majority in Westminster, and was soft-pedalling on the issue to avoid offending the Loyalists. Although there was a return to violence after the Docklands bomb, this was less marked in Northern Ireland, and focus shifted to a campaign of disruption on the British mainland.

There was another reason for going to Northern Ireland. I have an enduring interest in the Spanish Armada. It is one of the most romantic legends in British history. The story is of a great enterprise which foundered in the stormy seas surrounding this sceptred isle, after resounding defeat in a naval battle. One of England's greatest heroes, Sir Francis Drake, apparently vanquished the superior forces of an alien imperial enemy, after completing his game of bowls, of course. This schoolboy version couldn't possibly be true – or could it? History is written by the victors. Perhaps religious and xenophobic prejudices had twisted this story too?

I have another more personal interest in the true story of the Spanish Armada. My wife is Spanish, and our two daughters were brought up in England, bi-lingual, and with the benefit of the cultures of the lands of both their parents, enjoying frequent visits to their large Spanish family in Madrid.

One day, my eldest daughter's class was given the lesson of the Spanish Armada. She learned that the wicked Spanish Catholic King had set sail to invade peace-loving little England, contentedly ruled by their nice, new Protestant Good Queen Bess, and that the wicked Spanish King deservedly came a cropper, his fleet dashed on the rocks by the stormy forces of Mother Nature. Thousands of the soldiers and sailors of the evil invader met their come-uppance and drowned in the waters which protect our shores. My daughter was told that her beloved cousins in Spain were the descendants of rogues, and that thousands of those rogues had died miserably at the hand of the Protestant God. But this popular English version of events is not how it happened.

There are many interesting books on the subject. I discovered several histories, and a collection of correspondence of the time. I even discovered a contemporary personal account written by one of the Spanish survivors, Captain Francisco Cuellar. There I learned of survivors being sheltered and integrated into remote communities in Scotland and Ireland, where they were unfortunate enough to be shipwrecked. A different picture began to emerge.

It seems that Philip II of Spain was also King Consort of England. He was even proclaimed King of England in Winchester Cathedral. He was married to Elizabeth's half sister Mary Tudor, who was Queen Mary of England, daughter of Henry VIII, the man who invented the Protestant Church of England, allegedly because the Pope wouldn't give him a divorce from Mary's mother, the Spanish Catherine of Aragon. Mary was a bad lot, but being a good Catholic, she did what all good Catholics at the time did, and set about executing the heretic Protestants in her realm. This didn't go down too well with those in charge (who had only recently got used to the idea of being non-Catholics), and on Mary's death in 1558, she was replaced by her half-sister, Elizabeth.

Being a foreigner, Philip wasn't given another moment's thought, and anyway, he was kept quite busy ruling the Spanish Empire, the Americas, the rebellious Protestant Netherlands and any other parts of the world's surface which came his way. But on the whole he was not too pleased about the way things were going in England, so when the Pope asked him if he had any plans for asserting his rights, bloodying the English nose, and clearing up this tiresome Protestant business at the same time, Philip promised to give it some thought.

He was told he could count on the financial and spiritual support of Rome in what was in their eyes a Holy War, to re-establish the will of God in the British Isles. Typical of the time, politics and religion were inextricably linked, and Philip's career was marked by ruthless and vigorous activity in both fields. The Armada was seen in European quarters as a Crusade by the Old Religion against the Protestant heretics. It was of course much more than that.

Historically, invasion seemed a good idea. The Romans had done all right. The Vikings had languished for a long time in sizeable chunks of the East Coast and Ireland, happily collecting their Dane-geld. The Normans were still in place, so with God, the Pope, and Right on their side, why shouldn't King Philip and the might and wealth of the Spanish Empire succeed?

The operation was immense. Philip called on his advisers to come up with proposals. Among them was an outrageous idea of marshalling the largest fleet of ships ever assembled, by cobbling together all sorts of unsuitable foreign merchant ships and hulks to transport armies of men across the English Channel from the European mainland. The architect of this plan, the Marquis of Santa Cruz, rather inconveniently died suddenly before he could put the plan into action, and Philip singled out the talented but reluctant Duke of Medina Sidonia for the job of expedition leader. He did very well to make real what had been little more than an over-ambitious pipe dream.

The weather was bad from the start. The fleet of an ill-assorted jumble of galleons and galleasses (powered by sails and oars) included converted bulk carriers and scooters (not Vespas, but small craft for dodging around between the bigger ships to deliver despatches, personnel and other small items) and the departure was delayed while running repairs were carried out. The plan was to engage and inflict damage on the English fleet before escorting the hulks carrying the main invasion force, which was assembled at Calais, across the short stretch of sea to the shores of Kent and Sussex, the same successful routes followed by the Romans and the Normans.

The Invincible Armada engaged an elusive English fleet with unsatisfactory results. Manoeuvring in the storm-tossed Channel was almost impossible, and they withdrew after minor losses in order to re-group off the French coast. The English fleet unsportingly pursued and harried them, picking off stragglers, and setting a small number on fire. Communication with the forces waiting on shore was impossible, and they weren't even assembled where they should have been. Unable to hold anchor or stay together, the order was given for the Spanish fleet to call off the invasion, and to continue sailing up through the North Sea, beyond the top of neutral Scotland, around

Ireland to make their way home across the Bay of Biscay.

The existing maps of the Irish coastline were notoriously inaccurate, and special navigation instructions were given to avoid problems with the poorly charted West Coast by sailing further to the North before taking a southerly course home. In the event, the continuing storms and the un-seaworthy condition of most of the ships meant they were driven closer to shore than was intended. Some took refuge in Scottish ports, some were wrecked in the Western Isles of Scotland, many ships simply disappeared at sea, and many others were driven into the rocks of the Irish Atlantic coast.

The Great Invincible Armada was lost. Perhaps as many as seventeen ships were wrecked on the storm-ravaged coast of Ireland, with great loss of life. Another dozen or so simply disappeared in the stormy seas and were never seen again. Few of the survivors escaped execution by the English forces, or murder by the Irish pillagers. Some were hidden by the Irish outlaw bands, and over the course of time became absorbed into their society. A small number – no more than a few hundred – escaped to friendly, Catholic Scotland and from there to Europe and home to Spain. Captain Francisco Cuellar was one of these, and he provided a chilling first-hand account of his experiences. Of the estimated 30,000 men in the Armada, only 10,000 returned home to Spain

Some of the wrecks were accessible from the shore when the storms subsided. They were systematically stripped of anything of value. The positions of other vessels were recorded, but they were never found. Until quite recently, that is. Modern diving equipment has made possible the location of several of these wreck sites. After almost 400 years, there is little left of the original ships, but buried in the sands lie the fragments which an experienced archaeologist can piece together to form a picture. Everyday items such as plates and cutlery have been brought to the surface, together with military items such as canon, muskets, and swords.

And because the Armada was a Crusade, on a holy mission to restore Christianity to a heathen land, the troops were led by the finest noblemen of the richest Empire the world had ever known. They were dressed in their finery, wearing their best ornament and bejewelled badges of office. This was Spanish Gold, in short – treasure!

The most important of these wreck-sites are on the north and northwestern coasts of Ireland. The finds recovered from two of them are in the award-winning Ulster Museum in Belfast. One of these wrecks is the *Girona*, which is located on the Giant's Causeway in Northern Ireland, and the other is the *Trinidad Valencera*, located at Kinnagoe Bay in County Donegal in the Republic. I felt compelled to visit these sites and others, to experience the sense of place where these terrible events had happened. If I were to visit Northern Ireland, I would also have to overcome some of my preconceptions, and face up to the reality of the situation. In all, I was quite looking forward to it.

Chapter 2
Setting out: history

I have travelled a lot, probably as much as most people living in the age of jet travel. But I have never really toured, and I have never travelled any real distance on two wheels. My Vespa is strictly for trips into the centre of town, to avoid the parking problems. In three and a half years, I had travelled only 3000 miles, according to Ernest's speedometer.

It would be quite a challenge; there were lots of practical problems to solve; luggage was the most pressing. I am famous in my family for travelling heavy. It is not just that I want to take everything, short of the kitchen sink. I find it really difficult to leave out things "just in case". I like to think I am getting better over the years, for example, settling for a dual-purpose jacket rather than separate sets of casual and formal wear, for those dinner engagements which never quite materialise.

Gadgets are another matter. How can I leave behind my laptop computer, and what use is a computer without a printer? These items are designed for portability, but they go with a bewildering assortment of essential electrical adapters and chargers, which weigh a ton, and provoke embarrassing questions at airports. And books. I don't just mean a book to read (although of course you must have a couple of these, in case you finish the first one). No the real bulk lies in the reference books. I must have maps, and restaurant and hotel guides, possibly a foreign dictionary or two, and some notebooks. And I also need my cameras, plus a pair of binoculars.

And I haven't even considered what clothes to take yet! Fortunately, I do not have very strong views on what to wear. Of course I have my favourite clothes, but unlike my daughters who wouldn't be seen dead in last year's outfit, I am quite happy wearing a ten-year-old shirt – if it still fits. I have noticed in recent years that modern clothing has a marked tendency to shrink, and buttons to stretch, as time goes by.

I already had an excellent, rigid "top box" fitted to the rear carrier of Ernest. This could be unlocked and removed, so it would serve as a first-rate travel case. Lighter stuff could be carried in a rucksack, and after much research I bought one big enough to serve, but somewhat aerodynamic, as befits a high-speed traveller. Most importantly, it didn't have a high back which would impede my crash helmet.

The fitting session in a crowded London store was entertaining. The rucksack was of a type designed for downhill skiing, and felt very comfortable, but I jumped and twisted with it on my back just to make sure, jerking my head backwards. Fellow shoppers gave me a wide berth. The only worry was the colour. Bright orange is an excellent choice for speeding down the snowy slopes of the Alps, but orange has other associations in Northern Ireland, with Protestant Orange Orders taking their name from William of Orange. Would I attract a Republican sniper's gunsight? I had the inspired idea of covering the bag in a high-viz dayglow green reflective waistcoat as worn by motorway workers. This seemed both sensible and politically correct, to wear the colours of both sides.

Touring with a scooter, the experienced rider will also take a small stock of spare parts and tools. The Vespa is a masterpiece of design, and perhaps this would be a good moment to tell you about it. Vespa is the name of the model, not the maker: it means "wasp" in Italian. It is made in Pontedera, near Pisa, Italy by a company called Piaggio.

Piaggio was a manufacturer of aircraft, but as the Second World War drew to a close, Mr. Piaggio looked out of his office window, and realised that Italy hadn't done too well in the war. His lovely aircraft factory had been severely bombed, and even if the Allies would let him turn his hand to making military aircraft again – which didn't seem very likely at that moment in time – it would take a long while to join all the scattered bits of his factory together again. So he got on the field telephone to his chief aircraft designer Corradino D'Ascanio.

He came to the point very quickly. "Corradino, we've got a problem. There's no way we can go back to aircraft production for a while, and I've got the Bank Manager on my back, so you've just got to come up with a design for a small motorbike; you can call it a scooter, or something. And you'd better be quick about it." D'Ascanio said "No problem" in the local dialect, and went back to the drawing board. He carefully rolled up his drawings of a supersonic delta winged airliner, and a jumbo-sized four jet-engined people carrier, for another day, and set to work to design a multi-purpose two-wheeler that anyone could ride.

He had never before designed anything other than aeroplanes. Because petrol was in short supply, he decided on a small single-cylinder engine, and for low maintenance and more reliability, he made it run on a two-stroke mixture of petrol and oil. Remembering the times he had passed by motorcyclists at the side of the road struggling to remove a wheel with a flat tyre, soiled by chain-grease, he made several unusual fundamental design decisions.

He made an engine to drive a shaft direct from the gearbox to the rear wheel, with no oily Reynolds chain, and he mounted small diameter wheels on stub axles, so the wheels could be easily lifted on and off when they needed changing. He even made provision for carrying a spare wheel, so all the rider needed to do at the roadside was to remove the punctured wheel and replace it with the spare. He took the gear change mechanism away from the feet, and put it up on the handlebars, with the clutch. He put panels in the front to give the rider protection from the elements, and he put a saddle on top of the petrol tank, so the rider sat upright with his legs in front, like sitting on a chair. There was even room for a pillion passenger behind.

This basic design went into production in record time, and the birth of the Vespa was officially 1946. It is still in production more than 60 years later, although they make new fancy aerodynamic, automatic models in the main. Jealous rivals have pointed to the strange-looking offset position of the rear wheel, caused by the sideways drive shaft design.

To be perfectly honest, it is true that this may be described as a design fault. Mr D'Ascanio was mainly thinking of travel in straight lines at slow speeds, and the offset rear wheel presents no problems under these conditions. Even the most avid fan will admit wryly that a Vespa takes left-hand bends better than right-hand bends. Driving on the left in the British Isles, this means it is fine entering and exiting a roundabout, but things can sometimes be a bit unsteady while driving in the right-hand curve of the roundabout itself. This is only a matter of technique, and you soon get used to it. I have a friend who races Vespas – probably around circuits which consist largely of left-hand bends. In the days of the Mods, prowess was marked by the depth of the scratch marks the rider had inflicted on the underside of his machine by leaning over too far in the right-hand bends.

My own scooter, Ernest, is a model known officially as the Vespa T5 Classic. It has a sporty version of the early aluminium 125 cc engine fitted in a conventional frame. It still has the characteristic "blisters" on each side, reminiscent of an aircraft engine cowling. I have added a few tasteful extras, but stopped short of the banks of spotlights and bottlebrush tail on a long aerial mast, so popular with the Mods of my youth. It cruises happily at 45-50 miles per hour, but if pushed will turn in what the handbook calls "in excess of 100 kilometres per hour". It returns about 90-100 miles per gallon of petrol, which is about 35 kilometres per litre or 2.8 litres per 100 kms for those who think in decimals. Idling my time away on a rainy day in a bar in Donegal, I saw a notice announcing that the standard measure for a glass of wine served in that establishment was 125 cc. Imagine a small wineglass, filled with a mixture of air and petrol vapour. That is ultimately all that was propelling Ernest, me and all my luggage around Ireland.

The first motor vehicle I ever owned was a Vespa. It was the 1960s, and I was offered a second-hand 150GS by an assistant film editor, who was moving up to a small car to accommodate his growing family. He wanted £30. At the time, this was about a week's salary, and seemed very reasonable. I had no idea how to drive it, so he left it parked in the street outside my office. A friend offered to come and show me how it worked. He set the engine running by bump-starting it because the kick-start was broken. He then offered the machine to me, after a brief explanation of how the clutch worked. I jumped out the clutch with the engine revving too high, and with both feet firmly on the ground. The scooter responded by roaring forwards, but because I was holding it back by the handlebars, the scooter stood vertically on end, on its rear wheel, and then mercifully stalled. I was stunned by the power capable of whipping the machine through ninety degrees beneath me, and then I noticed that my instructor was rolling around on the pavement giggling insanely.

Over the next few days, my clutch technique improved. I was advised that there was a very long delay for driving tests, so I should put in my application at once, saying I was prepared to go anywhere, and accept any cancellation which might arise at short notice. Three weeks after my wheel-standing feat, I was given a test in Sevenoaks, a town 30 miles outside London. Although it was not a legal requirement at the time, I bought a crash helmet on the way to my appointment, and rubbed it with dirt in the car park to make it look more used. A very kindly examiner took pity on me, gave me second chances whenever I got things wrong, and I passed! I started to learn to ride properly after the Test.

With the impulsiveness of youth, I undertook most maintenance myself, although I was also lucky enough to find an Italian mechanic by the name of Mario Coco for the more serious work. It was rumoured Mr. Coco had worked on the original Vespa project, but he now had a small workshop in a mews in the posh part of Kensington. I think I was mainly attracted to him by his name. Although I relied on him to do the more complicated maintenance jobs, I felt quite confident about repairing punctures, changing the oil, adjusting cables, and tweaking the carburettor. I would often remove and clean the spark plug just for the hell of it. All this experience stood me in good stead in facing up to the prospect of 2000 miles or so alone on the road.

Chapter 3
Setting out: Watford and Liverpool

Bedecked with an orange rucksack and a green hi-viz jacket, the writer sets off: note the large top-box.

Ireland is well equipped with Bed and Breakfast establishments, or B & Bs, as they prefer to be known. In a country which used to have only a few hotels, mainly for the better off, there is a long tradition to provide travellers with accommodation in private houses. In recent years, with the worldwide increase in tourism, this has really taken off in Ireland, and new houses are often built with extra rooms added on for the B & B trade. Increasingly, these rooms are provided with their own bathroom facilities attached, or "en suite" as goes the preferred expression.

The prospect of staying in private houses fitted in well with my plans to "talk to the people", so I resolved to go with the B & B route, with occasional divergences and rare treats at superior establishments. When it was important to find particular accommodation at a particular time, I would book ahead to be sure. Otherwise, I would just check with a list of suitable-sounding B & Bs from the guides available and book by phone the day before. Only once was I unable to book my first choice. In retrospect, I now realise that perhaps the B & Bs that I chose reflected a very middle-class slice of Ireland. It was only in the streets and the pubs that I was able to meet working-class people.

I gathered about me a selection of books and maps to prepare myself for the trip. I should have prepared myself physically, but I have always found the idea of physical exercise faintly objectionable.

I worked out a route, and a time schedule which proved to be over-pessimistic in some parts, and under-estimated in others. I would start in Liverpool, take the overnight ferry to Belfast, stay there to visit the Armada exhibits in the Ulster Museum, and perhaps meet the ex-curator, who is the recognised expert on the subject. Then I would ride around the coast of Antrim, along a coastline described in many books as the most beautiful in Europe, until I reached the Giant's Causeway, where I would visit the wreck site of the *Girona*. I noticed that the nearest town to the Causeway was Bushmills, which is where they make the best Irish whiskey, a product I am very familiar with. From there I would make my way to Londonderry, or Derry, depending on your politics, to visit the memorial to the victims of the Bloody Sunday Massacre.

Under circumstances which have never been properly explained, in January 1972 a group of British soldiers opened fire on an unarmed crowd of demonstrators, and killed thirteen Catholics. Six of the dead were only 17 years of age. It was an incident which made me feel ashamed of my British passport.

From Derry I would cross the border into County Donegal, and visit the wreck site of the *Trinidad Valencera* at Kinnogoe Bay. While exploring the rest of Donegal, I would also check out some other sites where Armada ships are known to have been wrecked, and make my way down to County Sligo, staying near a bay where no fewer than three wrecks are known to lie, undisturbed. This is the spot where Captain Francisco Cuellar came ashore, and survived to describe the events in a letter to the King of Spain. I had the romantic notion of re-reading his account while I studied the landscape. From there I would make my way down through territory more familiar to me in County Mayo, County Galway, and across country to Dublin, for the ferry back to England.

My first problem was with transport to the port of Liverpool. I called to check out train services to take Ernest by rail, and was horrified to learn that all such services had come to an end with privatisation. It was explained that when Prime Minister Thatcher decided to privatise British Rail and turn it into 27 separate companies, Motor Rail was scrapped. So too was the Guard's Van which was previously attached to every train, and was available for the transport of bulky items such as bicycles, motorbikes and scooters. The same employee suggested I might try the newly formed Red Star Freight Company. The phone number he gave me was wrong, and when I finally battled through to Red Star Freight (which sounds vaguely Russian...) the woman who answered the phone said they didn't do that sort of thing any more. Mainly business packages, you know. She could suggest no alternative.

The Royal Automobile Club has enjoyed my patronage since the days of my first Vespa, and they have always proved very helpful. When I phoned, they gave me a list of local companies dealing in the transport of motorcycles by road. This seemed a good plan. After all, you see trailer-loads of bikes racing up and down the motorways all the time. The first quote I got was for £400 plus VAT, each way. By phoning around, I managed to get other cheaper quotes, but the least expensive was still £167. At these prices, I decided to give serious thought to driving myself all the way to Liverpool. I calculated that by avoiding motorways, and with frequent stops, I could probably cover the 230 miles between London and Liverpool in about 7 hours. The petrol would cost about £7. There was no contest. I would have to grit my teeth, and learn the techniques of riding a scooter long distances by jumping in at the deep end.

I cannot recommend Watford to anyone as a place to get lost in. At the first junction without a signpost, I made a guess and turned left instead of right, and eventually found myself in Watford. Ancient

Watford lies just to the north west of London, but the town planners decided some years ago to go for anonymity by knocking everything down and replacing the town centre with a one-way racetrack around characterless brick and concrete buildings, department stores, office blocks and multi-storey car parks. None of the road-signs in the racetrack system pointed to Liverpool, and once engaged in the one-way race, completing circuit after circuit, it was almost impossible to escape. I eventually managed it and dejectedly followed signs to the police station, to ask directions for the road to Liverpool.

A friendly sergeant took a deep breath, and suggested I go back home to North London and start again. When I insisted that this was impossible, because all the neighbours had waved me off with great ceremony and flowing tears only twenty minutes earlier, he grudgingly admitted there might be another way, but it required extraordinary skills of orienteering, and his look suggested that he doubted that I was in possession of such skills.

All directions in Watford start from the one-way system, so he re-directed me back to there, and counted me down to the exit I needed to take. From there on, it was up to me. I would be entirely alone on the highways and byways of the Watford countryside. The thought crossed my mind that my informant might be one of those desk-bound sergeants who didn't drive himself, and I was reminded of these thoughts a few moments later. I roared off into the now familiar one-way track, acknowledged my pit signals from the petrol station, and peeled off at the exit indicated by my police sergeant. This was more promising.

By this means, I was able to regain my planned route, and thereafter it unfolded before me exactly as I had visualised it from the road map - well almost exactly. I found that riding along at 50 or so miles an hour sitting on a high-revving engine was much less strenuous than I had expected. I only needed to stop every 100 or so miles for petrol, and every hour and a half for refreshment, and a rest from holding the throttle wide open. Real scooterboys call this a fag break.

Motorway driving in England is horrible. There are never enough traffic lanes to carry the volume of traffic, and there are always a lot of drivers travelling much faster than is good for them or anyone else. There are also lorries. The wind or back draught from a giant lorry travelling at speeds in excess of 80 mph is enough to shake a large saloon car. But it is capable of lifting a motor scooter up in the air and depositing it roughly on the nearest hard shoulder of the motorway. Having considered this prospect, I decided early on that I would not travel on motorways. Fortunately, the old network of 'A' and 'B' roads from the pre-motorway era still exists. These are well maintained, for the most part, and are divided into sections of dual carriageway or single carriageway. Where they used to pass through ancient market towns, allowing the stagecoach driver to feed his passengers and change his horses, now they often follow a diverted course around the local bypass. And bypasses mean roundabouts. The main attraction of these roads, as far as I am concerned, is that they carry very little traffic and hardly any lorries. The users of 'A' roads tend to be local. They drive carefully and respectfully, in case they happen to pass the local vicar or that nice Miss Pringle from the library. And they hardly ever blow motor scooters onto the hard shoulder.

At the Little Chef roadside restaurant where I stopped to have my first cup of tea, I impulsively bought an orange drink to take on the road with me. The cash register read my Kia Ora orange drink barcode as a Whispa Gold chocolate bar, and refused to take the going price for orange drinks (49p), settling instead for 36p. I had no inclination to argue with the cash register's version of events, and the cashier - obviously more experienced than I am in this puzzling type of encounter - was happy to accept my 36p. I suppose, if you start to work out the costing of re-adjusting the till balance, or (Heaven forbid!) re-programming the cash registers, just to recover 13p, the cashier's attitude makes sense. And multiply this by the number of all the Little Chefs all over the country, some with more than one cash register!

My mind boggled all the way up the next twenty miles of the A5. It was almost worth going into the next Little Chef and buying up their entire stock of orange drinks! I explored this possibility at the next Little Chef along the road, but they cunningly claimed to have sold out of orange drinks. At those prices, I was not surprised. I gave the bored cashier a knowing, confiding grin, but I'm not sure it was understood, because I had got my helmet back on again by this time. Anyway, she pretended not to notice. Perhaps she was under instructions from Head Office.

In agreeable weather, I sped through pleasant landscapes along good, uncrowded roads. Petrol station followed petrol station, and cups of tea became cups of coffee. Why were my fellow travellers in these refreshment places all so elderly? Were all the young executives elsewhere, busy speeding up the motorways, haranguing their secretaries on their mobile phones?

Suddenly, and quite unexpectedly I saw a sign to Liverpool, the city of the Mersey Beat and the Walker Art Gallery, home of a fine collection of Victorian paintings. I was ahead of schedule. Would I have time to visit the Walker? By the time I had battled with the central one-way racetrack (built in the style of Watford), I found Bootle Docks with an hour to spare. Not time enough for art, so I engaged the pickets in conversation instead.

I had heard about the striking dockers of Liverpool, and was uncomfortable to discover that the dock where my ferry was to leave was operated by "scab" labour, according to the pickets' placards. So I pulled over and immediately apologised for crossing their picket line, but what was the score?

In a perfect scouse accent, my informant told me, with an absence of passion to be expected in a dispute which had dragged on for years, that the Mersey Docks and Harbour Board had sold out under the rule of the Tory Government, and the docks had been privatised. There were no young men left in the dispute now, they had all moved on to other employments. But where was he expected to find a job a few years away from retirement? "Do you mean there was no redundancy, no compensation?" I said. "Oh there were offers, and some have taken them, but what's a few thousand pounds for a lifetime's work? The talks are going on, and with the Labour Government, maybe there'll be some progress all right. They have the power, after all they're still the majority shareholders. We don't want our jobs back, we just want decent compensation".

All the time we were talking, the others on the picket line chatted among themselves. They made no effort to join in to help convince me of the righteousness of their cause. Occasionally a passing car would toot its horn in solidarity, and they would wave back and give the car a half-hearted cheer. The severance pay offered by the Mersey Docks and Harbour Board to the 329 dockers who were locked out when they refused to cross a picket line was the princely sum of £28,000 per man. The pickets didn't explain to me why this was so unacceptable. Originally, they told me, they just wanted their jobs back, but that's not even a remote possibility now.

I have always been wary of dockworkers since the London dockers marched on Parliament in the 60s, in a disturbing demonstration of working-class racism, to demand immigration restrictions to protect their jobs. In one of those strange ironies which make you think that perhaps there is a natural justice after all, the London Docks, which at one time was the biggest set of Docks in the world, was closed down little by little, to be replaced by containers, channel ports, and airports. The community of the Docks and the Port of London was dispersed, and the huge conglomeration of crane-lined docksides and waterways was turned over to the developers. The idea of the grandiose scheme was to attract companies eastwards, away from the overcrowded City of London, to populate new forests of tower blocks and converted warehouses.

The enterprise was a financial and social disaster. The remaining working class residents were priced out and reduced to ghetto-like enclaves. It took a long time for any substantial companies to take up the invitation to move out of the centre of London, and the new buildings at the Docks stood largely unoccupied. The infrastructure of roads and public transport was woefully insufficient. The developers went broke, and the banks wrote off enormous loans which would never be repaid. The Government said initially it would all be financed privately, and then poured huge sums from the public purse into Docklands (as the PR company named the area) to prop it up. Viewed from Greenwich Park on the opposite side of the River

Thames, its vast extent can be appreciated. A monstrous White Elephant, a monument to the extravagant failure of Thatcherism.

It is unfair to be critical of these burnt-out Liverpool pickets, but it was also difficult to feel outrage at the way they had been treated, or any sympathy for their demands for fair conditions of employment when they were no longer interested in the right to work. I drove through the picket line with a cheering wave, and what was intended to be a spirited toot from Ernest's mini klaxon, and showed my papers to the disapproving security person at the gate. He clearly did not take kindly to those who consorted with the enemy.

The ferry route from Liverpool to Belfast was operated by a company which glories in the name of Norse Irish Ferries. I was half expecting the crew to be a wild bunch of redheaded Vikings, but they did not come up to these expectations. They were dressed in disappointing uniforms of white shirt and dark trousers, as one would expect to find in any neutral establishment. The service was operated by a single ship, recycled from other routes, sent here to end out its last days. It must have been one of the first RoRo's (Roll on Roll off ferries), and was probably considered the height of luxury by travellers of the post-war generation, used to huddling together in bomb shelters.

The service was overnight, travelling on odd dates from Liverpool to Belfast, and returning Belfast to Liverpool on even dates. A large part of the 12-hour crossing was taken up by waiting in the sea lock of the River Mersey at Liverpool for the tide to gain sufficient height for the ship to clear the river. There were faster crossings on modern craft, but these operate higher up in Scotland, on the much shorter crossing from Stranraer to Larne. A high-speed ferry makes the crossing in much less time, but for me it would have meant a further 200 miles of riding. To be honest, I was also attracted by the experience of an old-fashioned ferry trip, which must have been well known to so many returning emigrants.

CHAPTER 4
BELFAST

Ernest on the long avenue to Stormont, the handsome Parliament building of the Northern Ireland government.

We had arrived very early. The line of cars passing through the Customs shed was small in number, and I was surprised to see there was a cursory interview and examination in the style of the sort of Customs check one gets on the way to the continent of Europe. Weren't we travelling from one part of the United Kingdom of Great Britain and Northern Ireland to another? I greeted another motorcyclist on an elderly Honda 4 cylinder 400 cc F2 machine. I noticed London licence plates from 1981 - a machine held by some to be a classic. The rider had a pronounced Belfast accent, short hair and a Zapata moustache. His name was Robert McSomething - this isn't to hide his identity, I couldn't catch the rest. I was asked to show my passport at the same time as he was being handed back his papers, not a passport but an ID card of some kind. Why show a passport when travelling from one part of the United Kingdom to another?

We rode onto the ship together, and were directed to park over at the side, where our machines were tied to steel girders with massive ropes, next to a lorry. I wasn't happy about this crude arrangement, and insisted on extra padding, before making my way to the primitive single cabin I had been allocated. The loo was in the shower. When you used the shower, the floor filled up with water, and the loo got a soaking. The bareness of the cabin was reminiscent of a prison cell. I dumped my bags and got out.

At the bar, I was ignored while regular lorry-drivers were served first. This was a prejudice I hadn't expected to meet! I finally sat down with my pint of Guinness, and was joined by Robert McSomething. He was collecting the Honda for a friend. His own bike was a Kawasaki GT7000 XYZ fuel-injected Turbo-zapper (the bigger the bike, the longer the number). He had flown to London that morning to buy the second-hand Honda, bombed it up the motorway to Liverpool, and would deliver the bike the next morning to his friend. He didn't make a habit of this. It was the first time he had done anything like it. What was the ID card he showed the Policeman? He produced it and showed it to me. The Northern Ireland driving licences are the size of a credit card, and carry a photo. This is the ID Card by-the-back-door which all Civil Rights organisations were resisting in the UK for so long. A new UK driving license is only available now with a photo, and the old style photo-free license is no longer available, if it needs to be renewed for any reason. And of course the photo-card needs to be renewed at ten-year intervals, unlike its predecessor.

I said to Robert that on reflection I had been a bit dismissive of the Policemen's questions, over-confident in the knowledge of my own innocence. But perhaps they had been trained to look out for that sort of cover being used by the Bad Guys? "The average terrorist" (a Protestant word, I noted) "looks just like me. They'll take one look at you with your rucksack and your scooter, and they'll move on." He didn't mean it unkindly. "A Wally, you mean?" I suggested, and Robert nodded.

Robert was into big bikes in a big way. I asked him about a story I had heard that members of Hells Angels rode their bikes at midnight on a certain day every year, across a rope footbridge, the Carrick-a-Rede Bridge, near the Giant's Causeway on the North Antrim coast. He hadn't heard that one. A previous boss of his was leader of the Belfast chapter of Hells Angels. He told me of a group of six or so called the

Chosen Few. They were really mean. Stabbings were common, just for the hell of it. Did he work with bikes? I wanted to know. "I'm a prison officer" was the reply I wasn't expecting, and my jaw must have dropped.

It all fell into place. He even looked like a Northern Ireland prison officer. I could imagine a peaked cap covering that short hair on a round head, above that moustache. "But I'm not political. What do you do?" I mumbled something about advertising. He asked me how I came to ride scooters. I told him I was riding a scooter even before the Mods in the Who film "Quadrophenia" had been thought of. While still at school, I used to ride pillion with a group of early-leaver schoolfriends in the East End of London. One day, I was invited to go on a trip to the coast, to Brighton, a sleepy seaside town 50 miles south of London.

It was said at the time that Brighton had a police force of only three officers. I don't know if the leaders of the trip had seen the Marlon Brando film "The Wild One", which was banned in the UK at the time, but on arrival, hundreds of scooters rode through the town six abreast, terrorising the locals. It is said the three policemen went and hid. To be honest, I don't remember much about it. We went for a ride to the seaside, and met up with a lot of other scooters. I remember driving down through streets like we owned the place, but I don't remember any violence. I think we had to leave early, and it wasn't till we saw the next day's newspapers that we realised what we had been in. According to the press, Mods ruled, OK? I believe that was the first recorded Mod action. The date must have been 1958 or '59; the pitched battles between Mods (parkas and scooters) and Rockers (leathers and motorcycles) which took place in the 60s at seaside resorts around the South Coast, all this was much later.

As another couple of pints appeared, I found myself loosening up more. I continued: My first scooter was a classic, a Vespa 150GS. Then I moved onto cars, got married, and started a family. In the 70s I bought a second-hand Honda 70 from my secretary, what they called a Monkey Bike – small wheels, semi-automatic. Great fun. I used to wind it up on my way to work every morning, accelerating out of the Victoria Memorial roundabout in front of Buckingham Palace, down the Mall up to its top speed of 45 miles an hour. As I reached where the road narrows down through the Admiralty Arch, which was always blocked with queuing cars, I used to jump the bike onto the pavement and drive flat out through the pedestrian arch at the side, without slowing down. One day I nearly flattened a tourist!

Robert still looked interested, perhaps he was just being polite, so I went on about my life with bikes. My next bike was a silly mistake. In a local motorcycle shop, I saw a second-hand Special. It was a lightweight Greaves Silverstone frame, expanded and fitted with an old BSA 500 cc twin-cylinder engine. The expansion conversion had been beautifully and lovingly crafted with an aluminium plate and allen screw fixings. A huge extra-capacity petrol tank was fitted, with dropped clip-on handlebars, and the bike was converted to a single-seater by moving the seat back and extending the foot controls with rickety rear set rods. The straight through exhaust was beautifully noisy, but it was so highly geared that the only time I could get into 4th gear was down the long straight of Whitehall at about 60 miles per hour, for about 300 yards. Unfortunately, it wouldn't go around bends, only in a straight line. It was a pig. So I decided to leave it parked somewhere "unsafe" and wait for it to be stolen for the insurance pay-off. It didn't take long.

Robert nodded his agreement, and I carried on. Next I bought a new Honda 125 Trail Bike – pure marketing fantasy, with the standard workhorse 125 cc four-stroke single cylinder engine in a fancy sit-up frame. I used to do wheelies leaving the traffic lights outside the Houses of Parliament. Not enough power though, and then I heard of a Honda 250 Trail Bike going cheap. This was a proper bike with a wonderful four-valve single cylinder four-stroke engine. It belonged to a film director, who later went on to make Hollywood box-office busters. He was a speed freak, and his other vehicle was a Ferrari. He was never really happy with the Honda, and between the Ferrari and driving bans he was always getting, he hadn't put up many miles on two wheels. It was mine for a song. This one really went up Highgate West Hill like a rocket, although I still had to drop down into 4th gear for best results.

The answer to this problem was a Yamaha 500 XT Enduro. This

amazing 500 cc single-cylinder four-stroke had a valve-lifter to allow kick starting; the compression was so great, it couldn't be kicked over without it. The Yamaha handled beautifully, with a great torquey feeling of power. It was a well balanced, expressive machine and I often wish I had never sold it. But the writing was on the wall: in a two-week period, three motorcyclists known personally to me were killed in accidents. In each case, it was not their fault. As a father of two girls, I had responsibilities, so I sold my Yamaha to a very pleased New Zealander, and bought a cutting edge video recorder with the proceeds. I didn't come back to two wheels until I decided on my current Vespa for commuting. The Vespa is great fun in its way.

Robert McSomething listened to all this patiently. He said he liked to be able to climb on a bike and just go. He had enjoyed a string of big-bikes, and pranged a few, but apart from a few broken bones, he had had no serious problems. You're only young once. Who knows what's around the corner. He had collected the Honda for a friend, just for the fun of it. These cliché-sounding remarks were coming from a prison officer in Northern Ireland, who must expect to be a target for one reason or another, perhaps for the rest of his life; it could be from a personal grudge, or as a sectarian ritual execution. Whatever reason, the result would be the same. Who was to deny him the right to burn up the road at 160 miles an hour every now and again?

An uncompromising voice on the tannoy instructed us to be up at 6 am, and to be off the ship by 7 or else! This seemed a bit inconsiderate, but I had no trouble in complying, and after a troubled night's sleep, I shared a table at breakfast with an elderly couple who lived in a Belfast suburb. He had been raised in County Cork as the son of a vicar. They were frequent travellers to visit their children and grandchildren living in England. They were very critical of the condition and the cost of the Norse Irish ferry, which had a monopoly of the Liverpool-Belfast run. It was time the company spent some money and put on a new ship. Changes were promised for the end of the year.

In an obvious reference to the Troubles, they assured me the area where they lived was "quiet and respectable", and not far from Stormont. I told them I didn't yet know Belfast, but I had seen pictures of the Stormont Parliament, which must be the envy of all presidents the world over, with its remote park setting and unrivalled approach along a mile-long tree-lined ceremonial avenue. "We're not far from there." I found I was already falling into the Northern Ireland game of "What's your name? Where do you live? Where did you go to school?" the three questions needed to pinpoint the essential characteristics of the interviewee. I concluded that this couple, were Protestants, although he was from the South. Perhaps a mixed marriage? I was already making prejudiced judgements, and I wasn't even ashore yet.

In contrast to the run-down docks of Liverpool, the docks of Belfast were being re-developed for modern needs. Where was the Harland and Wolff shipyard where the *"Titanic"* was built, with "to Hell with the Pope" allegedly stamped on every steel plate? I rode on with apprehension through the early morning streets of Belfast. This wasn't just early: it was ridiculously early. I couldn't possibly call at my digs yet to leave my luggage, so I drove around the streets of the waking city with my green-covered orange rucksack on my back.

As I left the docks, shunning the short stretch of commuter motorway into town, I turned onto what must have been the old docks road. There I saw, on a petrol station forecourt, a military vehicle, a sort of a light tank, or what used to be called a Bren gun carrier. I realised I didn't know how to describe it properly, but it occurred to me that any Belfast toddler would know the current nickname for such a vehicle.

I drove on expecting to come upon a roadblock or some other evidence of military and police controls, but there were none. I took a more relaxed view of my surroundings, and discovered that Belfast is very like Watford in parts. Characterless red brick multi-storey blocks and one-way streets. The City Centre one-way system was very wide, and early rush-hour traffic was flowing normally. I went round the one-way system a couple of times, taking in what was left of the Victorian architecture. Were the people responsible for the gaps in the rows of Victorian buildings town planners or fire bombers? The result was the same, and much like any other provincial capital anywhere in the United Kingdom.

Where were all the armed police and the flak-jacketed soldiers I was expecting? Wasn't Belfast Centre the most heavily vigilated town in Europe, with video cameras, audio listening posts and spies-in-the-skies? It occurred to me that I might be arousing suspicion, driving round and round with what was obviously a gaudy bomb on my back. I might even be in a sniper's sights right now. There are no parking spaces for motorcycles, so I pulled over quickly onto a yellow line by a bus stop. I would buy a newspaper – that was an innocent-looking action. I remembered Robert's description of police reaction to my Wally-like appearance, and took some comfort. A sniper's bullet seemed unlikely. Belfast no longer fitted the description which I remembered of "a forest of factory chimneys."

I rode on, and pinpointed my digs, a grand-looking detached house on a main road near the University. It was still far too early to go knocking on the door, so I went back into the main part of town for more exploring. Over there was the Europa hotel – at the time, said to be the most bombed in Europe – and across the road was the Crown pub, recommended by a journalist friend. Nearby was the old Opera House, made famous by a Van Morrison album. I knew more about Belfast than I realised. I would stop for another breakfast, a coffee and a bun. The combination of a café that was both open, and had no yellow line outside, seemed impossible to find, but I eventually found one with an open car park opposite. I calculated that a car park attendant in Belfast must be a very nervous individual, waiting for the Bad Guys to leave a car bomb in his car park.

I rode up to the attendant's hut, trying hard to look as much as possible like a Wally with an orange and green bomb on his back. How much do you charge for a scooter? The attendant looked me in the eye. He was a veteran of many a march, and clearly well thought of in his Orange Lodge. "We only allow cars in here" he said sternly, "But if you would like to leave it just there in front of my barrier, you'll be all right." He had clearly not been trained to look out for bombs in rucksacks, or in sinister black scooter top boxes. I thanked him profusely, pointed out I would be having a coffee in the shop opposite, and parked where he had directed.

Eventually, when I considered the hour to be acceptable, I went back to my magnificent digs to ask if I could leave my luggage. Mrs. Ruby Miller couldn't have been more welcoming. As soon as I had introduced myself and apologised for my early arrival, she asked me the question I would become familiar with in the next few weeks: "What time would you like breakfast tomorrow and what would you like?" It took me a while to start thinking about tomorrow. "Oh I don't mind. What's best for you?" "Any time at all." "What about 9 o'clock?" "That's fine, but could you make it 8.45?" "Of course, or I could make it later if you like." "No, not later. You see, breakfast is between 7.30 and 8.45."

Mrs. Ruby Miller was new to the job. I learned later that the previous owner, a retired nurse, had sold up the previous year. The new owner was a friend of Mrs. Miller, and had asked her if she would take on the job of landlady. She was recently retired, and took to the prospect of a second profession "at my time of life" as an enjoyable challenge. She fitted into the house well, occupying each room with a comforting presence. Later, when I saw her out of doors, she looked much smaller. My room was already prepared, so I left my things, and set off to visit the Museum.

CHAPTER 5
TREASURES OF THE ARMADA

My first digs in Northern Ireland.

After my problems with parking, I decided to walk the short distance down the hill to the Botanical Gardens, where the Ulster Museum occupies a tranche built into the lawns and footpaths of a typical Victorian park. I was comfortably early for my appointment with the ex-curator, writer of several books on the subject of the Spanish Armada and Ireland, and formulator of the permanent exhibition of items recovered from wreck sites. It was a great coup for him to get the authorities in the South to agree to gather the finds from various sites all over Ireland together in this one museum in Belfast, not without some resentment being expressed in some quarters of the Republic.

The Museum was well attended by groups of school children, all neatly uniformed and worryingly well behaved. There are many exhibits obviously aimed at informing as well as showing, with models of Bronze Age villages, and a life-sized wattle-and-daub hut which inquisitive young eyes can peer into. In the room immediately next to the Spanish Armada exhibition, a group of twenty or so 8-10 year olds was seated attentively on the floor while a teacher incongruously gave them a lesson about health and hygiene.

The Armada collection lived up to the pictures in the ex-curator's books. There is a great deal of excitement in a medal or an item of jewellery which can be clearly traced to an individual. Here there are gold chains from the *Girona* which can be attributed to persons who were known to be on the ill-fated vessel, but there is also a gold ring which can be identified as having been in the possession of a young nobleman who sailed with the Armada and was never heard of again. Until the ring was found, it was not known that he was on that particular ship.

Most impressive of all is a jewelled clasp of the chivalry Order of Santiago. There was only one Knight of Santiago who sailed with the Armada, Don Alonso de Leiva who took over command of the fleet when it left the English Channel, and was shipwrecked on board the *Sancta Maria Encoronada* at Blacksod Bay. He got most of his crew ashore, consolidated a force with other survivors in a small fort, set sail again on a second ship the *Duquesa Santa Ana*, which in turn was shipwrecked. So he moved to a third ship, the *Girona*, which was tragically wrecked at Lacada Point on the Giant's Causeway with great loss of life, including that of Don Alonso de Leiva. Almost 400 years later, his Cross of Santiago was found on the seabed, and now sits in a display cabinet in the Ulster Museum.

There are other personal items on display, but I was very impressed by the cannon. I must have passed by several hundred cannon in my time, without a second look. In the period of the Armada, there was great inconsistency in the manufacturing process. A poor one could explode at any time, killing the poor unfortunates who were crewing it. When a cannon-maker established a reputation for standards of care and quality, he was much sought after, and he could ask high prices for his product. His guns were all individuals, and were hallmarked with pride, showing the maker, the date and the client who had ordered it.

One of the best makers of cannon was Remigy de Halut of Malines in Flanders. He had a more or less permanent order from King Philip ll.

of Spain, who took all the cannon Master de Halut could supply him. Some of them were still in use more than 200 years later in Wellington's Army in the Peninsular War. On display in the Ulster Museum are two matched cannon recovered from the *Trinidad Valencera*. They bear the insignia of the maker and of Philip ll, and are marked with their individual weights. It is known that the missing third one, with its identifying weight mark, was recovered from the wrecksite later in 1987, and found its way into the possession of a private individual from the Republic, who kept it. I only hope he is as proud of it as the Ulster Museum is of its two sisters.

Laurence Flanagan is the most likeable ex-curator I have ever met. He is a man of two marriages, two families, two careers and two historical study periods. Laurence's first subject is prehistory, and he has just written a major work on the subject. He suggested a liquid lunch, and led me to a nearby pub which had recently been refurbished. I feared the worst, acres of plastic surfaces, mock wooden beams, loud music and plastic food. In fact it wasn't too bad.

I learnt that Ireland is one of the richest parts of Europe in sites of Stone Age, Bronze Age and Early Christian civilisations. It was from Ireland that Saint Columba took Christianity to the British mainland. Parts of Ireland are littered with the remains of early communities, providing evidence of a sophisticated lifestyle while elsewhere the rest of early mankind was barely emerging shivering from caves. Laurence became an expert on the Spanish Armada by reason of his position as curator at the time that the wrecksite discoveries were made between 1967 and 1969.

In the absence of any other candidate, he took on the task of taking charge of the period, and fought hard and successfully to achieve the finest exhibit of Armada relics in the world. He has collaborated on several television programmes about the Armada, produced a definitive, highly informative and readable catalogue, and a stunning smaller book packed with high-quality photographs. Although he is proud of being an Ulsterman, I sense his rivalry with the South is more to do with academic prowess than politics.

The ruin of the island fort in Donegal where de Leiva gathered his forces after being shipwrecked for the second time was equipped with a small cannon salvaged from the shipwreck. At the time of the discoveries in the late 1960s, and the subsequent publicity, this cannon was still in place, but it disappeared mysteriously, and is now known to be in the private possession of a local, let us say, professional person. As an academic, Laurence is of the opinion that this relic should be on public view, but there is no sign of any action from the authorities in the Republic.

Largely as a result of his efforts, there is an embargo on unauthorised diving on the wrecks at Streedagh Strand in Sligo. As an historical site, any investigation must be undertaken along strictly archaeological lines, centimetre by centimetre carefully recorded. So far, the vast cost of such an operation, running into 2 or 3 million pounds and rising, plus an annual maintenance cost of about £250,000, has proved prohibitive. It doesn't seem so much to me, as the price for preserving the records of an event equally important in the history of Ireland, Spain and England. I would have thought that someone out there could see the value of such an operation? Laurence Flanagan would like to hear from you, care of the Ulster Museum.

I was watchful for any telltale signs of religion and politics in our conversation. I suppose the second marriage could have been a clue suggesting non-Catholic, but this isn't always a reliable indicator.

Good Catholics in Spain leapt at the opportunity of divorce when it became legal again in the post-Franco years. The Pope had to issue a stern warning over the number of "annulments" issued in Spain to devout Catholics who didn't consider the law of the land sufficient authority to grant a divorce. But they were happy enough to enjoy the benefits of a divorce blessed by the Pope on the shaky, and often improbable, grounds of annulment.

There was nothing in my conversation with Laurence to suggest anything more than a frustration at the political situation and the unwillingness of the politicians to seek a solution to the Troubles. My impression is that Laurence doesn't have room in his life for the demands of devout religious practice, or for extreme political action. His passions lie elsewhere, and there are few passions as intense as an academic passion.

On my stroll back up the hill, I took more notice of the surroundings of the broad avenue in which Malone House is situated. I imagined this was once the district of the wealthy burgers of Belfast, the shipyard magnates, the merchants, and the gentlemen farmers. There were large houses set back from the road in ample grounds, often served by a driveway. A couple of them were in a state of abandon, another was being extensively rebuilt as a conference centre, or a private nursing home. On this slight rise above the city, with the University and Botanical Gardens at its foot, removed just far enough from the more sordid side of town where the money was made amid swirls of belching black coal smoke in the days of industrial prosperity, I could imagine the finery of Protestant Belfast living out their social hours in an endless string of dinner parties and elegant ballroom dances.

As I drew nearer to my digs, now almost modest by comparison with most of the houses I was passing, I noticed one large house in particular was surrounded by an unattractive high fence. I couldn't see beyond to the house and gardens, but on the corner was a sort of buttress, a mock castle perhaps, with a narrow slit window, like a medieval archer's peephole, but horizontal, like a pillbox. As I examined it from closer, I realised with a shock that there were two eyes peering back at me from the slit: the eyes of a British soldier. This was some kind of an army post, just a few yards from where I was staying. This was the only sign of army or police activity I saw in Belfast all the time I was there.

CHAPTER 6
AROUND BELFAST

A statue of Carson, in typical belligerent pose, dominates Stormont.

I collected Ernest and rode out to visit the Somme Heritage Centre, some distance from the city centre, I was told. Nobody I spoke to seemed to know for sure. I have a long-standing interest in the Battle of the Somme 1916, and have been fortunate enough to have known a large number of survivors from that most terrible moment in the history of the British Army. A handful of incompetent Generals sacrificed the nation's youth for what they mistakenly thought would be the most glorious victory of all time. Most of the country has forgiven and forgotten the mistakes (not me!), but in Belfast that memory is kept alive in the banners paraded every year by the Orangemen. Here's why.

In 1914 plans for the independence of Ireland were finally agreed, and the Home Rule Bill would be passed to establish direct rule from Dublin. Resistance to this idea among the Ulster Protestants was total. Under powerful, rich political masters such as Lord Carson, they formed into militant groups and prepared to fight for their own independence from the Catholic South. They bought arms from Germany, who - on the eve of the First World War - was only too pleased to provide weapons for the rebels.

When war broke out, Westminster reacted by suspending the Home Rule Bill "for the duration of the hostilities". When the War Office called for volunteer battalions for military service, they were overwhelmed with the response from young men all over the country. They were quite unprepared, and had neither uniforms nor weapons, nor accommodation for so many. In Northern Ireland, Carson stepped forward offering not just a battalion, but a whole division of more than 10,000 Irishmen. And what's more, his Ulster Division would be armed and uniformed by himself, ready to serve. Effectively, he simply converted his band of Ulster Volunteer Force rebels into British soldiers, needing only a minimum of training.

Together with all the other volunteers forming the New Army, these troops were moved into the front line in Picardy, North France, where the German, French and British armies had reached a stalemate in trenches. Under political pressure for some action, the Generals prepared to send the willing but inexperienced volunteers into action in the biggest attack in history, the Big Push, which would drive the Germans back to Berlin. But history shows that the Lions were led by Donkeys. On 1st July 1916 the Generals sent their New Army over the top, with orders to "walk, not run", and in a single day the Army was destroyed by the German machine guns and artillery, which should have been destroyed by the biggest artillery barrage ever seen. With about 70,000 casualties the first day of the Battle of the Somme was the biggest single disaster in the glorious history of the British Army.

No Division fought harder than the Ulster Division. Theirs was the only sector where the attack objectives were achieved, but nevertheless they were forced to withdraw because the assaults on either side of them were driven back and failed. The Ulster Division suffered 5104 casualties, more than half of those who went into action, and they shared countless awards for bravery, including four Victoria Crosses. When news of this great tragedy reached home on the mainland, it was accepted by families with both private and national mourning in a spirit of intensified patriotism. In Ulster, the attack was seen as an act of betrayal. To their minds, the brave youth of Ulster had been sacrificed by their English field commanders on the instructions of the Westminster Government, to rid them of the threat of rebellious insurgence after the war, when the Home Bill was due to be activated.

Ironically, the decision had already been taken that this would never happen. After the Easter Rebellion in Dublin in April 1916 by a small group of Irish patriots, the paranoid British High Command were led to question the loyalty of all Irish troops, even the most experienced professional soldiers from Irish regiments – among the oldest in the British Army. The Irish Divisions saw service on the Western Front, but were quickly moved away to less sensitive zones like India and the Middle East. Some say it was because of the Easter Rising that the Home Rule Bill was shelved. Tragically, the post-war discourse between the British Government and the Provisional Irish Government produced the division of the Six Counties and the Twenty-six, which is the source of the current Troubles.

Just as Australia has never forgiven the British for the sacrifice of young Australians at Gallipoli, Northern Ireland has never forgiven the sacrifice on the Somme. Its memory is kept alive in the paraded faded banners, and in modern street graffiti. "Remember the Somme! No Surrender! Carson was right!" Some of these modern graffiti items require a sophisticated knowledge of politics and history to be interpreted. An outsider is left puzzled by their message. I rode past one of these on my way towards the Somme Heritage Centre.

The Centre is a modern building in a spacious setting in the Ards Peninsular, about 10 miles out of town. On my way, I passed through an obviously working-class Protestant area with graffiti like the one already mentioned. The houses gradually became more middle-class, and then I suddenly passed a grand entrance to what I took to be a building of some importance. The view up the tree-lined avenue to Stormont was breathtaking. I would have a closer look on my way back.

I arrived at the Somme Heritage Centre just after four, parked carefully, and was told the Centre had already closed at 4 o'clock precisely. I enquired about what the Centre offered. I learned that individual visits are possible, but it is really geared to guided tours. If I wanted to come back tomorrow, I should make it early, because two school parties were booked in for the morning. "What did they have by way of exhibits?" "There's the Trench Experience, and other displays relevant to the Battle of the Somme". Although the literature talks about "bringing the two traditions of Ireland together to learn about their common heritage", I rapidly formed the impression that this wasn't for me, and I thought my time would be better spent in the morning pushing on up the Antrim Coast.

The view along the broad avenue to Stormont Castle is immensely impressive. At the barrier, I was told I could ride along to the imposing statue of Carson in front of the main house to take my photographs, but I should go no further. Ernest looked very smart as I snapped him in the afternoon sunshine with the towering façade behind. The building was created at the time of the Treaty to satisfy Carson's demands for a Northern Ireland Parliament, but became a white elephant when the Northern Irish Assembly was suspended and Direct Rule from Westminster was re-imposed in 1973, and again in 1974. For 50 years, it had represented Protestant rule from which Northern Irish Catholics were effectively excluded. I saw no obvious signs of heavy security in the deserted, immaculate park surroundings, although I could feel the CCTV cameras following my leisurely progress.

With the University so close, it is not surprising that the area at the bottom of my hill was bustling with crowds of far-too-youthful students. They queued at the cash dispenser machine by the pub, they dashed from group to group, late for a date, they half-walked half-ran down the road, in that excited way of the young. There is something about being in a crowd of young people which is very stimulating. There was an air of bubbling enthusiasm. They paraded, they swaggered, they embraced, they giggled and they roared, just like kids anywhere. But I learned from the next day's newspaper that just down the road a young unfortunate, judged and found guilty of some social crime by a band of self-appointed thugs, was at that moment being kneecapped with a sawn-off shotgun.

I found a restaurant, and enjoyed a beer while I thought about what to order. The music was soft rock, and moved from likeable standard to likeable standard. Nobody stood up and cheered when Elton John moved on to "Benny and the Jets". All the songs were comfortably familiar, and not one of them had the slightest edge whatsoever.

On the walk back up the hill, I called in at an off-licence for a small bottle of mineral water. The place was packed with students preparing for a Wednesday night of revelry in Belfast. My request was treated with disbelief. It was as if I had asked for a pound of pork sausages in a kosher delicatessen. "You will find your water" I was told pointedly "across the road at the supermarket", and she served the next customer who was struggling with a wire shopping basket overflowing with sweet cider and Coke, obviously the in-drink in student circles. On the late BBC Radio News I heard that a supermarket chain was withdrawing a range of children's drinks because they contained 4.6% alcohol. That's above the average strength of a pint of beer. I also heard that a RUC policeman had been kicked to death in County Antrim.

CHAPTER 7
A RIDE UP THE COAST

The following morning, I said goodbye to Mrs. Ruby Miller (I love that name!) and set off with my orange and green bomb up the Antrim coast road. Belfast-born poet Louis McNeice spent his childhood in Carrickfergus; his career was later carved out in England, mainly working for the wartime Third Programme of BBC Radio. I always thought he was an anglicised Scot, until I met Mrs. McNeice. She used to run an eccentric restaurant in Kinsale, County Cork, staffed by a collection of well bred Surrey girls, all of them gushingly well intentioned, but definitely not in control of the situation. The restaurant was called "The Spinnaker", but it was never referred to by this name; it was known universally as "The Widow McNeice's".

Louis McNeice was a fine poet, and one who contributed a great deal to the spread of culture at a popular level during the War years and just after, along with Dylan Thomas and a strong BBC team of socially committed individuals. His work has since been eclipsed by shooting stars such as W. H. Auden, but I suspect that with time, his greatness will be recognised again. Apart from the church where his father was the priest, there didn't seem to be much else of note in Carrickfergus, apart from the imposing castle, once taken and held briefly by the French, I am told. I hurried on my way up the coast road.

Larne was a different matter. The town was bustling with a pleasant mixture of locals and holidaymakers, brought there by the ferries which serve the Scottish mainland just a few nautical miles away. I couldn't resist a look at the port where an illicit load of arms from the Kaiser was brought ashore in 1914 to feed the Protestant rebellion. We were led out from the town centre on sweeping new roads and interchanges to the port area. The high-speed ferry connections to the mainland are a great success, bringing day-trippers as well as other tourists to the Antrim coast and beyond. These vessels are modern, and look forward to the 21st Century, rather than backward to the early 20th, like my overnight ferry to Belfast. The port installations are modern too, designed for large-volume traffic, no doubt with an eye to the future development of this traditional route between

Ireland and the Scottish lowlands. Scotland was the homeland source of most of the current population of Northern Ireland, ever since the Plantations of the 1600s, when the Protestant Scots were brought in to occupy the lands evacuated by the evicted Irish residents.

Outside the port area, I spied a teas-and-hamburger caravan, and I rode up to within a few feet of the counter. I was the only customer. I enjoyed a hot cup of tea, taken in that unusual position associated with such establishments; my elbow resting at right angles on the high counter bar. The Tea-man was a well-built, well-fed 20-year-old. He recognised the obligation of a person in his isolated position to engage his customers – however modest – in conversation. It was a bit like being at the barber's. "Not bad weather for the time of year", always a sound opener, guaranteeing a response of some kind from the customer. "I see United are after signing up the Italian then" (a question designed to sound out the customer's own interests and affiliations, without revealing your own). When I made it clear that as an Arsenal supporter, I was blissfully ignorant of Manchester United's plans, he replied: "Well, Arsenal had quite a good season too, didn't they". (More complicated this one: the subtext is "I'm going to change the subject, because you're not one of us, but I just want to remind you that your lot only finished third in the League, and our boys finished top").

At this point we were joined with a nonchalant swagger by the driver of a huge corporation dustcart, which he parked on the roundabout a few feet away. "The full whack, Michael" was swiftly interpreted as a request for a full, cooked Irish breakfast. Bacon began to sizzle, bread began to brown, sausages gurgled and eggs metamorphosed into perfect half-apricots in opaque white circles. Michael was in his element.

The dustcart driver wanted to know about Ernest. How fast would she go? What was the fuel-consumption like? Was I planning on going far? I gave him satisfactory answers, interjected with approving remarks by Michael, as he practised his conversation skills. "Really! As much as that! That's really something". He was only going through the motions though. I don't think he had forgiven me for being an Arsenal supporter. I certainly hadn't forgiven him for being a Manchester

United fan. How can you pretend to support a team which is 300 miles away? That's not support, its just blind follow-my-leader. What's that dubious statistic? That 98% of all Manchester United supporters have never even been to their Old Trafford ground?

The dustcart was diesel, I was told. Fuel consumption and speed didn't come into the equation. Now that was odd, because Michael's Dad drove a diesel Peugeot, we were told. I left the dustcart driver to his breakfast, and Michael to his conversation skills, waving farewell as I rode off in what we fondly considered to be an impressive display of blistering power and jaw-dropping fuel consumption.

There is an album track by Van Morrison *"In the Days Before Rock 'n' Roll"* in which he sings of his days as a youth, spent along this coastline, and it came into my head as I rode along. And wasn't St. Patrick brought to Antrim as a boy-captive from the Scottish mainland, and made to work as a swineherd on the slopes of the hill known as Slemish, to the East of Larne? Or was he a shepherd? That was at the end of the 4th Century. He escaped, but driven by a vision, he returned to drive out the snakes and bring Christianity to Ireland.

You can't blame him for the modern troubles though. The responsibility for that must surely lie with whoever it was who had the crackpot idea of expropriating the lands of the Catholic Irish in Ulster, and bringing in Scottish and English Protestant "Planters" at the beginning of the 1600's. The acts of the incomers in consolidating their position have passed down the centuries, and flowered as the cultural differences, and violence and loathing in the Province today. Massacres of Catholics, like the one on the cliffs at The Gobbins in nearby Islandmagee in 1642, set the tone for a religious persecution which has continued ever since, in one way or another.

There are salmon cages in the bay at Glenarm. On the deserted quay, a fisherman was repairing one of the salmon cage nets. There isn't much of the traditional fishing industry thereabouts nowadays. I tried to visualise the map showing the short distance across the Irish Sea to the ocean dumping grounds used by the

Atomic Energy Authority for radioactive waste material – "All perfectly safe, of course". For years the AEA claimed it was only used for relatively harmless waste, like chemicals and explosives, which they couldn't deny because from time to time canisters are washed up on Scottish shores. They kept up their story and denied they ever did anything really wicked, and have only recently admitted the truth, that they had been dumping nuclear waste all along.

Incongruously, in the maritime setting of Glenarm harbour, there was a nearby hut for racing pigeons, a popular sport locally. I asked about the salmon cages. Was it true that such concentrations of salmon brought an infestation of sea-lice, which attached themselves to other fish? Is there any truth in the story accusing them of ruining the sea trout fisheries of the West Coast? I was told they had no sea-lice problem in Glenarm. The cages are some distance from the shore, located in an area of strong currents, which scour the fish and keep them clean. Disease was unknown in the cages here. They didn't even have to use chemicals like elsewhere. He had heard that the bosses had gone so far as to apply for "organic status" for their salmon here.

I had obviously met a loyal employee, so I changed the subject, and asked about the two churches I could see, one on each side of the river, one Catholic, one Protestant. The fisherman told me that there is a local saying: When the Devil is in Glenarm, he can't get out. When he is out, he can't get in. There is a church of some sort on every road in and out of the village, to keep the Devil at bay. And that's a lot of churches! He pointed out the Castle, the seat of the Earl of Antrim, and then he asked did I know anything about fossils? He could tell that I was an educated man. He showed me one he had in his pocket, a whorl-like shape resembling a flattened snail. He had found it higher up the coast where numbers of them are washed into the sea in a mix of clay. I said it was very pretty, but couldn't tell him any more. He looked at me with disappointment: I had let him down.

The village of Glenarm is very pretty too. It has a pretty village street, rising up to a pretty Castle. Set back from the High Street is a pretty bridge across the pretty river to what was the old main gate to the Castle, bearing the inscription: "With the leave of God, this Castle was built by Sir Randall MacDonnell, Knight, Earl of Antrim, having to his wife in the year of Our Lord 1636." The MacDonnells came here from Scotland, at the end of the 14th Century. John More MacDonnell of Kintyre, Lord of the Isles married Margery Bissett, daughter of an O'Neill, and ruler of the Glens of Antrim. Their descendants still live in Glenarm Castle. As I rode over the main bridge leaving the village, I passed a heavily laden touring cyclist coming in the other direction. I fancied he looked at me with an expression of desperation. Could it have been the Devil, trying to escape from the church-defended streets of Glenarm?

The Londonderry Arms in Carnlough is famous for once having belonged to Sir Winston Churchill, and there is a portrait of the old chap himself in the bar. The other pictures are devoted to a curious cult, the worship of a racehorse, Arkle.

For those of you to whom the name is only vaguely familiar, Arkle was the greatest steeplechaser of all time. He won the Cheltenham Gold Cup three years running. Not only that, he had personal charm. There grew up an enormous Arkle fan club, and people sent him presents on his birthday and at Christmas. He appeared on television and at opening ceremonies for garages and supermarkets. He was a real celebrity. He paraded at race meetings, and was always the main attraction. He had star quality, and he knew it. He acknowledged the cheers of the crowds, rather like a royal personage, with an inclination of the head, and - I fancy - a gracious smile. When he died in his 20s, a fine old age for a racehorse, he was mummified and stuffed, and still attracts a string of visitors, rather like Lenin in his mausoleum. The landlord at *The Londonderry Arms* was a fan, and gathered around him a group of fellow fans. They would meet regularly to talk about Arkle, and from time to time they arranged visits to his stables. The happy photographs in the bar record their activities.

All along this coast there is a series of glens or valleys which run down at right angles to the coast. The much-admired coast road itself was built as Relief Works during the mid-19th Century Famines, but before the road the only access in or out was by sea. The Glens of Antrim have a long and violent history, which is reflected in their names. Glenarm is Glen of the Army, and Glencorp means Glen of the Slaughter. Because there was no access by land, these Glen communities were very insular, looking more to their close by Scottish neighbours across the water than to their inland routes. My other grandmother was a Ramsay, from the Ayrshire seaport of Saltcoats. There was certainly a lot of traffic between the Scottish coast and the nearby Glens of Antrim, and I may be more closely related to these people than I realise.

Perhaps more than anywhere else in Ireland, here history goes hand in hand with legend and myth. Was it here that the giant Fionn MacCumhail scooped out a handful of earth and flung it into the Irish Sea, thus creating both the Isle of Man and Lough Neagh at a stroke, before moving on to create the Giant's Causeway? The grave of his poet son Oisín near Cushendall has recently been identified as a megalithic tomb and stone circle. Another curious fact is that the whole area has maintained a high level of Catholics in spite of their persecutions, in some areas as high as 90%. An important enclave this, a very long way from the border with the Catholic South.

CHAPTER 8
CUSHENDALL, NOT CUSHENDUN

...high up on the ancient tower at the crossroads...

Ernest was eating up the miles past the Glens, and in what seemed no time at all, I had reached Cushendall, where I had planned to spend the night. But I was very early, and it was only 2 in the afternoon. If I pressed on to Bushmills, I could gain a day on my schedule. I rode through the town, vaguely looking for the B & B which I had booked the day before. Before I knew it, I had passed through, and emerged on the other side of town. I decided to press on to Bushmills, so I phoned the Cushendall landlady, and guiltily invented a story about having been unavoidably delayed. Would it be ok if I cancelled my booking? She didn't seem to mind, so I made another call to prepare for an earlier arrival at Bushmills.

Petrol was low, and I checked the map for the next town. The map didn't make sense, so I just carried on anyway, down a wonderful but narrowing road, no houses, but long and straight across hilltops and swooping down the other side. No other traffic, just a young couple walking along in the middle of nowhere. (How did they get there?) When I came to an unexpected junction, not on the map, I realised I had clearly taken a wrong turning. I dismounted and worked out that I was somewhere up the Glen of Cushendale itself, and the petrol gauge was showing "Empty". My first Vespa had a reserve tank, but Ernest doesn't go in for such things, and I had no idea if "Empty" really meant empty or not. I made a mental note that I really should carry a spare bottle of petrol for such moments. According to the map, there was nothing much ahead of me, but the road I had joined went back to Cushendall, where I could at least get back on the right road.

I had other pressing matters on my mind, and looked around for a hedge where I might have a pee. Suddenly, the previously deserted junction became filled with vehicles. Cars whizzed by, a family saloon turned into the gateway where I had just selected to relieve myself, and I returned to the junction. Peeing on the nice man's garden was not acceptable. A tractor roared past, and I spotted an overgrown ruined house on the opposite corner of the junction. I waddled across with my bomb on my back and contemplated the thicket of branches which separated me from a suitable spot. The lane had recently been hedged, and the farmer had dumped all the trimmed branches on this triangle of ground. How long before the strolling couple would reach this spot? If I hurried, I would have time to pee, surely? I stepped forward onto the branch-strewn verge, and almost immediately disappeared into a hidden ditch. I was lying on my front, head facing downhill, a few inches from a stinging nettle patch. I was pinned down by the weight of the rucksack on my back, and I couldn't get up. Eventually, I wriggled onto my side and managed to struggle insecurely to my feet, chuckling foolishly.

There was no doubt in my mind that I was being punished for telling the landlady in Cushendall a fib. She was clearly protected by special powers who saw to it that transgressors were chastised according to the severity of their offence. I had been let off comparatively lightly, with no bones broken, and no sprained limbs. As if to apologize for their zeal in throwing me into a briar patch, the mystery powers magic-ed up a petrol station just around the next bend. I filled up Ernest's tank and resumed our journey; when I arrived back in Cushendall village, the powers pointed out the signpost I had missed previously, high up on the ancient tower at the crossroads. I continued on my way with little more than a mild slap on the wrist for telling a fib, and a reminder that in Ireland there are forces at work which we poor mortals can hardly begin to know about.

Mrs. Wilson didn't have a problem in accepting the story of her houseguest that his previously unavoidable delay had suddenly been overcome. Yes, she still had the room available. She was a thin woman, about 40, with wispy hair, and her eyes kept darting towards the clock. She was constantly on the move, picking things up and putting them down again, adjusting the position of an ornament, touching with her fingertips the walls and banisters as she passed. She seemed to have more important things to worry about than my on-off arrival, and she quickly showed me to my room with no questions. I noticed that she had a pronounced upper lip, which scarcely moved when she spoke. This gave the impression of her being unfriendly, but the tone of her voice was very warm and welcoming, and she smiled with her eyes.

It was a small terraced house – some would call it a cottage – built for estate workers at about the turn of the last century. But it was cosy inside, homely, with every modern convenience. I parked Ernest outside the front door, and unloaded my gear. Mrs Wilson re-appeared, looking more relaxed, and remembering her duties as a landlady. "You'll be wanting some tea" she told me, "just make yourself comfortable in there. I won't be but a minute." She indicated the front sitting room, and I was happy to settle into an armchair, and look around me. As in so many homes today, the television set dominated the room. All the chairs and sofas were turned towards the grey, blank screen with a vase of plastic flowers on top.

It was a room of knick-knacks. Cherished collected figurines of all shapes and sizes covered every available flat surface. They jostled for position with the clocks (why three clocks?) and they peeped from behind more dust-free artificial flowers. There was a small collection of family photos, weddings and christenings. Above the tiled fireplace, which housed a gas fire, hung an attractive river scene print. I peered at it trying to make out its origin, at least the artist, but I could find no clues. As well as the river landscape, on other walls there was a still life of a bowl of fruit, an idyllic country cottage with roses round the door and chickens in the yard, and a more serious-looking group of familiar figures.

A red-coated soldier wearing a three-cornered hat was peering at a written note offered by a woman in a long tartan shawl, holding a baby. Another soldier buried his face in her shoulder. He was wearing a kilt, and his right arm was in a sling. The family dog was standing on two legs, reaching up to greet him. I couldn't remember the name of the Victorian artist, but the scene represented a wounded Highland soldier returning home to his young family. The note was being shown as proof to the military official that he had been discharged, and the Army could not touch him. It was called something like "The Discharge Note", a fine sentimental picture, very popular in Victorian times.

Mrs. Wilson caught me studying the print. "Do you like Private Wilson then? It was a present from my in-laws, and I always liked it; not to everyone's taste, but I like it. I call it Private Wilson after my husband. His grandfather was in a Highland regiment, and I like to think it could have been him. Silly, but there you are. I didn't put the sugar in, in case you don't take it. Choose yourself." The cup and saucer shared a small tray with a sugar bowl, and there were some sugary biscuits besides. "I won't be long now – just got to pick up the kids from school. Make yourself comfortable. Shall I put the tele on?"

There are moments when there is nothing like a cup of tea, and this was such a moment. I relaxed back in Mrs. Wilson's armchair and sipped the strong workman's tea she had given me. No teabag infusion this. There were tealeaf fragments swirling in the cup, and the strong flavour was enough to tell me it had mashed well in a dark brown, rough china teapot. It was the sort of tea they served to National Servicemen in the NAAFI on their first night away from home. It was the tea they served in the air raid shelters during London's blitz. It evoked smoky taxi driver shelters, and factory canteens before they introduced individual packets of everything – sugar, butter, jam, and teabags.

I must have nodded off, because I woke suddenly to the sound of the front door being kicked in. My first thought was of a terrorist attack – I might even be taken for Mr. Wilson, probably a well-known Protestant activist. The door opened and three small faces peered in, and stared at the stranger in their front room, giggling. I was introduced to them in turn, two girls about seven and eight and a boy of about five or six. Mrs. Wilson bundled them away upstairs and told them to come down for their tea when they were changed out of their school things. They were lucky to have a good village school, she told me, but they would have to travel ten miles for a secondary school, when the time came. There used to be a school in the next town but it closed down after a fire, and has never been re-opened. "Dissidents" she said, a word which sounded out of place in that comfortable living room. "Do you mean Catholics?" I asked. "Oh no, there's enough factions on our side to make up differences, without need of outside help." She didn't offer any more explanation, and I didn't like to ask. I was going for a walk, I said, was there more to the village in the other direction?

There was a lot more to the village. On the other side of the crossroads extended a fine traditional village high street, dotted with shops and houses of all types. This was a high street that had grown over the years, no town planner had homogenised the jumble of buildings, but the natural pressures of commerce had squeezed the outline into an amorphous shape. It was lovely; old shop fronts of old-fashioned butchers and family grocers, even a proper hardware shop. Inevitably the fast food revolution had given rise to instant, uniformly plastic facades, proclaiming "take out" and "hamburgers" with the same enthusiasm as in the American Midwest towns that inspired their design. I would mooch about for a bit, have a drink, and find somewhere to eat an early supper, probably fish and chips. Big mistake.

There were several pubs, but in choosing the most rustic-looking, the Antrim Arms, I made a bad mistake. The barman was obviously a grump, suspicious of jolly-faced strangers who rolled into his bar in the early evening. The bitter was off, and the Guinness was playing up. He grudgingly opened a bottle of Guinness for me with a tacit disapproval he made no attempt to conceal.

There was one other customer, who could have been a retired farm worker. He was perched on his stool at the bar with a sour expression, rivalling the barman's temperament. "Don't tell me" he addressed to the bar grump, "I've never liked it". He supped his pint. It must have been the last pint of bitter drawn before it went "off". "But what can you do about it? - Nothing!" replied the barman. "We're not responsible, they are." "That's true enough", his customer paused, "But I don't have to like it though, now do I?" I couldn't work out what they were talking about, but I got the message that they didn't like it much. "I don't even want to carry on with this when they bring it in, and that's a fact" continued the barman after a long pause. "What d'you mean then - retire?" "Well you tell me - instead of charging £1.50 for that pint there, it'll be 100 euros, or summat. Would you lay out 100 euros for a pint? It's a fortune." "Not as bad as lira, mind. Buy a drink in Italy and it's so many thousand lira they'll be asking you for. Outrageous, I call it, downright outrageous, and you never know if they're takin' you for a mug or not." They both paused here while they contemplated the outrageousness of the concept of a common European currency for a moment, and I grasped the opportunity to drink up and leave. "Have a good evening, sir!" said Grumpy brightly as I reached the door. I think he was being ironic.

The fish and chip shop was promising. There were three formica tables with spindly, chrome-legged chairs alongside the counter, and there was an expectant buzz as queuing customers waited for their orders to be freshly fried. I could imagine the fishermen from the village saving a box of the best of their catch for their local chippy, and I agonized over a choice between super-fresh cod or succulent haddock. Cod had to be the most popular choice, so I went for that. Bread and butter, yes, pickled onion, yes, pickled egg, no thank you. By the time my plate arrived at my table, I was full of anticipation. How would this compare with my local fish and chip shop? Was the fish more fresh? crisper chips? and what about the batter? It is no exaggeration to say that although the pickled onion was a bit soft, it was easily the best thing on my plate. The fish was grey and pappy, tasteless. The chips were soggy, the bread was limp and factory-sliced. I finished my meal in great disappointment, glancing occasionally at the eager faces in the queue at the counter. Perhaps I should have had the haddock?

I strolled around the town a little more, and then decided to head back to my digs, and read my book before an early night. I soon realised I was lost. The streets at the crossroads looked completely different now, and I wandered around skulking, and looking very suspicious. Somehow I had turned around and lost my sense of the way north. I recognized none of the buildings, and the streets all looked the same. Fortunately, I spotted Ernest parked outside a familiar house in a side street.

Mrs. Wilson opened the door, and invited me to sit with the children in the television room. "Have you eaten?" she asked. There was still no sign of Mr. Wilson. I told her about the fish and chip shop, and she said she didn't go there. If I had said, she would have been happy to cook something. She had to give the kids their tea, and one more wouldn't have made any difference. Remembering the grey cod, I thought a plate of spaghetti hoops on toast sounded quite a good idea, but I said I was fine, thanks. The quiz show on television came to a sudden, triumphant end, and as if prompted, the three children got up without a sound, said a very polite good night to me and went upstairs to bed. "I have to tell them a story in a minute" said Mrs. Wilson, turning off the tv set. "And then I'll make you a cup of tea?"

There was an unusual air of calm about this house, considering it was home to three young children, and I kept wondering about Mr. Wilson. Was he a shift worker? or working away from home? perhaps in prison? - or had he abandoned his family for a scarlet woman? As if on cue, the front door opened, and Mr. Wilson came in. At first I thought he was a security guard in his strange uniform, but then I realised that Mr. Wilson was a member of the Royal Ulster Constabulary. He was very unconcerned to find a stranger in his front room, and introduced himself with a warm handshake. He wasn't as tall as most policemen, and he was very friendly, asking me questions about Ernest, and where I had been, and where I was going to. Was the family upstairs? Then he disappeared to the kitchen to "have his tea and a scrub up."

I had a brief internal struggle with myself. This was a golden opportunity to find out what made a RUC man tick, but he was my host, and there were certain rules to be observed. I decided to wing it, and not press the questioning if I met with resistance from the Wilsons. I heard Mrs. Wilson come downstairs and go to the kitchen. She re-appeared shortly after with a pot of tea for the three of us.

When Mr. Wilson joined us, he had changed into normal clothes. "Hard day?" I asked. "About average. Not every day's like the ones you see on the tele" he joked. "How long have you been in the force" I said, trying not to make it sound like Star Wars. "A good few years now - I'll be taking early retirement in two years. Then I'll be off. All sorts of opportunities in security these days, and enough is enough." Mrs. Wilson agreed, nodding solemnly as she sipped her tea. "He's done his bit" she said. I decided to go for it: "What made you take it up in the first place? Was it in the family?" Mr. Wilson became very interested in his tea suddenly, and I thought I'd blown it, but then I realised he was only thinking.

"It was a long time ago, and it was, well, easy to join up. I knew I wanted to do my bit for the community; I wanted to do a good job, and this one sounded exciting. It's been that all right. But now I'm mainly in the office, and that's all right too, because I'm looking after the younger men, my colleagues out there on the streets. I'll have no regrets when I hang up my hat though." I've always had a healthy mistrust of policemen, especially of what motivates them, but I couldn't see any chinks in Mr. Wilson's argument. Was he then truly concerned only with making a contribution to this rural community? For all I knew he might have taken as many liberties against Catholics as any of his colleagues. I wasn't going to find out either way over a cup of tea in his front room.

Mrs. Wilson asked me if I'd had a chance to look around the village? I gave them both a run down of the bars and the chippie I'd visited. At the mention of the Antrim Arms, Mr. Wilson chortled over his tea. He clearly knew Mr. Grumpy and could imagine the scene. "It's better a bit later on" was all he said, enjoying the thought. I looked at the clock and knocked back the remains of my tea. Tomorrow was a busy day, and I would take an early night. There was a brief discussion about the all-important subject of breakfast, and I took my leave. The television clicked on as I left the room.

I left at a decent hour with Mrs. Wilson's continental breakfast inside me. She was unhappy about me not having a fried breakfast, and didn't think a bowl of cereal was enough for a "grown man". But she waved and smiled as she showed me which road to take out of the village. There was no sign of Mr. Wilson, or the kids.

CHAPTER 9
CUSHENDUN, NOT CUSHENDALL, AND ROUND THE TOP

"I will not be a-riding across that thing!"

The village of Cushendun (-dun not -dall) has the distinction of belonging to the National Trust. Unfortunately, when I arrived the village was being rebuilt. I was keen to visit the pub owned by the National Trust, called Mary MacBride's, but its windows blanked out with white paint announced the fact that it was being "renovated" from top to bottom. I studied with narrowed eyes the idle workers from the window of the National Trust Tea Rooms across the road.

Ernest was admired by a much-tattooed biker in fading black leathers, and we got into conversation about bikes. His current machine was "waiting for parts". This is an expression which I have learnt to interpret as "waiting until I can afford the parts", and such seemed the case here. He was the proud owner of a superbike, a hybrid between a Triumph and a Norton. The normal arrangement is to put a Triumph engine in a Norton Featherbed frame, and the result is known as a "Triton", he explained for my benefit. He confessed he was a compulsive tweaker, always looking for the last ounce of power from what was, after all, an engine originally designed for more sedate days. He had over-cooked it, and the engine had blown up, stripping the timing chain cog, wrecking the gearbox and driving bits of engine out of the side of the metal casting. A major re-build was the only answer, and it would have to wait until he could afford it. Would I like to see it? I made my excuses and said I was expected elsewhere. I suppose it didn't occur to him that I might not be interested in looking at a pile of wrecked engine parts.

The euphoria I had felt flying along the narrow country lane, when I took the wrong turning in Cushendale, returned when I left the main road to drive by a winding hilly lane out towards Torr Head. The tight bends and steep slopes tested Ernest to his limits, and with no other traffic around, we enjoyed a spell of wild riding in low gears with a screaming engine. The wind was off the sea, and as we twisted around it was alternately in my face or at my back. After a few days in the saddle, and a long spell of riding, I felt I was recovering the feeling of oneness with the machine that I had when I rode more regularly, and this was the ideal road to put it to the test.

The feeling of riding on two wheels, powered by a motor, is very different from driving a car – except perhaps a single-seater racing car. A rider leans into a bend, often turning without need to move the handlebars. He sits upright to create air resistance for better breaking when approaching a bend, and will hunch down over the handlebars to create a more aerodynamic shape for cutting through the wind on a straight. Experienced riders will sometime use only the rear break to drift a bike slightly sideways in a manoeuvre.

When I left the right angle of Torr Head behind me, with the shoreline of Scotland clearly visible in the distance across the water, the road speeded up. That is to say, the curves were more gentle, and the rises and falls were hummocks which we flew over, going up on the suspension at the top, and bottoming in the dips. The wind was behind me, and I fancy it must have taken my broad shape and flat rucksack to be some kind of a sail. I felt like a windsurfer, impelled forward by this friendly wind, and when I looked at the speedo, I was surprised to see that I was doing 60 miles an hour! This was a silly speed for a road where sight of oncoming traffic was limited. But fortunately, there wasn't any traffic. Just a series of clippy little bends asking you to use the whole roadway, and steer by leaning your body weight, as you flicked through the curves.

I rejoined the main road just south of Ballycastle. This is an area of serious history. From here a ferry runs out to Rathlin Island, where King Robert the Bruce is said to have sulked in a cave licking his battle wounds, only to be inspired not to give up by the example of the existing spider tenant. He returned to defeat the English in the Battle of Bannockburn. But the victory was all a waste of time, because thereafter things went from bad to worse, and in no time at all there was the Act of Union, which condemned all Scotsmen to go through life correcting people when they were described as "English" instead of British. And they don't themselves say "British" in reply; they say "Scottish". But they produce good fiddle players, and they ran the British Empire for Queen Victoria, and every good English football team has at least one Scots player, so perhaps Robert and the spider were right.

One of Ireland's great mythical sagas was acted out at nearby Fair Head. This is the Irish version of the Tristan and Isolde story, which exists in so many other cultures too, and tells of the return of Deidre of the Sorrows, the revenge of King Conchobor against Naisu and his brothers, and of Deidre's defiant suicide by dashing her head against a stone to cheat Conchobar of the fate worse-than-death he planned for her. Death before dishonour! All these characters have many different spellings, according to which telling of the story you are reading or hearing, but the spelling doesn't seem to worry the Irish much.

The late 20th Century has put its heavy stamp on the area of Ballycastle, and created the Ballycastle Experience. My impression was that the entire surrounding countryside has been turned into golf-courses, and all the inhabitants – locals and visitors alike – are obliged to dress up like mannequins in the golf department of Lillywhite's. You don't even have to play golf to do this. I saw normal passers-by, taking the afternoon air in a teatime stroll, looking as if they had just come off the 18th green - well perhaps they had. I didn't stop in Ballycastle to muse about Robert the Bruce, or Deidre of the Sorrows, or to catch up on what the well-dressed golfer is wearing.

I knew that Carrick-a-Rede Bridge was not far, and I wanted to recce the bridge for a possible midnight drive across it, in the style of the Hell's Angels I had heard about. I was worried about the weight. If the Angels could do it with a Harley Davidson, I should surely be all right with Ernest, but I would leave off my rucksack and top box, just to make sure. I might even do it without a helmet, because if things did go wrong, and I was dashed on the rocks hundreds of feet below, a helmet wouldn't make much difference. I have never really taken to a crash helmet. I didn't use one before it became compulsory by law, and I was half hoping to discover that the law was different in Ireland, but of course it isn't. So I toe the line, and accept feeling claustrophobic and hearing-impaired whenever I put on my helmet. I hope I never need its protection.

I didn't want to miss the turning for the Carrick-a-Rede Bridge, so I pulled off the road and got out my large-scale map. I carelessly left the lid of the top box open, and the wind began to rustle the inner plastic bag. I was absorbed in sorting out the footpaths from the tarmac roads on my map, and didn't notice the arrival of another motorcyclist until he pulled up alongside with a whooshing sound. This was a serious biker, in full leathers and blacked out helmet visor. He lowered his huge, expensive Japanese machine onto its side-stand and removed his expensive helmet.

I began to feel uneasy. Had I done something wrong? Had he been following me? "You all right, mate?" he asked, ruffling his hair in the way of all bikers released from their helmets. "Broken down, or what?" He was about 30, short, fair, spiky hair, and I couldn't catch his accent. "No, no, thanks mate. I'm fine - just checking the map" I answered, waving the map limply. In stopping, he was fulfilling the two-wheeled brotherhood of the road. When you see a fellow biker in trouble, you stop and help. "Where you going then? Where you from?" He had heard of London, but he hadn't heard of Carrick-a-Rede.

He was from near Edinburgh, touring, headed for Derry to see some mates. He was in no hurry to carry on his way, and I wasn't going to be rude enough to leave first after he'd stopped to help. "Never had one of these" he continued, almost regretfully, indicating Ernest with a neatly black-booted foot. "What'll it do?" The answer of 65 miles an hour in good conditions did not impress him enough to make his eyebrows lift. About 100 miles to the gallon was better received, but then it would impress a man on a machine capable of doing speeds of at least twice the legal limit, and guzzling petrol at the same rate as a family saloon car. "My old Dad had one once, before my day of course. He still gets nostalgic when he sees one go by. He keeps saying he's going to get an old one and do it up. I wish he would! So you're all right then, mate?" he asked again, remembering the two-wheel code, as he picked up his helmet. With a multi-cylinder roar, he disappeared from sight even before I had folded up my map.

I found the track to the National Trust car park, and had an enjoyable chat with the cheery lady volunteer who tried to sell me NT membership. It was a long walk out along the coastal cliff-path to the Carrick-a-Rede Bridge, no motor vehicles allowed, and I felt it was safe to entrust my orange and green bag and helmet to the nice lady, and she agreed to look after it for me. "How far is it?" "Just a quarter of a mile or so", and off I set.

The walk along the cliff was bracing. The weather was fine, and the views breathtaking. Among the several fellow walkers, I came upon a Japanese couple. They were taking video shots of each other with alarming energy, dashing up the side of the hill, hanging over the handrail, doubling back for the reverse angle. I walked through their shot, but they hardly seemed to notice me. Eventually, I reached the steep path leading down to the Bridge. I was consciously recce-ing the path from the point of view of returning clandestinely on Ernest at dead of night. This looked the least passable section so far, very steep with rough-hewn rocky steps.

Halfway down, an elderly lady had stopped for breath, on her way back up. She greeted me in a Lancashire accent, full of the joys of life. "Not far to go now, lad!" It was nice to be called "lad" again. The Bridge came into sight. The bright sunlight and the blue sea far below picked out its spindly structure, acid-sharp. It looked like one of those rope bridges in a Tarzan movie, spanning an impossible chasm, usually with one rope half worn through. And as another strand snaps!

In fact, the ropes of the Carrick-a-Rede Bridge are made of steel, and it is a very firm structure indeed. Access to the landside end is down a near vertical wooden ladder, and at the other end it leads onto the top of a steep-sided pillar of rock, used by fishermen who have a permanent salmon trap there. There was no way you could get a motorbike down to the level of the bridge without a crane, so the Hell's Angels myth bit the dust. I was secretly relieved I wouldn't have to attempt a crossing by starlight after all. Defying the vertigo, I gritted my teeth, jutted out my jaw, took a breath, and struggled across on foot. An idle youth was draped nonchalantly across a rock on the far side.

He watched unmoved as I crabbed cautiously across, clutching the cables, and then went back to his paperback. He blended in with the setting too well to be a visitor, and I asked him if he was a fisherman. "You could say that" he replied. "Do you work the salmon nets then?" I wasn't giving up easily. "That's right." "And what's the fishing like?" I added brightly. "Bloody awful", and sensing an unavoidable conversation imminent, he carefully marked the corner of his page and put his book aside.

"It's not really worth doing it any more, but my Dad's got the license, and doesn't want to give it up. It's gone to pot. It's the salmon farms - must be! We used to get a fair living here, must have been 10 of us about ten years ago, before they put the cages up in the bay. Now there's barely a living for just my Dad." "I've heard there were problems," I ventured, "what's the cause?" "I dunno. Some say disease, some say it's the chemicals to treat the disease. Fact is, before the farms we had stacks of fish, and now there's hardly any. I'm just helping my Dad out while I finish my exams, then I'll be off.

Have you been to America? I've got a mate says there's no trouble getting bar work, things like that, no problemo over green cards, that kind of thing." I agreed with him that I'd heard that too, especially on the East Coast. Where was he thinking of? "Well, I wanna see it all, don't I. But I'll start in New York, then Boston, then see what turns up on my way to the West. I'm in no hurry."

I wanted to know why he was thinking of emigrating, when there were so many opportunities in the modern Ireland. But he wasn't emigrating, he answered quickly: he was travelling. He clearly associated the word "emigrating" with something unpleasant that had happened to older generations. His instincts were no different from any other young man who wanted to see something of the world before settling down to a more regulated lifestyle. "I'll be away about a year, and then come back and take up my college place – that's in Computers. No problemo with getting a place on the course I wanted, and I might even manage to save a few dollars to come back with. And they all queue up to give you a job straight off the course. I can pick and choose."

He told me that officially he was there sitting on his rock to help anyone who might get into difficulties when crossing. People panic on the bridge and freeze, petrified. He was there to give them a helping hand and return them to the mainland. I wished him good luck and walked back over the bridge, trying nonchalantly not to look as if I might panic any second. I even stopped halfway and pretended to look down to the waves crashing on the rocks far below, but I've never been good at heights. I was secretly very pleased to regain the terra firma on the other side.

The Japanese couple had left the path and they were now photographing one another standing on the very edge of the cliff. They passed each other their own cameras for even more risky pictures. I decided I would like to be back on the other side and gone, before they progressed to hanging upside down from the Bridge. The friendly volunteer lady was still in the car park looking after my luggage, and she fully understood that I would like to think it over before deciding to join the National Trust. "That was a long quarter of a mile," I said. "Didn't I say it was a quarter of an Irish mile?" she smiled. It was late, but I still had enough daylight to call in at The Giant's Causeway Centre on the way.

The car park attendant looked at me hard. "Is that a motorbike?" he asked. "Not really; it's a scooter" I offered. "Only if it's a motorbike, we charge a pound, but I don't think we charge anything for scooters. Park where you like." A very Irish remark. In the Causeway Centre, I was told the lower cliff path was closed, impassable and dangerous, but I could still go out by the cliff path, and look down on Lacada Point if I wanted. It was late, and I suddenly felt tired. I wanted a hot bath and a slap-up supper. I would come back in the morning. At least I didn't have to ride Ernest over the Bridge at midnight.

CHAPTER 10
BUSHMILLS

The Bushmills distillery – not to be missed.

Bushmills is a serious little town. I was once more pleased to see a war memorial in the centre of the crossroads, dating from the First World War. A fine figure of an Irish Tommy in full kit stands above a column on which is inscribed the names of all the local dead. Another smaller group of names remembers the casualties of the Second World War. It's the same story on all war memorials: the fallen of the Second World War are tiny in number, compared to the losses of the First World War. A local survivor of the Ulster Division who was awarded the Victoria Cross on the first day of the battle of the Somme 1916 is commemorated separately. He lived out his days nearby, and died in 1955 after nearly 40 years of nightmares.

On one side of the crossroads now sat the old men of the town, discussing the day's events, and how things are not as they used to be. On the other side sat representatives of the town's youthful unemployed, idling with their bicycles and discussing the scores from the American Football games on television. The space between the two groups is known as the generation gap; the Irish Tommy memorial held the centre ground. I pop-popped past on Ernest, taking in the scenery and looking vaguely for my B & B, attracting feigned disinterest from the youth, and curiosity from the old men.

I was now used to seeing the local police stations fortified against terrorist attacks, but in Bushmills, another fortress concealed the BT telephone substation. I wondered if this was usual, or special to this town for some reason. Perhaps it is one of those special communications centres.

Finding one's digs is an important part of the touring game. By the time I had paraded my orange and green luggage past the war memorial for the third time, even the idle youth representatives were beginning to take notice, so I stopped next to a farmer with his head under the bonnet of a car to ask the way. "It used to be called the Auberge until last year" I offered when my enquiry was met with a blank look. Light dawned. "I have it! Weren't they French or foreign or something?" He gave me directions which ended with "and then keep going. Youse can't miss it." I have learnt to mistrust this last phrase. "How far is it?" "Oh, a good mile or so" he said in a reassuring tone, taking pity on someone who worried how far away places are. I also knew that "a mile" in these parts means at least two, and that "a good mile" means more like four. For "or so" you can add at least an additional mile – so, a total of five miles then!

Killen's was a pleasant surprise. I just kept going like the farmer had said, and after exactly five miles, an isolated sign appeared at the side of the country lane. As "The Auberge" it was built up into a successful business by a French couple, and had then been sold on to a young couple starting their first business together. He does the cooking, and is Scottish, she is from Derry. The establishment is a very continental model of a good restaurant combined with half-a-dozen comfortable rooms. The bath water was hot and the food and wine were excellent. The remote situation is not a drawback for clients looking for what is on offer, and cars began rolling up as dinnertime approached.

Youthful, attractive Mrs. Killen apologised for the Troubles, which she said in her view, were only caused by a few hotheads. Events were always exaggerated out of all proportion by the press and the television. She had grown up in Derry, which together with Belfast is considered the centre of most of the disturbances. She was very chatty: she had been to London to visit her sister, who had been working there as a teacher at the time. In two or three years the sister had worked her way up to Assistant Head of Year in a busy London Comprehensive. With an impressive c.v. she easily got a job in a school back home, while her fellow graduates who had stayed put were still unemployed and looking for their first job in an overcrowded profession.

Mrs. Killen was pleased to exchange the sometimes violent atmosphere of Derry for the more peaceful surroundings of County Antrim, but she admitted that the Derry people were more liberal and more fun loving. Antrim folk are more strait-laced, and serious.

I was still trying to guess which camp she was in, although she gave the impression of being apolitical. "Is it true" I asked "that in Derry the Catholic population is very high, did I see a statistic of 87% somewhere?" "Sure now we're never just so few as that!" she said, answering my unspoken question at the same time. Mr. Killen was a good cook. He had learned his profession thoroughly, from the bottom up, working in international kitchens in Ireland and on the mainland. He met his wife while working in Derry. As a Scotsman he was a foreigner, and his situation and beliefs were considered irrelevant to the local situation.

On the BBC Radio news in the morning, I heard that the RUC policeman, Gregory Taylor, had been killed in very disturbing circumstances.

He had been drinking in the early hours of the morning in a bar in the village where he lived and worked. There was a discussion about the government's proposals to restrict the annual Orange marches throughout Northern Ireland. Feelings ran high, and he found himself in a minority in a group of fellow villagers, good Protestants all. When he realised the situation was getting out of hand, he left the bar, but he was followed into the street by a group of eight or ten drinkers. They caught up with him and gave him a beating. They kicked him to death in the street, and left him there.

Such brutish violence is hard to take in from a riot-torn Third World hot spot, but when it happens in a village in the Northern Irish countryside, it is something else. These men were respectable, god-fearing fathers and sons, like anyone else. The newsreader gave the name of the village as Ballymoney in County Antrim. When I looked at the local map I discovered it was only about eight miles away; while I was tucked up in a warm bed, foul murder was being committed.

Chapter 11
The Wreck of the Girona

To the left of the writer can be seen the finger of rock against which the Girona is said to have foundered.

After a stormy night, the next morning was unpromising. When the rain showed signs of slackening, I pulled on all my wet-weather gear and set off for the Giant's Causeway. The wind was gusty, and seemed to blow the rain away, but it made for very uncomfortable riding. Sr. D'Ascanio's Vespas were not really designed for strong winds, and the low centre of gravity means there is a pronounced tendency to wobble.

At the Causeway Centre, there was a warning sign that because of the strong winds it was dangerous for visitors to take the cliff path. I hadn't come almost 400 miles to be put off by a little wind, so I tightened my anorak, pulled up the hood, and set off on the long walk to Lacada Point, the site of the wreck of the *Girona*. In good weather, this must be a very popular walk along the cliffs to Dunseverick Castle, and the footpath was very eroded by the passage of thousands of feet, no doubt wearing sensible, stout walking boots.

The National Trust was giving the usual path a rest: it was fenced off, and they were directing walkers to a new path closer to the cliff edge.

This didn't do much good to my vertigo, and as the grass grew more slippery, and the winds began to blow offshore, driving me ever closer to the edge of the cliff, I began to have second thoughts about the wisdom of undertaking this risky walk. I was quite alone on the cliff-top. I realised that other, more sensible (and probably better equipped) walkers had read the warning notice, and decided to have a cup of tea until the storm moved through. They were no doubt even now trying to decide whether or not to have a second slice of toast. "Well, I will if there's some blackcurrant jam. I didn't care for the raspberry." Meanwhile, I struggled on against the elements, slipping on the wet grass, and keeping as far away from the edge as I could.

I rounded a headland and saw Lacada Point in the distance; I was probably the only person mad enough to be outside on a day like this! I gradually made out the shape of a small tractor in a field by the cliff-top, and then the figures of two workmen. They were improving the footpath, and as I drew level I realised they were erecting a handrail on a particularly slippery slope overlooking Lacada Point. With obvious disregard for their own safety, they were working on the outside edge of the cliff path itself. I exchanged a greeting and hurried on. I didn't want to be around when one of them was blown over the edge to the rocks below – as seemed inevitable and imminent! When I reached a point where a photograph was possible, the wind was at its strongest. I dropped down to my hands and knees, to take shelter from the typhoon-force winds, which were plucking at my clothing, anxious to hurl me into the sea to join the ghosts of the Spanish sailors.

I recovered my breath, and some of my composure, and took stock of the scene. Lacada Point stretches out from the headland like a finger. The overloaded and weakened *Girona* had been travelling from West to East, in an attempt to get back to the more friendly shores of Scotland. This was a galleass, a sailing ship with additional power provided by oars manned by up to 300 galley slaves, designed to give greater manoeuvrability in the close combat anticipated between the two great fleets in the English Channel. The normal contingent of 120 sailors and 169 soldiers was swelled by the crews of the two other wrecked ships who had squeezed aboard. The storm would have been driving them from the Northwest. They were closer to the shore than they thought, and they must have been looking up fearfully at the towering cliffs and headlands before them. If visibility were good enough, they would have seen the shape of Rathlin Island 7 miles to the East. Some 20 miles beyond that lay the coast of Scotland, but they were damned by the long, curling finger of Lacada Point, which hooked in the *Gerona* and dashed it against the rocks.

Within only a few feet of the shore 1300 souls were drowned; only 9 reached the shore. Evidence of their fate lay on the sea bed long after the fabric of the ship was dissolved away by the waves, but it was not until 1967 that the remains were found by the Belgian nautical archaeologist, Robert Sténuit. The very remoteness of the site had prevented earlier discovery by the looters.

In lousy weather, I took photographs of the site, and quickly withdrew. I could hardly hold the camera still in the fierce wind, and my glasses needed windscreen wipers. By most standards, I knew they would be lousy photographs, but at least they were <u>my</u> photographs. I held onto a clump of grass as I leaned forward and clicked the shutter.

"Did youse get a good view of the Point" the workmen wanted to know, still oblivious to the fact that in a matter of seconds they might be blown onto the rocks below. "If youse had gone a bit further round, there's a fine view from there all right." "Good enough! The pictures I got are good enough" I called into the wind in their general direction. I grew in confidence as I made my way back.

A bunch of big black Irish choughs were hanging in the wind on the edge of the cliff. They were performing aerobatics, turning complete somersaults in a Victory roll, like Second World War Spitfire pilots. This must be the closest choughs get to having chough fun. There was no other logical explanation for the behaviour of these birds.

In the distance I saw other walkers venturing out on the cliff-top towards me. Leaning forward into the wind, I noticed for the first time the hosts of tiny flowers at the side of the path. White and yellow star-shaped dots vibrated in the wind. Heathers of different shades. I wish I knew more about the names of flowers. I passed a young couple, with the man waiting patiently while his companion crouched low down, the macro end of her camera lens fully extended as she poised only inches above a cluster of the tiny star-shaped scrubland flowers. motionless, and deep in concentration. There were cliff-top flowers like miniature cowslips, and scaled-down lilac poker-shaped foxgloves. And there were bright yellow gorse with gnarled, bare roots exposed above ground.

Another couple had left the path, and they were standing perilously close to the edge of the cliff, holding each other in a close embrace, as if they were planning to leap off in a suicide pact. A middle-aged couple strode resolutely past, clearly determined to reach the end of the walk at Dunseverick Castle before anyone else that day. They were dressed in the walkers' uniform of matching Rohan jacket and trousers, and Brasher boots. I was prepared to bet their sensible knapsacks held a packed lunch, a warm drink, and a small medical kit in case of accidents.

Chapter 12
A noggin in Bushmills

I parked Ernest with his black top-box explosive device opposite the fortified British Telecom substation in Bushmills, and decided to test the reaction of the three-star Bushmills Inn to a scooterist in brightly coloured wet-weather anorak and over-trousers. This old inn is being renovated. The interiors look authentic, but are far too clean. The floors are carpeted. There is an enormous, cavernous restaurant, as if they were expecting any minute the arrival of a wagonload or two of hungry American tourists (and they probably were). I was greeted warmly by a uniformed work-experience trainee, who could only have been 14 years of age. I was informed that I might have a bar snack in the bar or a meal in the restaurant, if I preferred. A smoked salmon sandwich and a glass of Guinness suited me just fine.

This was obviously the pre-dinner drinks bar for the well-heeled restaurant customers, but where did the locals drink? The front part of the building was in the hands of the decorators, so the answer was probably that the locals drank in the next bar down the road until they could have their bar back. Still, I enjoyed my light lunch in the posh bar, read my *Guardian*, and enjoyed a well-presented glass of Guinness. After another couple of circuits of the war memorial, I went home, to change before setting off for a tour of the Bushmills Whiskey Manufactory.

Whisky consumption is a subject I know something about, and during my periods of informal painstaking research in the Highlands and Islands of Scotland, I have pieced together more than a little knowledge about how the miracle of turning water into the water of life takes place. Bushmills is the world's oldest whiskey distillery still in production. Confusingly, although the date 1608 appears everywhere as the year in which the distillery was founded, I discovered this refers to the origins of production in the region. There has been a whiskey distillery on the site of the present building only since 1784, which takes us back to a time before the French Revolution.

I should perhaps explain here that whisky without an "e" is the spelling which can only be applied to whisky made in Scotland. American and Irish whiskey must have the "e" to show they're different, but there is also a Spanish whiskey which spells itself without an "e", and a Welsh whiskey which is made from Scotch whisky, so heaven knows how that is spelt. It is probably safe to say that if you are worried about how to spell Japanese or Chilean whiskey, you will probably not offend anyone if you give them an "e" just to make sure.

To complicate matters further, the Irish are very pleased with their "e", simply because it helps to distinguish their product – superior in their opinion – from the product across the water. What's more, the Bushmills distillery in Northern Ireland belongs to Irish Distillers, the Jameson group from Southern Ireland, which in turn belongs to Ricard, the French pastis group. In a situation as complex as this, I hope it becomes clear that my initial motives for a visit to the Bushmills distillery arose from a genuine desire for a knowledge which can only be obtained from dedicated first-hand research.

They are very well organised up at the world's oldest working distillery. There is a team of uniformed hostesses who conduct visitors around the plant for a small fee, explaining the miracle of the water of life as they go. A very mixed bag of tourists was assembled. I suppose elderly American couples were in the majority, and I was worried about some of the more frail ones making it all the way round. There were a few feckless youngsters too, and even some genuine foreigners. One oriental-looking couple was probably a team of Koreans bent on industrial espionage, I concluded. They couldn't fool me! Nobody goes to look around a factory unless there's something in it for them. Most of us settle for the reward of some free samples at the end of the trip.

Our guide, whose name was probably Margaret, was at pains to explain that she was also prepared to answer questions, should there be any. By her manner, she made it clear that she didn't expect anyone to be so presumptuous as to ask any questions.

The first thing she explained was that the distillery works a four-day week. This being Friday afternoon we would see no workers in the plant, which contributed an eerie emptiness to the scene which met us as we moved from room to room. The product of the Bushmills distillery is proud to be northern. I was therefore surprised to discover that the barley from which the malt mash is made is brought up from the South. Even more surprising was the discovery that the grain spirit with which the malt whisky was blended in a ratio of 70% grain to 30% Bushmills malt, also comes up from the Jameson distillery in the South. So what is considered in some exotic circles to be the best known product of Northern Ireland is actually largely Southern. This is an excellent example of cross-border trading between members of the EU community.

However, to continue, as I was saying, basic Bushmills (orange label) is matured longer than basic Scotch, and once-used American bourbon whiskey wooden barrels are used for the purpose. Black Bushmills (black label) is probably the world's finest affordable whiskey, and is matured for longer, after being transferred into old sherry barrels. In recent years, the distillery has begun marketing a 10-year old pure single malt product with no blended grain spirit content. There is also a small production of 12-year old single malt, and an even more special 16-year old brew, which goes through three barrels in its maturing process, ending up feeling rather smug and superior in the depths of an old port barrel.

Anyway, I think that's what Margaret said. To be honest, I was by now feeling figure fatigue. When we were led into one of the storage warehouses we were advised to take a deep breath. It was worth it. I asked if there was somewhere I could sit down, because I really felt quite happy close to so many hard-working barrels. I sensed I could even hear the miracle taking place. Margaret said that no I couldn't sit down just yet, and in answer to my next question she said there was long waiting list for jobs in the warehouse. She explained that what we could smell was known as the "Angels' Share" (I may have got the apostrophe wrong here; I really don't know how many angels are involved.) This is the term they apply to the 2% of the whiskey which is lost annually through "evaporation".

I asked if we might be allowed a little "evaporation" ourselves, and Margaret patiently explained that we would first have to visit the bottling and labelling plant, after which we would be invited to take part in a tasting session, provided we could behave ourselves. I think she may have been a little cross because she was hoping to keep the final stage of the tour as a surprise, delivering us into the bar as a dramatic *coup de théatre*. Old hands of such tours around breweries, wineries and such knew that we could rely on some "hospitality", included in the price of our ticket, otherwise there wasn't much point in going.

We dutifully grouped around Margaret finally in the hospitality and rest room area, while she told us what she had in store for us. She wanted three volunteers to take part in an experiment. Hearing the word "volunteer" we all instinctively took a step backwards, but eventually, three of us willing souls were encouraged to take part in a tasting session of different types of whiskies or whiskeys.

They were urged to compare Kitchen Scotch with samples of American Bourbon, Southern Irish Whiskey Ordinaire, and their Bushmills Orange Label. Under the watchful eyes of the others, the volunteers agreed that Bushmills was definitely the Best. Next, de luxe Scotch and something else (I can't remember what) were compared with Black Bushmills. No surprise here when Black Bush won hands down – well I think it was down. So finally the Single Malt Bushmills was compared with a Highland Malt, and there may have been a third one, but the details are a bit hazy.

At this point, there was a clear division of opinions. The American taster held out for the third one, thinking it was a bourbon, the German insisted none of them was as good as a good schnapps, and I said the only way to be completely sure was to start again at the beginning. I thought this was a very amusing suggestion, but Margaret had had enough of me by now, so the other two lads and myself just finished off what remained of the samples and agreed to leave it at that.

I asked my new friends if they would like to go over the road for a drink, but it seemed their wives had something else planned for later, and they were steered firmly away in the direction of the exit. Fortunately, I had arranged for a lift back to Killen's, where Ernest was wondering what I had been up to. Even Vespas can look reproachful.

Chapter 13
The road to Derry

After a restorative siesta, I made my way downstairs for dinner. While seated in the lounge, enjoying an aperitif and trying hard to look as if I belonged there, I became aware of sounds of activity in the bedroom immediately above the lounge. The floor must have been excessively thin, because the activity could clearly be heard to develop into sounds of passion, and it became obvious that a session of pre-dinner rumpy-pumpy was in progress. I discreetly opted for a stroll outside, and went to visit Ernest to see if his mood had improved. I even managed to push him under cover in case it should rain again.

When I returned, some of the other guests had already been called into dinner. During dinner, I tried to guess which of my fellow diners had the room over the lounge, but this was impossible, because they were all couples, and they all had smiles on their faces. It was some time before I realised they were probably smiling at me, because I had forgotten to take my hat off after my pre-prandial stroll. I reasoned that the figure of a grizzled, portly old man, wearing a baseball cap at dinner, staring quizzically at each couple in turn as they toyed with their *vol-au-vents* would have brought a nervous smile to most faces.

On the radio later that night, I heard that the police were interviewing ten suspects in connection with the murder of the RUC policemen. Among them was a part-time policeman, a colleague of the victim.

The next morning I was cross with myself for settling for "good enough" on the gale-blasted cliff-top, and not pressing on the perilous 300 extra yards over the slippery grass for what had been described as a better view. As a penance, I decided not to take the easy, direct, main road route to Derry, but that I would make a less comfortable diversion inland, dropping down into the countryside lanes to take in the town of Ballymoney where the RUC policeman had been kicked to death.

The name of Ballymoney is rather more glorious in its history than in its present, although some would say that it is the same violent energy which drives its townspeople today as in the past. Ballymoney was one of the centres of the Rebellion of the United Irishmen led by Wolfe Tone in 1798. At the time, there was some confusion about where the confrontation was to take place, and the rebels requisitioned large quantities of ham and wine as provisions for the future conflict, but unfortunately consumed large quantities of it on the spot. The town was burned to the ground by government forces.

I learnt that on the first day of the Battle of the Somme on 1st July 1916, this small town lost 29 sons of Ulster, serving equally in both the Protestant and Catholic regiments. As I cautiously rode into town with my full regalia of top box and orange and green bomb, the town seemed normal enough, no checkpoints, no police tape with through-traffic diversions. Inevitably, I got lost. The road numbers didn't correspond to those on the large-scale map I had, and the signposts were unhelpful. I stopped to ask a passing postman. He didn't know the way. He wasn't from these parts. He accompanied me across the road to ask directions from a face at a small window by a solid-looking gateway.

As I stood there listening, I slowly realised this building was the heavily fortified station of the Royal Ulster Constabulary, no doubt staffed by colleagues of Gregory Taylor. The officer whose face was at the window left his post and came out onto the pavement to give me directions to the road I was looking for, although he wasn't very sure himself. Where did this road end up? He couldn't say. Road numbers meant nothing to him. If I went down here and turned right, I would come to Coleraine and the coast. And if I turned left? He couldn't rightly say, now how could he?. During this conversation, there was no indication of any unusual tension at all. Everything seemed unexpectedly normal, although I later learnt that the funeral of Gregory Taylor was to take place that day. The RUC man didn't even look at my orange and green bomb, just scratched his head as he tried his best to guide me on my way out of town.

~☆~

There were strong winds blowing, and my cross-country route along minor roads turned out to be a good idea. The trees gave some protection from the worst gusts, and although at times there was rain in the wind, it wasn't enough to make life uncomfortable. There was very little traffic on these roads, and I felt much safer without having to worry about the danger of a sudden gale-gust blowing me into the path of one of the lorries on the coast road.

I thought about Gregory Taylor and his killers. I grew up in a community where street violence was only just under the surface. You developed a sense for when it was about to break out, and you reacted accordingly, either braving it out, or backing down and clearing off. The subject of the annual Protestant marches, organised by the Orange Lodge, is a thorny one where both sides hold their own traditional, entrenched and passionate positions, and somewhere between the two lies the middle ground of the majority, most of whom are just hoping for an equitable solution.

These were some of the thoughts which accompanied me on my ride across country to the city of Derry, via Ballymoney. Just before Derry, I began riding past the stragglers of a long trail of mothers and small children walking along the roadside. Their numbers grew, quite out of proportion to the sparsely inhabited townships through which we were travelling. I decided it had to be some sort of peace-march, a well-organised demonstration by tomorrow's generation against the sort of events that had been precipitated in Ballymoney.

I remembered the Peace Movement of mothers and children from both factions in Northern Ireland, which after initial success had fizzled out in the late 80s. The long roadside string of mothers and children – with the occasional dad – seemed endless, in good spirits but without banners of any description. Soon I could see ahead that they were turning off the main road down a country lane. I would follow them to try to find out more. As I drew level with the point at which the immense crocodile swung abruptly through 90 degrees, I saw a banner across the road under which they were marching. "Jogger Trail". It was some kind of a fun-run, a day out for the kids. Another demonstration of the acts of community bonding, like the school parties one sees everywhere, the Somme Heritage Centre, and the Orange Order.

The showers became heavy, and the winds became stronger as I approached Derry, but I tucked my head in and was soon through the worst of it, and puzzling over the roadside directions into Derry itself.

The city of Derry was founded by St. Columba in the year 546 AD, and in 1614 a group of London guilds provided the resources for re-building it as the last walled city in Europe, ironically as a haven for the newly arrived Protestants fleeing religious persecution in Scotland. They changed the Irish name *Doire* to Londonderry. It was the scene of repeated major sieges in the mid-1600s, with the Protestants on the inside and the Catholics on the outside. A Protestant told me with a desperately serious look in his eye, as if he already knew I wouldn't really understand what he was telling me, that: "At the Siege of Derry, the Protestants saved the British Empire from the threat of Catholicism."

Nowadays, the current Catholic population is in a majority of more than 2:1, and after the large number of infamous examples of anti-Catholic discrimination in the 20th Century, it is natural that it should have become a focus of Irish Nationalism. That doesn't mean that the liberal Derry Catholics want to be subjected to the rigid prohibitions of the South. They feel themselves above the old Roman dictates about sex and marriage which were built into the Republic's constitution, and they have priests who are more flexible in their approach to the problems of everyday life than some of those who wear the cloth in the South.

CHAPTER 14
REMEMBERING BLOODY SUNDAY

These were some of the views I had gathered before I entered the city limits, but I had no idea where the memorial to Bloody Sunday was located. Was it something one could ask about at the Tourist Office? All I knew was that the site of the massacre was overlooked by the old walls of the city.

One Sunday in January 1972 soldiers from the Support Company of the 1st Battalion of the newly arrived Paratroop Regiment (the "Paras") fired on a group of protesters, killing thirteen of them; a fourteenth died later. New evidence suggests that Army marksmen were called in to open fire from high up on the battlements, causing most of the fatalities.

This contradicts the official version that the Army patrol returned fire in self-defence, when IRA gunmen shot at them over the heads of the demonstrators, from the rooftops of the Catholic council flats nearby. An anonymous Para with a troubled soul, referred to as Soldier 027, has told how he and his comrades were encouraged by an officer to "teach these buggers a lesson. We want some kills tomorrow". His statement was changed by army interrogators before being presented as evidence to the Widgery Tribunal, which reported their findings on the shootings six weeks after the event.

This report has been accepted to be a whitewash, an attempt by the Conservative government and the British Army to sweep the incident under the carpet, and to move on. It has subsequently been shown that those killed during the massacre did not start a fire-fight, as claimed: no trace of arms was found. The Army maintained that the IRA weapons were 'spirited away'. It was a confused situation, but no evidence of fire from the direction of the demonstrators was ever found – no injured soldiers, or even bullet-holes in the ramparts.

A brief summary of the later Saville Enquiry Report would not go amiss here:

When Tony Blair led the Labour Party to an election victory in 1997, ending 18 years of Conservative rule, one of the first actions he took was to commission a highly respected High Court Judge, Lord Saville, to hold an enquiry into Bloody Sunday, and to consider new evidence that had come to light following the 1972 Widgery Report. Neither knew then that the hearings would last for 434 days between April 1998 and January 2005, and examine 900 witnesses, at a cost of £191 million; it was finally published in June 2010, just 38 years after the events, 5000 pages long, in 10 volumes, weighing 20 kilos, and costing £572 per copy. It was also available free on the internet. The Widgery Report was 60 pages long and copies cost 36p.

Saville concluded that the killings were "unlawful", that "no warnings were given", that "no soldiers were under threat", and that "soldiers were the first to open fire." Exhaustive forensic tests showed that none of the victims had fired weapons (contrary to the claims in the Widgery Report), and there was no evidence of nail-bombs among the fallen – soldiers had clearly lied to Widgery. Saville also warned that the PPS (the Northern Ireland Crown Prosecution Service) might look into the evidence of unlawful killing, and perjury, and consider bringing criminal prosecutions against the perpetrators. Two of the soldiers were responsible for most of the killings, and one has since died, but Soldier F might still face charges of unlawfully killing up to 6 victims.

It was said that the thoroughness of the enquiry was without precedent, with "every single shot recorded, every single soldier's actions gone over." It was also revealed that in another incident a week earlier, a demonstration against an illegal, secret internment camp at nearby Magilligan Strand was broken up with "extraordinary, unjustified physical violence" against the protesters, by soldiers from the same Paratroop Regiment. Despite this, the officer commanding the unit involved in Bloody Sunday, one Lieutenant Colonel Derek Wilford, ignored the instructions of his Brigadier to hold his men back from the Bogside. He was subsequently severely reprimanded.

Apart from the tragic deaths and traumatic injuries of the innocent, and because of the whitewash and the refusal to hold a proper enquiry before 1998, a large number of British families in Derry had to endure the accusations that their relatives were criminals and terrorists; their relief at having their reputations cleared by Saville can only be imagined.

The *Guardian* journalist, Simon Winchester, who broke the story in 1972, continued to follow events closely, including the Saville hearings, after which he described Lord Chief Justice of England Widgery as "a man of shameful memory".

The shootings happened during the watch of Conservative Prime Minister Edward Heath, and ironically it fell to the new Conservative Prime Minister, David Cameron, to announce the bones of the findings of the Saville Enquiry to Parliament and to the nation. He did so with complete contrition, apologizing on behalf of the nation for an act that was "unlawful and unjustified". In three words which meant everything to the families of Derry he said: "It was wrong."

In its immediate aftermath, the blunders of Bloody Sunday and Widgery served to spur recruitment to the IRA for years after.

On arrival at Derry, I rode straight into the city centre (passing another First World War memorial) and on towards a gateway in the city walls. The road was narrowed by a fence made of boards and scaffolding, and ahead was a no entry sign. The building on my right was the Victorian Courthouse in Classical Greek style. That building struck a chord, and I remembered that a few months previously a woman RUC member was shot down in front of this Courthouse. I quickly turned Ernest round and drove back. There was a street map in the window of the Tourist Office; there was no arrow indicating the "Site of the Bloody Sunday Massacre", so I went inside to ask. My enquiry was dealt with as politely as if I had asked the way to the nearest shopping mall.

The estate of council houses was not as I remembered seeing it in television reports. They were more modern, small, red brick houses, neat and tidy - probably more recent. I parked Ernest outside someone's front garden, and walked across to look at the obelisk.

"Murdered by the British Army" was written at the bottom of a list of 13 names, with the date of their deaths. Six of those named were 17-year-old boys on a peace demonstration; a 59-year-old died later.

I was very affected by the stark simplicity of the memorial, and the message it bore. I looked up resentfully to the battlements, from where some of the shots had come. The distance was not far; it was not a hard shot for a trained marksman. They must have shot to kill, because at that distance they could have chosen to wing their victims if those giving the orders had wanted them to.

This was not the inevitable result of the accidents which happen when an armed force is dispersed in a resident civilian community. Nervous, inexperienced fingers on the trigger, army standing orders which are too rigid, hotheads on both sides, and the constant threat of death at the hands of the terrorists, all these things lead to killings which are accidental or unavoidable.

Weighing up the evidence of my own eyes, I concluded that the killings on Bloody Sunday were acts of murder, designed to set an example and to intimidate. This was a case of the Army of a sovereign state killing its own citizens. It may have been treated by the establishment as just another unfortunate incident in the long and glorious history of the British Army in defence of law and order; but the families and friends of at least six 17-year-old boys, and eight others, will not forget or forgive the events of that day.

A few yards from the Bloody Sunday memorial is the painted wall which tells the traveller "You are now entering Free Derry". The rundown area of Bogside in Free Derry was a landscape of boarded-up buildings and graffiti, burnt-out abandoned cars. I ventured in cautiously, and then had second thoughts about the wisdom of what I was doing, taking Ernest's British number plates into such an intimidating area of vandalised cars, unswept streets and accusing looks from passers-by.

I pulled over at a small neighbourhood newsagent, to have a look inside and buy a fruit drink. Immediately, I was surrounded by at least ten tiny children who appeared from nowhere. They reminded me of Roman street urchins, except they were all cleanly dressed and rosy-cheeked. A four-year-old boy asked me a question, but his accent was so thick I couldn't understand a word from inside my crash helmet. I removed the helmet and spoke to him with the combination of unintelligible and noncommittal "ums" and "ahs", and meaningless gestures, which normally works in such circumstances. This seemed to provoke another intense question in equally indecipherable brogue from a three-year old girl, so I waved vaguely at the shop and went inside, looking back and gesturing as I went. I was followed into the shop by a middle-aged house-husband, who noticed my concern and assured me my "Bake would be all raight, raight enough".

By now Ernest was surrounded by hordes of little people; a small girl climbed up and sat on the saddle while another shook the handlebars. "I'm only worried that it doesn't fall over and hurt them" I explained, and the man in the shop made reassuring noises, dismissing any need for concern. It was taking a long time to serve the customers in front of me, so I took a drink from the chill cabinet, and offered to pay. The shop-lady noticed my nervousness, and took the money.

When I got back outside to Ernest, the first four-year old was tapping the saddle with a large hammer. The house-husband appeared at my side, and thinking the boy had taken the hammer from somewhere in the scooter, instructed him to "Give the man back his hammer, now!" The boy's five-year old sister explained it was his own hammer, and told the boy crossly to stop hitting "the man's bake". I didn't like to ask why a four-year old should have his own personal hammer as a plaything, so I lapsed back into what I hoped were friendly-sounding grunts. Order was restored, and my saviour went off, leaving me to kick-start Ernest into life. This impressed the crowd of midgets greatly, and the four-year old boy demanded to be taken for a ride, but I politely refused. I carefully picked off various children from the different parts of the "bake" they were hanging on to, and drove off past the barricaded Bogside Inn on the corner, whose front wall used to carry the slogan "Informers Will Be Killed". It didn't seem to be open for business, so I felt no obligation to stop.

Taking stock, I realised I had just been frightened – "terrorised" is far too strong a word – by a gang of likeable four-year old urchins. I was also aware that my over-anxious reaction to them was my fault, not theirs.

Back in the other part of Derry, I felt twitchy in the petrol station as I filled up. I felt the security cameras on me as I paid at the cash desk, and wondered how many times they had been robbed at gunpoint. I felt anxious when I stopped at the roadside to consult my map for the route into Donegal, and as I crossed the road bridge outside the city, I looked back at the large dock area which had seen so many emigrations in harder times.

The city of Derry has attracted enormous investment incentive payments from the central British Government, and many foreign investors have set up factories in the area. Only that morning it was announced that a Derry-based American company making computer hard disks was expanding, and 1200 new jobs were to be created. The same company has another factory in Cork, in the Republic, and there were to be another 1000 jobs available there too. Ireland was booming, and the "Celtic Tiger" was a tangible fact, bringing new industries to enthusiastic, well-educated workers, eager to join the consumer revolution.

My visit to Derry was very short, but very impressive. Why had I spent so much time looking over my shoulder? It wasn't just because of the reputation of Derry as the seat of Nationalism. The surroundings of fortifications and graffiti gave an air of genuine menace, and I had reacted to it. People who lived there had come to terms with it all long before, and were no different in their manner than people elsewhere. Was it just my imagination, or were they perhaps even a little more jolly than in other parts? I was reminded of the light-hearted breeziness of Londoners during the Blitz, the community spirit of a people under attack.

~☆~

CHAPTER 15
NORTH INTO DONEGAL

Ernest at the front door of our B & B – a rebuilt Planters house.

My journey of transit through the territory of Northern Ireland should have been a rite of passage, but I felt no change. Instead of being more sympathetic to the Protestant argument, I felt that knowing more, I now understood even less. The time was historic. The new Labour Government in Westminster was showing every sign of a genuine desire to find a solution to the Irish Problem. I hadn't gone out of my way to solicit and confront any strong opinions, but I had been expecting to have my own prejudices broken down by contact with the people. In a time of hope the Protestant arguments as presented in the media had served only to confirm those preconceptions about the weakness of their cause, and to underline the apparent justice of the Catholic demands.

I heard a suggestion that the source of the intensity of Protestant passion is the desire to defend the traditional freedoms of non-Catholic Christianity. They are prepared to fight to maintain Lutheran ambitions, a return to the authentic religion of Christianity before the Church of Rome got to change the rules, and bend the essential principles of the teachings of Jesus of Nazareth. But the racist rantings of preachers at Ian Paisley's Martyr's Memorial Free Presbyterian Church do not argue the case for freedom, quite the opposite. The passion and the brutality shown by the gang who kicked Constable Taylor to death, seemingly in defence of their right to hold parades, must arise from the fears of an isolated community in danger of losing its privileges, its superiority. Nothing had shown me otherwise.

It seemed to me that the hardy warriors, resolute men of the medieval poem had become desperate men, sensing the imminent danger of the loss of advantage, and perhaps worse. Thousands of British citizens were living in the shadow of sectarian murder, and history has shown the reality of what can happen. It is said that during the build up to the Peace Talks, applications for membership to the Orange Order soared to unprecedented levels; stocks of orange sash material were sold out, and replacements were rushed into the tailors to meet the demand. These hardy warriors will not surrender just because someone in Brussels tells them that they are all Europeans now.

While I was in Ireland, population statistics were published showing that the Protestant-Catholic split in Northern Ireland has continued to narrow, and it was predicted that early in the 21st Century the Catholics will be in the majority. Protestants have always found comfort in the repeated Westminster promise that no change in the status of the Province can be made without a majority vote in a plebiscite, on the basis that no Protestant turkey is going to vote for Christmas. But that victory now seems less certain. Several times I asked the question: "So, do you really think Ireland will still be divided in 100 years? - And in 50? - And in 10?" What is certain is that it is only a matter of time before Ireland is reunited, and in their hearts the Protestants know it. The hope of us all is that a formula can be found where that inevitable unification will come to be accepted by all. Otherwise we will be back to the lawless and rebellious days of 1914, but with Uzi machine pistols and Semtex explosives, rather than Mauser rifles.

The dual carriageway out of Derry became a country road. The direction signs turned into the names of Donegal towns, and I prepared myself for a border crossing. Where were my papers? Passport? Ernest's insurance? Vehicle registration? And then a larger sign came into view: "Welcome to Donegal". I felt relieved. Contrary to my fears, I hadn't been blown up, shot at or stoned in my passage through the province of Northern Ireland. At the border there was no red-and-white frontier pole, no Checkpoint Charlie, just empty southern Irish countryside. Not so much as a hut.

The first village was called Muff, and it was recognisably Irish, with a bar or two, a B & B, a modest shop, and a small police station. Unlike police stations in the North, this police station wasn't a barbed wire bedecked Beirut fortress. It was an ordinary old village house with a single sign "Gardai". An Irish Gard in uniform walked briskly up the pavement towards his front door. He didn't seem surprised at my enthusiastic wave, and he waved back. It was like being on holiday. I felt I was home again. Northern Ireland isn't home: it is somewhere else. The phrase "a place apart" came into my head from I don't know where. To underline my feelings of exhilaration, the sun shone and the road stretched up before me. I passed a petrol station with a sign "Discount given for sterling", and I was reminded that I was in a foreign country and didn't have any local currency. It was Saturday, so the banks were closed.

It is at times like this I feel extremely grateful to the inventor of the hole-in-the-wall machine, the humble ATM. The idea of being able to put a plastic card in a machine almost anywhere in the world and withdraw money seems little short of miraculous. Just because I tap in my magic, secret, personal code number, the machine not only feels justified in helping me out with a small advance, it even notifies the man sitting in the National Westminster Bank in Muswell Hill, the one who looks after my money for me.

He opens the ledger, turns to the page with my name at the top, dips his quill pen in the inkwell, and writes down that I have withdrawn £50 from that little bank in Kowloon just across the road from the Red Dragon Pub. And he doesn't bat an eyelid. If I may confess a secret wish, it is that I am convinced that one day he's going to make a mistake. He will be interrupted by a phone call just as he picks up his quill pen. When he resumes work on his pile, he will pass by my withdrawal from Credit Lyonnais in St. Tropez, and start writing up the £25 taken by the boy at the greengrocer's for a few beers and a curry last Friday night. It hasn't happened yet, but I live in hope.

We bowled into Saturday lunchtime Moville, and I nonchalantly pulled up on the yellow line right next to the only hole-in-the-wall on Lough Foyle, outside the Allied Irish Bank. I confided my secret number, and asked for a small advance in Irish money, please, if it's no trouble. To my horror the machine replied "The service you require is not available at this time". Consternation! I silently withdrew my card, and thought of alternative action. I could go back to the petrol station and change some sterling, or there might be somewhere else in Moville.

I found the post office, fifteen minutes before closing time. Do you do exchange? Could you change £40 for me please? The reaction of the counter clerk was surprising. He could indeed change the £40, but the rate of exchange was so poor, he felt too embarrassed to tell me what it was. After some encouragement, he confided that only last week, he had changed some sterling for himself, and he couldn't believe how little he got for it. Was I certain I wanted to do it? Did I really need the money? I would get a much better rate back in Derry. I explained that the machine at the Allied Irish Bank and I weren't on speaking terms, and with lunchtime slipping away, I was desperate. "Well if you have to, so you have to" he said with profound sad wisdom, and he took my £40 and gave me a handful of strange bank notes and some coins. That should get me a glass of Guinness and a sandwich all right.

I thanked him, and he closed up the shop behind me as I left. I thought about the bank machine's stubbornness. It was very early in the weekend for a machine to have already given away all its money. Perhaps there was a limit per transaction? I went cautiously back to the Allied Irish Bank, and this time halved the amount of my request. Old Faithful kicked in, and spewed a bunch of brand new bank notes out of the slot before me. It even gave me back my card, and a receipt. I hastily lifted the curse I had earlier placed on the heads of families of the directors of the Allied Irish Bank, and chose a pub.

I got into conversation with a youngish chap, from his clothing I would guess he was a labourer. He was rolling a cigarette. The usual stuff of opening questions, but now without the sectarian sub-text of such talk that you find in the North. Where was I from? He asked. What did I do for a living? Advertising is it? Now he could tell me something about that.

Had I come up along Lough Foyle there, from Derry? Did I notice a place called Red Castle? Well just along from there one day a few years back, he was out walking along the shore, down by the rocks and all, and he came into a bay there, and he couldn't believe his eyes. There in the middle of the beach, perched high up on a rock on the shoreline was a television set. Yes, a television set! And he immediately thought of the advertising campaign for Benson & Hedges - so, did I remember it? All those funny images of flying ducks and God knows what else. Surreal was it? There you have it. And he thought to himself - that's just like one of them Benson & Hedges ads. No, he didn't know how it got there. No, it was an old tele, just the outside case and the screen really. No, he left it there, and carried on his way. But he often thinks about it. Did the tide put it there? Was it some lads having a laugh? You get some strange things happening on the shore. The big house is a posh hotel now. Very dear, no sense going there unless you've pots of money.

My sandwich arrived, and I thanked him for his story. It was timed so beautifully, it was as if he had been employed to fill in the time while I waited. I have a theory that all those country people you see leaning over a gate all day long, nodding as the cars go past, are actually employed by the Tourist Board to provide local colour. In their right hand - which you will notice is always out of sight - they carry a counter which they click as every car goes past. At the end of the day, they are paid on a piece-work basis, according to how many cars they have nodded to in the course of their day's work.

I noticed something odd about the signposts. The distances were all given in kilometres, but the speed limits were still in miles per hour. This avoids, no doubt, a situation in which an Irish motorist might assume he can drive at 50 miles per hour in an area subject to a 50 kilometre per hour speed limit.

With a pocketful of Southern Irish cash, a tank full of Northern Irish petrol, a good road and in high spirits, I bowled along the road to the village of Culdaff. I stopped to ask a roadside gardener for directions to Culdaff House, and passed through the large gates and up the long un-made up drive to the Big House. It was a very imposing Big House, the remains of one of the original Planter's Houses built in the style of an elegant country mansion by the Scottish Presbyterians drafted in to take over the lands from the Irish when the O'Neills fled to France.

I parked Ernest by the majestic front stairs up to the main doors, and was thrilled to notice two cannon balls at the foot of each stairpost. Were they from the nearby wreck of the *Trinidad Valencera*? In the hallway was a massive rusting iron sea chest, rumoured to be a relic from the Spanish Armada. This house was built only a few years after the Armada sailed, and it was perfectly reasonable that there should be relics from the wreck taken up to the Big House. In answer to the ancient doorbell, I was at once met by the daughter of the house, who un-questioningly showed me to my room, up a grand staircase and along a lofty corridor. The room was light and airy, but treasure fever was upon me, and I hastily dumped my luggage, and set off again with all haste for the wrecksite.

CHAPTER 16
THE WRECK OF THE TRINIDAD VALENCERA

Close to the beach at Killagoe Bay lie the remains of the Trinidad Valencera.

Driving in the West of Ireland requires a certain etiquette, but the rules are easy to learn. Drivers who cross with another vehicle coming in the opposite direction are expected to give a short wave of the hand in greeting. Perhaps the origins lie in the idea of a blessing for a safe journey. In West Cork and Kerry, this is done by lifting one hand from the steering wheel and showing the open palm to the other driver. As you move northwards, the hand is no longer required to leave the wheel, and it is considered enough just to uncurl four fingers and raise them towards the other car. By the time you reach Connemara, these fingers may be reduced to one solitary index finger. In Mayo and Sligo, it becomes noticeable that this is generally accompanied by a slight nod of the head. In Donegal, all that is needed is the nod.

I tried all sorts of combinations of hand salute, but taking one hand off the handlebars of a two-wheeler may cause a wobble. Raising a gloved finger was pointless, because the hand was concealed in the handlebar faring. The Donegal nod suited me better, but I observed that the true practitioners of this skill nodded with an additional screwing action, twisting the head upon the neck, right to left, through an angle of about 35 degrees horizontally. After a period of practise I felt I had mastered the technique sufficiently to blend in with the locals. My Donegal nod was universally acknowledged and returned.

~☆~

Killagoe Bay is at the end of a long straight cross-country lane which doesn't seem to lead anywhere. Halfway along this road, I passed a small girl and her baby brother, seated at the gate of their cottage. She was giving him lessons in waving at tourists, and it was evident that there couldn't have been many along that stretch of road, because he hadn't got the action right at all yet! His arm movement was far too vigorous, and his sister tried in vain to demonstrate that all that was need was a slight flick of the wrist. I responded with a knowing nod, screwing my helmeted head through no more than the regulation 12° segment I could manage. I fancied she felt slightly embarrassed by her young brother's excessive arm movement, and her flick was accompanied by an apologetic shrug, as if to say "What can you expect from kids today?"

I was happy with my map-reading skills, having joined this road by a series of even smaller lanes which wound their way across the countryside from Culdaff to Killagoe Bay. I knew that the road ended in a sharp hairpin which dropped down to the bay itself. When this hairpin duly appeared, and Ernest dipped immaculately into the steep curve, I was surprised to see two cars had followed the same route before me, and were already in the small car park overlooking the beach.

Slightly above the beach, and with the best view, was a bench by a small brass relief map, installed there by the Irish Tourist Board to commemorate the wreck on the occasion of the 400th anniversary of the Armada in 1988. It showed other known wrecksites around the shores of Ireland, and highlighted Killagoe Bay. It described how 400 sailors and soldiers on the *Trinidad Valencera* had sought shelter from the storm in Killagoe Bay on September 16th 1588, but unfortunately the ship became stuck on a rocky reef. After two days trying to re-float the ship by offloading all weighty items such as people, ballast and cannon, the ship broke its back. Only 40 lives were lost in the wreck, but the rest were saved. Many of them were murdered at Derry by the English forces. Most items of any value were salvaged from the wreck at the time. In 1971 divers from the Derry Subaqua Club located the exact site again after a storm shifted the sands. In the archaeological operation which followed, many items were discovered, and now most of them are installed at the Ulster Museum in Belfast.

The poor old *Trinidad Valencera* was typical of many of the ships which made up the greater part of the Armada fleet. Of the 130 ships of all shapes and sizes, only about 30 were warships. The rest were merchantmen or packet boats, hastily equipped with a few cannon. These cannon were often defective, and the roundshot (cannonballs) were poorly modified to the calibre of the unusual variety of guns. So when fired, if the barrel didn't explode, it was quite possible that the extra covering to pack the roundshot up to a size to fit the gun would strip off in flight and cause it to fall hopelessly short. There were many reports from the English of ineffectual firing from their Spanish adversaries during the confused combat.

Trinidad Valencera was a merchant ship from Venice, taken by the Spanish and conscripted into service in the Armada. She was cheaply built, to deliver merchandise all around the Mediterranean, not to stand up to the weather in Atlantic storms. She was quite a chunky tub, displacing 1100 tons, manned by a crew of 79, and carrying an extra 281 soldiers on the expedition; 42 mixed obsolete cannon were awkwardly distributed about her decks, wherever they could be accommodated, and each gun was allocated 50 bodged roundshot. As if this wasn't enough, her cargo was a collection of items of siege materials, for the expected Siege of London. When she became stuck on the rocks of Killagoe Bay, she stayed there, with no hope of getting off.

I saw Killagoe Bay at its best. In bright sunshine, white puffball clouds skated across an intensely blue sky. The sunlight and the clear sky reflected in the sea gave the scene a Caribbean look, and I was able to take a number of panoramic photographs in a wide variety of lighting conditions. From where I stood a rocky outcrop pointed outwards, like a giant mailed fist, to the spot where the ship had foundered. An orange buoy seemed to mark the site.

I could clearly see what had happened, and imagined the events in my mind's eye. The sandy strip between the sea and the land below the cliffs of the bay stretched almost as far as the headland at the far end, and I could now make out the figures of three youths walking along the strand. Closer to where I was standing, a small family disgorged the paraphernalia required for an afternoon on the beach, with buckets and spades, an umbrella, a cold-box and folding chairs for the adults. Did they know of the significance of this beach? They needed only to read the plaque thoughtfully provided by the Irish Tourist Board to learn the whole story.

I rode down the last bit of the slope to the car park, and climbed down over the rocks onto the beach. Close up, the rocks which had claimed the *Trinidad Valencera* looked very fierce, jagged and volcanic. On the beach side, they were levelled off with sand, and there were tidal pools filling the depressions in the rock.

I was suddenly filled with a mad and illogical urge to look for treasure from the ship. Here were some tiny slivers of wood, over there a rusting piece of metal, and those seashells looked very old indeed! By the time my frantic searching had calmed down, I realised the slivers were in fact sea-worn roots from a recent gorse bush, the metal was probably no more than a couple of years old, and the seashells had probably been inhabited until quite recently. So I reluctantly put them all back. "Take nothing but photographs. Leave nothing but footprints" came to mind. But I kept a super-smooth periwinkle just as a keepsake.

Next to the parked cars was an old bicycle, one of those upright roadsters with over-large wheels and wide-spread handlebars. Looking around for the owner, I spotted the figure of a man close to the family group, but not part of them. He was moving around on the sand, and seemed to be taking sightings out to sea. As I strolled further down the beach, I began to notice the markers he was using, piles of stones with red and white striped sticks standing vertical above them. As he scampered up and down, he appeared to be taking sightings along the aligned sticks and taking notes. I could now see he was very odd: eccentric-looking, mid-thirties, gaunt with unkempt, almost shoulder-length hair and a one-week beard. He wore a faded all-in-one boiler suit. His bearing reminded me of the castaway Ben Gunn from "Treasure Island".

As I watched him, he watched me back, suspicious and annoyed by my attention. Eventually he spoke, answering my unasked question. "Calculations, I'm making important calculations, that's what." His accent was not local. If I had to put an identity to it, I would have said: Nottingham. When I asked him calculations about what, he snapped, "That's for me to know and others to guess at." "Does it have anything to do with the Armada wreck?" I asked, trying to sound off-hand and politely interested at the same time.

He stiffened, stopped scampering and stood up. He was surprisingly tall. "What do you know about it?" he quizzed. "Not much more than it says up there on the plaque" I said. "What can you tell me?" He moved towards me as he spoke. "I can tell you they've got it all wrong, that's what. There were two wrecks, not just the one they found. I figured out where the other one lies with my calculations, and I'm going to find it. I'm just waiting for the right tides." He was now uncomfortably close, and he lowered his voice as he said in a conciliatory tone "It's buried under the sand, you see, so I'm just waiting for the right tides to uncover it."

I was beginning to feel nervous, standing so close to a man who was obviously raving mad, so I quickly came back with "What do you hope to find? There won't be much left, will there?" I was remembering the display cabinets in the museum filled with all sorts of personal artefacts. "It's spread out. The wood's all gone long before. There's no wreck as such, just the site really. I'll settle for a few pieces of gold, a few coins, a few trinkets. But I'm the only one who knows where and when. It's all down to my calculations, and the weather, and the tides." I fancied his eyes widened in that unwashed, weathered face, and he made me more nervous, so I withdrew hastily, wishing him well, and leaving him to his search.

The three youths were coming back. I noticed their car had a Bushmills number plate. The family on the beach had reached the point where they were just making their Grandma comfortable on her folding chair. Her son was pouring a cup of tea from a thermos flask for her. His wife was showing the two very small children how to make a sandcastle.

I sat on a rock for a while, and thought about the wreck of the *Trinidad Valencera* and the strange man who sought her treasure. As far as I know the word "Valencera" only means "from Valencia", so what was the significance of a "Holy Trinity from Valencia", I mused. Was it a painting? Or a vision? The question hung in the air, and as far as I know, it hangs there still, in the bright blue air above Killagoe Bay.

I noticed a slight improvement in the baby brother's wave as I passed by a second time. The word was clearly out, and as I passed the next group of cottages, two ten-year-old lads ran into the lane cheering Ernest and me on our way. I lifted my gloved hand from the handlebars in a Queen Mother salute in reply.

Back in the village of Culdaff, I stopped at the pub for refreshment. A poster on the wall announced a concert that night by a Beatles sound-alike group called Beatlemania. Tonight was Saturday night! The gig began at 12 midnight; late starts for dances are customary in the West of Ireland where the agricultural working day is determined by the hours of daylight, plus an hour or so to have something to eat, get changed into more appropriate clothing, and get in a few drinks before the serious business starts.

Gigs at McGrory's Pub in Culdaff attract the Youth from all around, some from as far as Derry. There is a tradition of folk and showband music here, but tonight's Beatles concert given by an English group from Newcastle was sure to be especially attractive. I opened a conversation with the pub landlady, behind the bar, and she told me about some of the previous performers whose photographs were all around the bar. Was the Beatles group any good? They were very good. I could hear sounds of sound-balancing coming from the dance hall at the back of the pub. The boys had already arrived. They would be through in a minute.

One by one, a string of young and not-so-young individuals filtered through to the bar from the dance hall area. There were also a couple of girls, and some obvious road manager types. I tried to work out who the musicians were. It wasn't difficult - they had to be the ones who were asking for food and drink. They looked nothing like the Beatles. There was a short redheaded one, a tall gangly one with a skinhead haircut, another with pale skin and blonde eyebrows. They wore modern clothes, bright sweatshirts and baseball caps, bomber jackets. Was this the group that launched a thousand hits? I told the landlady, without much enthusiasm, that I would come back later.

CHAPTER 17
A Beatles concert

The Lady of Culdaff House was very friendly. She called me by my first name, which was a gesture I appreciated, in her own home. She said she was a "returned emigrant", since her family had emigrated to Scotland from these parts in search of work. After working as a nurse in Scotland, (where she probably picked up the habit of calling people by their first name), she had returned here to Ireland, and settled down She loved her big house, and saw sharing it with paying guests as a logical way of helping to pay for its maintenance. She quickly got through the preliminaries of landlady type questions about the time and content of the next day's breakfast, and then invited me to sit with her family in the sumptuous living room.

Her husband was a quiet-spoken, gentle-mannered man. He showed me a heavy book which contained the family history, written and privately published by one of his female ancestors. He indicated her portrait on the wall, and another of the founder of this latest chapter of the dynasty. The original house was burned down during the Troubles of 1922, and was re-built to a similar design but much smaller, effectively just one wing. He didn't know if the cannon balls at the foot of the staircase were from the wreck of the *Trinidad Valencera* for sure. They probably were.

He had been out looking for the wreck himself in his youth, but it seems they were looking on the wrong side of the bay. The Derry boys found it quite by chance after a storm had shifted the sand around in the bay. He had heard about the wild-man treasure-hunter, poor soul. He wasn't sure about the iron sea chest in the hall. It had the seven bolts commonly associated with most of the artefacts connected with the Armada, but someone else had said it was German. In the grounds there was a small folly, built like a fort. He was told that there used to be cannon arranged there on the battlements, but they were taken away and melted down in the last World War, when scrap metal was wanted for munitions.

The home farm was only 100 acres now, and he didn't farm it himself. He rented it out to someone who knew more about those things than he did. He had tried several jobs, and was presently driving lorries all over Europe. It was only a small business, but it helped keep the house going, he explained. He spoke very quietly, in an accent with an almost imperceptible burr, and he always listened carefully for the next question, his head slightly to one side.

His twelve-year-old son drove around the grounds at demon speed astride a four-wheeled Yamaha motorbike, a quad. He told me the original 350 cc engine had been changed for one of 250 cc, but he didn't explain why. Perhaps it was to encourage him to keep his speed below 50 miles an hour along the winding rutted driveway. He pretended not to seem very interested in the Vespa in a superior sort of way - after all, his machine was twice as big as mine in every respect - but I later caught sight of him sneaking an admiring look at Ernest, parked outside his family's baronial front door.

I walked down the drive to the village for a few jars in the pub, and for the Beatles concert. The bar was hotting up, and I was lucky to find a table for a light supper of salmon and baked potato. Potato in some form or another is to be expected with every meal in the Irish countryside.

There were crowds of excited young people in the bar, drinking youthful drinks such as Martini with Coke. One group was obviously dressed up for the occasion; they wore clothes which would be considered unusual, verging on the outrageous, in almost any setting, but in the West of Ireland they looked positively weird. Black tights with a black body stocking is not that unusual nowadays, but one of the girls was dressed up as a bride. The others - all girls - fussed around like a bridal group, wearing veils and clutching purses. In addition to a wedding veil sprouting from the top of her head, the bride wore demonic makeup, a pink tutu and ballet tights, and she carried a small posy of artificial flowers. She had difficulty balancing her posy, a lighted cigarette, and a pint glass of blackcurrant cordial and vodka, and loud, quite unladylike guffaws of laughter were interspersed with the most shocking swearwords. We could have been anywhere. The surprise was that we were in a remote part of the West of Ireland. It couldn't have been a genuine hen night, could it? Or a spoof?

This custom of a pre-nuptial night of freedom, a female stag night, has been spreading in recent years, partly through the influence of American television series, where it is a favourite soap opera theme, and partly through the greater freedom enjoyed by liberated women. It is no longer unusual for women in Ireland to go out alone or in all-girl groups to pubs, restaurants and dances, as it was not so very long ago. I was puzzled by the bridal party, and couldn't work out if something else was going on. They looked more art student than soap opera. Was it some kind of social comment? They were certainly enjoying themselves.

I went next door to stake out a good place by the bar in the dance hall. The place was already packed, and I was the oldest one there by a long chalk. The DJ was good, and the kids were all dancing. I like the modern anything-goes style which allows individuals to dance on their own if they want to. There were also groups of five or six friends all dancing together, boys and girls mixed. The old-fashioned arrangement of one boy, one girl, only seems to happen on the slow numbers, and there weren't many of those. Frantic is a good word to describe the evening's proceedings: frantic dancing and frantic drinking.

The same barman who had served me a drink in the main bar only a few minutes earlier served me again. He didn't seem to recognise me, but since he couldn't hear me above the music, I think he did pretty well to work out what drink I wanted by reading my lips. It must be quite another matter to communicate that you want a vodka and lime with a slug of orange cordial, emptied into a pint of sweet cider and Guinness, mixed. Maybe all these modern combination drinks have abbreviated names, like "fruity vod in a black-and-gold".

While I was musing about this, and enjoying watching the latest dances performed, the DJ wound down his record player and shouted into the mike. He was obviously very excited too, and because he shouted, his voice was completely distorted. The result was as unintelligible as a British Rail announcement, but the content was irrelevant, because his voice reached a pitch as he introduced what must have been "The Beatles!" and the Fab Four trotted out onto the stage at the end of the room. The scruffy musicians I had seen earlier in the bar sipping mineral water and eating veggie burgers were now transformed: they all wore black Beatles wigs and Beatles suits. By their energy and attack, they really had become the Beatles, and as they let rip with "Please Please Me" the entire roomful of next generation dancers became transformed into 60s screaming Beatles fans.

The noise was deafening, and the effect was great! The girls screamed, the boys screamed, the bride screamed, I must admit that even I screamed – well, it would have been churlish not to. The Stage Beatles went banging on without a pause through three straight numbers, and the mystery was explained of how the real Beatles got started and took off with the speed they did. The sheer energy of this music in a confined space is mighty powerful medicine. Between numbers, the right-handed bass player gave us a passable impersonation of a Liverpuddlian Paul, and there was a wry sense of humour in his links, which reminded me of the irony of John Lennon. The sound was fantastic. I could swear that they had original 60s amplifiers to capture that authentic crushed and distorted sound which is several centuries removed from today's over-perfect digital quality. It sounded like vinyl played at full volume on a Dansette record player, and then up a bit.

The crowd rocked and danced and screamed and sang along with every verse. I couldn't see a single one of them who might have been born before the Beatles' final album was published, first time around, but they knew all the words of all the songs, word perfect. After forty minutes of a wall-to-wall set of the early numbers, "Paul" announced a short break, after which they would return with some "psychedelic numbers", and the dancers rushed for the bar, as Beatlemania played out with "You Know I'm Down".

It was very hot, and once the barman knew what I was drinking, I only had to wave an Irish five-pound note to guarantee a non-stop flow of pints of the black stuff. The excitement was all a bit much for me, and the rush of sweaty young bodies to the bar obliged me to retreat from my privileged position. I was feeling tired and emotional, as well as hot and sticky, so I stepped outside to take the night air. As I emptied my glass, I caught sight of Ringo slipping into a kaftan and a long hippie wig, and I decided that a psychedelic trip down memory lane was probably more than would be good for me at that precise moment. I cut short my Beatles concert with the sounds of "You Know I'm Down" still ringing in my ears. It had been a night of great "crack", which is the word the Irish use to describe that sort of a night. "Fun" doesn't have the same impact.

I never went to a real Beatles concert. The quality of the sound systems was so poor in those early days, and I just didn't fancy trying to hear them over the desperate screams of the audience, when I could listen to them perfectly well over my headphones. I didn't realise then that pop concerts are about more than sound quality. I now regret turning down a chance to see the Fab Four's penultimate full concert in the UK at the Rainbow, which was previously known as the Astoria cinema in Finsbury Park; as my local cinema it was also where I saw my first ever film – but that's another story.

From my season ticket seat in Highbury, the Arsenal Football Club Stadium, I could see my infant school, my junior school, and the school I went to for school dinners outside of term time. I could also make out where the roof of the house I grew up in was, just concealed behind a slight rise. To my left, on the other side of what I now know to be the main railway line to the North, was an enormous slab-sided brick building – the Astoria Cinema.

It was built in the 1930's in the days when a visit to the cinema was to be considered a trip to a palace of dreams. Purpose-built cinemas sprang up all over the country, exotically equipped with gilt paint and burgundy-red velvet seating. The proscenium arch was always far grander than was needed to accommodate the projection screen, in keeping with the massive sweeping scale of the interiors of the auditorium. They were given names like Regal, Grand, Super, and

Palace, and someone recently returned from a visit to Granada, in Spain, came up with the name Alhambra after the Moorish palace in that city. There were Alhambras all over the British Isles, and a few still survive. The architect of the Astoria Cinema Finsbury Park must have been on the same trip: he designed an interior which was like a Moorish palace.

After queuing in the rain under the unfriendly eye of a splendidly epauletted commissionaire, members of the North London public were allowed through at the prescribed time to shuffle up to the ticket office and buy a ticket to paradise. On the way to the auditorium they skirted a magnificent marble Moorish fountain, complete with genuine, languid goldfish. As soon as the punters sat down in the tip-up maroon and gold seats, their necks rolled back and their eyes went upwards to the screen, and onwards and upwards past exotic mock fronds edged terracotta-tiled roofs and turrets. And above all this was the architect's pride and joy!

The ceiling was as dark as an Andalusian night sky, and was peppered with thousands of twinkling stars, as if the cinema were open to the sky above the Palace of the Alhambra in Granada itself. A post-war child living in fog-bound London rarely saw the sky, and I had certainly never seen any real stars. The effect of such a spectacle was breathtaking, and I have never forgotten it. It must have contributed a great deal to my love of going to the cinema.

Thinking these thoughts, I skipped and bounced up the long drive to Culdaff House by the light of a silvery moon, but the songs which drove each step and echoed in my ears, which were still ringing from the concert, were nothing to do with Moon and June. They were from a very precisely definable period of just a few years when four Liverpool lads took the world by storm, not long before they discovered fame and psychedelia.

I've always been an Elvis man, and I expect I always will be. The truth is: like most people, music is very important in my life, and I honestly enjoy all sorts. People with less catholic tastes find it hard to believe that I can enjoy both Bach and Little Richard, but I do.

To appreciate the revolution that Elvis brought to popular music, it is necessary to be able to remember the desert of dreary and banal cover versions, which was the sole output of the British pop music scene before the King. Listen to Young Elvis (preferably the '56 recordings) and you will still hear the tremendous, fresh energy of youth. As I speak, there are very few examples of that freshness to be heard today. Most new music is immediately swamped by the heavy hand of big business which controls the modern pop scene through a handful of powerful multinational companies. We hear what they want us to hear, and we pay dearly for it.

My mother's younger brother was my Uncle Walter. He took us into his house for a time when my own parents' marriage fell apart, and I was able to study him at close quarters. His head held thousands of popular songs from the past, many of them unknown to me. He would start singing when a word triggered a memory, so if for example, someone said the word "bird" in conversation, Uncle Walter would start singing *"There'll be blue birds over/The white cliffs of Dover"*. I can't remember him ever singing a complete song, just couplets. He also carried a bag of boiled sweets which he offered to everyone he met. He was very popular on the bus, where he was known as the Sweets Man. On another occasion, he offered a sweet to a policeman in a difficult moment on Remembrance Day in Whitehall, and it was gratefully accepted, breaking the tension immediately. Together with my mother's other brother, Uncle Walter served as a fireman during the Blitz in London in the Second World War. When I see newsreel footage of firemen struggling with huge water hoses against a background of streets of houses in flames, I still wonder if it is my two uncles I can see there.

The next morning, I heard on my Walkman radio that the fresh grave of Gregory Taylor, the RUC man from Ballymoney, had been desecrated. An act of grave desecration can only be seen as a demonstration of extreme hatred. The message was not just that Gregory Taylor had overstepped the mark, but that his murder was justified, and he was to be pursued beyond the grave. A nearby Catholic church was described as having been "stormed", and the Protestant attackers attempted to set fire to it. At Ballymena 27 RUC officers were injured in disturbances surrounding a march. All the signs were of tension building up to explosive levels in preparation for what many had previously hoped would be a peaceful marching season. The other news was of the parliamentary elections in the South, which looked like ending in a minority coalition, and a change of government. The greatest excitement was that a Sinn Féin representative had been elected in the border constituency of Cavan-Monaghan. The political arm of the IRA was to have a voice in the new Irish Parliament, the Dail.

Chapter 18
Malin Head

There were two late middle-aged couples at breakfast, and my highly trained senses detected Advertising Man. Well yes, they had both worked in advertising, how did I know? They were originally from Columbus, Ohio, but now lived in Atlanta, Georgia. That's right, Columbus, Ohio was the hometown of the great humorist, James Thurber, how did I know that? My informant's grandmother had known Thurber's mother, quite a character. I told them I had probably read everything ever written about Thurber's mother by her son. Having established such close links between us, my American friend felt sufficiently emboldened to reveal the reasons for his presence in a Donegal breakfast room.

He was touring Ireland in a clockwise direction, looking up the roots of his family, the Irvines, who had emigrated to America from hereabouts. He was now retracing their footsteps in the company of his present wife and two friends. The manner of the friend's wife suggested that she was a third wife: insecure and over-protective. She interrupted the storyteller to ask what I was doing in Donegal?

My first informant was the veteran of many an unruly marketing meeting, and his technique was impeccable. He resolutely fixed my eye, and while he distracted his friend's third wife by asking her to pass the butter, he told me that they had just visited the old family home in Dunfanaghy, near the Bloody Foreland. I asked him to tell me more, sir. He explained that he had been this way before; he could remember accompanying his father on a similar visit in search of his roots way back in 1954.

After the War, his father was stationed near London, and he determined to visit the house in Donegal from which his own grandfather had emigrated to America, and the father took his own small son with him. That small son was my informant. In 1954, father and son had flown to Belfast, where they had booked a car with a driver. In those post-war days, the only persons who arrived by air and ordered a car and driver were persons of quality, or of great wealth. The car provided by Hertz was a huge, black Daimler chauffeur-driven limousine, and father and son were solemnly driven across the byways of agricultural Ireland to the old homestead.

My informant had a dim memory of the house, and the people living in it at the time, and of waiting while all the villagers had a drink with them in the pub, before they were driven back to Belfast again. He had managed to find the same house again on this trip, and had introduced himself to the people who live there now. The present inhabitant was the son of the previous one who had received the visitors in 1954. He was only a youngster then himself, but he remembered some Americans arriving one day in what the family described as a fine Rolls Royce, with a uniformed driver. Yes there was a boy with his father, and was it really yourself?

As on the previous occasion in 1954, there was no escaping the obligatory visit to the pub, and if it wasn't for the fact that my informant was teetotal, denied the consumption of alcohol in any form by serious-faced doctors, the evening might have ended for him in a smoky blur. As it was, he had shot a good video of the whole visit, to show to the folks back in Atlanta. He couldn't show it to me because American TV is different from European TV, but I could look at a replay through the black-and-white viewfinder screen if I liked?

I suspect that he was quite relieved when I declined, saying I would soon see Dunfanaghy for myself. I had very few commitments on my trip, but one of them was to visit the cousin of a London friend; the cousin lived in the coastal village of Dunfanaghy, and he was a fiddler. "His name isn't O'Rahilly is it?" trembled my informant from Ohio. "I believe it is!" I replied, and we exchanged "Goddams" and "Shuckses" and "Would youse evers?" as we wondered at the remarkable qualities of coincidence, and how small the world is.

Today was due to be my first day as a real tourist. My mission was to tour the Inishower Peninsular. Suitably dressed in all-weather clothing, I set off to do just that. I bent my head into the wind and rain, and pointed Ernest towards Malin Head. There wasn't much to see when I got there, the rain was coming down in a swirl which reduced vision to little more than the length of a football pitch – a Gaelic football pitch, of course.

The Malin Head made famous by a thousand shipping forecasts was an uninspiring sight, huddled against the uncomfortable weather. There was a good but twisting road curling out to the Head itself, and little sign of civilisation after the village of Malin huddled round a neatly mown, bright green grass triangle. At Malin Head itself there was a scattering of abandoned concrete blockhouses, where sat a young couple in their parked car, Belgian by its registration, staring out fixedly at the lowering clouds.

The ride improved as I turned my back on the Head, and pop-popped through the awful weather down a series of minor roads and lanes along the Northeast shore. I was relieved to find myself back in Culdaff, bought a newspaper and made for the pub to warm up and dry out. The news was of the hung parliament, and the prospect of a fresh coalition. The landlady was in good spirits, and was happy to explain the political scene to an outsider.

There's no real difference between the two main parties now, she said, which seems to be the way things are going all over. She broke off distractedly to give instructions to a very young girl with a worried expression, about putting out the lunch menus. When she returned to the conversation, she continued, "Around here the people vote for the candidates, not for their parties."

Donegal East had just voted into the Irish parliament the seventy-year-old brother of the previous representative, who had died, causing a new local election. The new member of the Dáil had never been involved with parliamentary politics before, I was told, but he lived locally, and was well liked, so people voted him into office anyway. "The young people have no interest at all. They've no idea who's for what, so they leave it alone. Dublin's a long way off from here, and we just get on with our lives without them. That's not to say we wouldn't like to get this business with the North sorted out, all right, but they seem to be getting on with it at last. It's been going on that long, it's hard to think of it without the troubles they've been having. We've no time for all that now, ourselves. Now, how's your drink?" I returned to my *Irish Times*.

I read the official statement by the Irish National Liberation Army about one of their number who had been shot dead during a raid on a general store in the South, in an unsuccessful attempt to steal £457 from the till. The INLA spokesman confirmed that at the time of his death, the shot man was "on active service in the struggle against British imperialism and Irish capitalism". The breakaway INLA is described as Marxist, but Trotskyist better describes this attitude. There was no mention of the objectives of the unification of Ireland (IRA) or the protection of minorities (Provos) in the sectarian struggle in Northern Ireland. The shopkeeper himself was unlikely to have been either an imperialist or a capitalist, and it is difficult to see how the untimely death of the INLA man could have contributed to the struggle against imperialism.

I had been spending a lot of time recently with my maps. I enjoy maps, and I was very pleased with the series of large-scale Irish Ordnance Survey maps that I had bought for the trip. As I studied them, and struggled with some of the names, I was reminded of the early days of map-making, as reflected in Brian Friel's play *Translations*.

An English mapmaker employed by the Ordnance Survey is given the task of recording local place-names. His orders are to translate the Irish names into English, but he is himself taken over by the charms of the Irish people, by the language, and by the poetry and the meaning of the Irish place-names. As the job progresses, he becomes more romantically "Irish", and his Irish assistant becomes more unimaginatively "English". The mapmaker concludes it is his duty to record names as closely as possible to the Irish. On one level, the play may be seen as an allegory about the nature of the relationship between the English and Irish peoples.

Not all the employees of the Ordnance Survey were as conscientious as Friel's cartographer, and in some parts of Ireland the place-names are still shown as ugly-sounding English translations from the Irish. Other districts are more fortunate, and the local folk history embodied in a place-name has been preserved for posterity. Irish is a rich language, in many aspects. The poet Aidan Carl Matthews wrote of *"Thirty-one names for seaweed/Written on the shore"*.

There is a spot on the map of Donegal which is peppered with megalithic remains and standing stones. Impressive archaeological statistics about North West Ireland abound: the longest barrow, the oldest cross, the biggest tomb, and the densest grouping of Stone Age relics in Europe (or is it the world?)

The rain was weakening, and I felt sufficiently fortified to launch forth with Ernest into the elements again. We picked our way down glistening lanes, with raindrops quivering on the leaves waiting to drop off as we disturbed them in our wake as we drove past. The sun made a re-appearance, and the wet landscape shone like liquid silver, mercurial. There were no other vehicles on the road but us, and in high spirits I encouraged Ernest to swing and sway as I flipped him along the lanes; he needed but little encouragement.

As I neared the megalithic playground shown on my map, I saw a rough, hand-painted sign at the roadside which said simply "Stock Cars" with an arrow pointing to the heart of what I knew to be downtown Megalithia. I ignored the archaeological riches on either side of me and followed an earthen track across a farmyard down to the seashore. In the middle of an estuary marsh, someone had built a concrete race circuit, no bigger than a speedway track.

A large crowd of spectators was gathered, and I parked Ernest on the grass and joined them. On the track, three or four "old bangers" were being coaxed into life by their boy drivers. The average age of the drivers was about 15, but there were grey heads among the mechanics, tweaking and teasing as they squeezed the last ounce of power from the ancient family saloon cars. The cars had been stripped of their doors, seats and windows, but oddities remained, like the occasional rear light cluster, still clinging like a limpet.

The bizarre contrast of wild landscape and industrial debris was heightened by the presence of a tightly penned-in herd of commercially reared deer just a few hundred yards from the racetrack, peering out through the chain fencing at the spectacle of automotive Sunday afternoon entertainment.

One stock car gave up the ghost, and was wheeled into the centre of the circuit. Another spluttered and died. Of the remaining three cars, one was obviously quite sick, and another was clearly much faster than the third. Nevertheless, when the signal was given by dropping a grubby chequered flag, all three cars roared off, and the race began. The drivers were learning fast, despite their youth. They hung out their rear ends on the bends, and they twitched their way up the straight, releasing a gush of power.

The faster car bumped into the slower ones a few times, and the driver of the really slow one pulled off the road, leapt round to the front of the car, and frantically made a show of pretending to fix the problem to get right back into the race. After some more circuits, the other two pulled off alongside the first, and joined him in anxiously examining the dead engine. This wasn't a race about winning; it was about taking part.

I left them to it, with an eye on the sinking sun, and went back to Ernest, now surrounded by an admiring group of 6 or 7 small boy racing enthusiasts. The leader was about 10, and he took a step forward and said with a knowledgeable air, "How big's your engine, mister?" I told him in a matter-of-fact manner, as if talking to an acknowledged expert, that it was 123 cc, with a bore of 55 mm and a stroke of 52 mm, it was a two-stroke engine, with a high compression ratio of 11.3:1 "Of course," I added in a confiding tone, "You'll probably know that the T5 stands for five transfer ports." He said "Oh right!" and swaggered off to tell his pals, and I started up and rode off past the deer and the standing stones.

The weather had improved to leave us a bright, warm evening, with a low orange sun. I rode through an empty landscape and came upon a deserted coastal gun fort which had been made into a military museum. The site dominated the sea approaches to Lough Swilly, and I was reminded of the Guns of Navarone. This must have been one of the forts which remained on lease to the British after the Treaty. The museum was closed, so I didn't have to struggle with a choice between continuing my ride through a summer's evening, or making an educational visit to the historical gun fortress.

Ernest needed petrol again, and we stopped at the next service station, in a small village called Creeslough. After the usual polite conversational introduction, the proprietor told me he had been to North London himself. In fact, he had even been to the Arsenal Stadium at Highbury. We shared a moment idly trying to recall the members of the team he would probably have seen when he was there, starting with the goalkeeper and finishing up with the centre-forward. I think we got them all right, and we felt quite pleased with ourselves. But all the while his ten-year-old son scowled at us from behind his Manchester United shirt.

Back in Culdaff, I decided to eat in the Village Café, but that was another bad mistake. How is it possible that people living so close to the sea have no idea how to fry a bit of fish? It took a pint in the pub to wash away the taste. Was there no decent fish-and-chips shop in Ireland? The crowd of customers in the bar was very different from the Beatle fans of the night before. Middle-aged and jolly, most of them, and one very elderly, frail lady who must have been 90 something. She was accompanied by her sixty-year-old daughter, but they didn't speak to one another. Each stared at the wall in front of them, lost in their own thoughts.

The daughter was uncomfortably thin. She was a serious smoker, of which there are not many left. She inhaled deeply, lifting her shoulders with a conscious effort, and then she held her breath, with the smoke locked in deep down inside her. Over the course of the next minute of so, the smoke escaped in curls and licks, from her mouth and down her nostrils. When you thought there couldn't possibly be any more smoke left inside her, she blew the last puff out from between her lips, and instantly raised her hand and took another deep drag. The tip of the cigarette glowed long and bright, and wickedly.

CHAPTER 19
LETTERKENNY AND BEYOND

The interior of the ancient fort of Griannan Aligh.

The next morning I said goodbye to Culdaff House, and made my way the short distance to Letterkenny, which was to serve as my base for exploring the next peninsular. On the way, I had to pass an ancient fort called Griannan Aligh – a variety of spellings exists. The fort is located high up on a hill, dominating the nearby main road and the surrounding countryside. It is said to have been a Stone Age fort, before it became the seat of the Kings of Ulster, the O'Neills. The last building was razed to the ground many centuries ago, but from an ancient ruin it was restored by a well-meaning Victorian gentleman to its present splendour.

I rode up to the top, and parked Ernest in the Stone Age car park. It was deserted. The rebuilt circular stone fort was very impressive, and the views were astounding. It was easy to stand alone on the ramparts, blasted by the winds and to imagine how things once were. I looked eastwards to Northern Ireland, and westwards towards the Atlantic, and America beyond. I scampered about the neatly piled stones, taking photographs and enjoying the views.

A German-registered camper van drew into the car park as I returned to Ernest. The retirement-aged driver and his companion immediately started to tidy up their vehicle, as if they couldn't bear to wait a moment longer. They swept the floor with a dustpan and brush, and they gathered microscopic fragments of detritus into tiny heaps. I felt like going up to them and saying "Never mind that. You really should go up to the fort, you know - it shouldn't be missed!" But then I thought they might be alarmed at being thus addressed in an empty car park by an apparent madman wearing a crash helmet, sailing waterproofs, and a green and orange backpack, so I left them to it. They were making a very thorough job of spring-cleaning their car, obviously enjoying it, and there are worse places to do it.

Further along the road, I saw a lay-by with a large vehicle parked, apparently serving refreshments to passing motorists, although I couldn't see any customers. A cup of tea sounded a good idea, so I pulled in and began to remove the more bulky bits of my driving gear, before approaching the mobile canteen.

The Asian proprietor was busy re-arranging his stock of snacks inside the open back doors of his van, and didn't notice me, so I called out "A cup of tea, please!" but I could tell from his reaction that something was amiss. He turned to me and looked quizzically at the figure before him. "Good idea" he said, with a brightening smile, "I'll put the kettle on!" I looked at the side of the van behind him and read "P. Patel & Son - Oriental Goods". No counter, no flap, not even a serving window. "I'm sorry, are you not a tea-caravan?" I said accusingly. "A conveyor of oriental delicacies, more like, but I can manage a cup of tea. I was going to take a breather myself. Just adjusting the load." He indicated the inside of his vehicle, which I now realised was a walk-in travelling shop. Saris and other cotton clothes were hanging cheek by jowl with cardboard boxes of groceries, and shelves of carved wooden figures and alarm clocks.

My companion produced an electric kettle from somewhere within the driver's cab, and poured two mugs of tea. "Only powdered milk, I'm afraid - sugar?" It always surprises me to hear a broad Yorkshire accent coming from an exotic, noble face from the Indian subcontinent. He smiled constantly, often breaking up a sentence into short phrases, interspersed with a friendly grin. It must be impossible not to buy something from this man, who was completely likeable. To dispel my obvious embarrassment, Mr. Patel began his story.

He started his mobile shop when business in Barnsley got a bit slack after the coalmine closures in Yorkshire in the 80s. At first, he just travelled with the usual grocery goods on the East Coast of England. Then one day – he couldn't remember why – he caught the ferry to Ireland, and has been coming back ever since. Over the years, he began to introduce more and more Indian items, spices, chapatis, clothes and ornaments. "People look out for me now, to stock up when the curry powder runs low. We don't make a fortune, but it makes a change from Barnsley three or four times a year. I sleep in the van, and it's made out real nice" he said. "And there's no one as friendly as the Irish" he added, "well except for us Yorkshiremen, of course. We're the friendliest folk I've ever met" he grinned broadly. "I've been away three weeks, and I've one more to go. Get back while there's still some decent cricket on, I hope, as soon as the stock runs down."

He looked across at Ernest, and asked "Are you a tourist then, on holiday are you, like?" I gave him a short version run-down of my circumstances and told him I was from North London. His face brightened: "Do you know Barnet? I've got folk living there. Never been down there myself – well you know what they say about softy southerners" he grinned broadly, and took my empty cup. I thanked him for his hospitality, and resisted the urge to apologize again for taking him for a tea-stop. He seemed a very happy man, but out of place in this land of bogs and empty spaces. I don't know though – a bit like the Yorkshire Moors, perhaps.

My digs in Letterkenny were in a modest end-of-terrace house on the outskirts of town. I was warmly received by a lady whose first name was Majella, which I thought was a lovely name! After leaving my bags in my room, I set off with Ernest, heading north again, up the opposite bank of Lough Swilly. The day had now decided to put on its best face, and a bright sun shone from a blue sky, broken with luminous cumulus clouds.

The seawater in Lough Swilly was as blue as the sky it reflected, but unfortunately the surface was broken by a clutch of at least twenty circular salmon cages. I knew that it was from somewhere near this point that the Earls of Tyrconnell had sailed away into exile. Close by, a devout and gifted Victorian churchgoing lady had dedicated herself to the writing of hymns. Among the hundreds she produced were three which were to be the most evocative in the memories of several generations of children brought up in the British Empire: *"Once in Royal David's City"*, *There is a Green Hill Faraway"*, and that all time favourite for weddings *"All Things Bright and Beautiful"*.

I sang the last one to myself as I pressed on until I arrived level with the gun fort museum at Dunree on the far side, which I had almost visited the day before. I could make out the details of the fortifications quite clearly a mile or so across the blue water. The mouth of Lough Swilly is a vast natural harbour where it meets the sea, capable of sheltering the entire fleet of the Armada many times over. If the Spanish captains had only had the sense to anchor here and wait for the storms to pass by, many of them would have been saved: perhaps some of them did.

Around the next bend, I came upon a small lay-by, thoughtfully situated for touring motorists to look at the view, open their thermos flasks, and eat their jam sandwiches. And the view was truly stunning. Miles below me was a long empty strand by a cobalt sea. Gradually, as I watched, two or three figures became discernible on the beach, one with a dog, and another braving the intemperate waters of the North Atlantic, taking a swim.

It was a grand view, and I slowly became aware that I was sharing it with another almost motionless person, cloth-capped and thornproof jacketed, probably in his late 60s. His most noticeable feature was a very red nose. He told me he was a retired hospital porter, with a small thirty-acre farm just down the road, beyond. He often came up here for the view. He didn't really farm to make a profit; he just kept a few sheep and some ponies, but not to make a living from them. He was worried about the foxes. Couldn't he call in the local hunt? I asked. "Foxes are a protected species hereabouts now, so there's no hunting allowed, and every year they come along and play havoc with my lambs, just as soon as they're born. And what can I do to protect them? I'm no hunter. I don't know how to kill a fox. But I'll have to do something to save my lambs. Maybe I'll get a gun."

He wanted to find out more about me. Had I come along the shore of Lough Swilly? Had I seen the salmon cages there? "They belong to one of those international corporations, yes - a multinational. The locals hate them because they look so ugly, and they're poisoning the natural wildlife. I used to have a hundred swans at the bottom of my land, just beyond there, and now there's only a few left." He didn't explain the connection between the swans and the salmon farm; he left it unsaid, as if further words of explanation were unnecessary. We stood quietly for a while contemplating the sadness of this news, and wondering what to do about his fox problem, and then he said he had to go and make his tea. "Do you like it here? Yes? it certainly is a lovely spot. I'm pleased you like it here, and thank you for the conversation."

As I rode into the village of Carrickart, a figure of a man ran out from the petrol station, darted across the road in front of me, and disappeared into a brick building on my left. He was carrying a dark coat and some kind of a hat in his hand. A few yards further along, another man came running up the road straight towards me, as if he wanted me to stop. A car stormed into the road 100 yards ahead, flashing its lights and sounding its horn. It stopped with a squeal of brakes and picked up the running man, now wearing a helmet, then roared on, almost without stopping, and disappeared. It had to be some kind of emergency call.

I carried on cautiously, in case anyone else was lying in wait, and stopped at a crossroads to check my bearings, comparing the names on a finger post with my map. A small fire engine came roaring past, ringing its bell, hogging the road, and disappeared up the road I had already decided not to take. The mysterious emergency was explained: I had seen the scramble of the local fire brigade.

On the other side of the road, in a field, I noticed a strange pile of what looked like pinkish sacks. I crossed over, and heard a buzzing sound and the bleating of sheep. Looking over a stone wall I saw a burly sheepshearer at work. The pile I saw was a pile of newly shorn fleeces. The unshorn sheep were huddled into a corner, nervously awaiting their fate. My greeting was not returned by the shearer nor by the boy helping him. The shearer looked about 30, with a mop of blond hair and a weathered complexion. He pretended not to notice me peering over the wall, and the boy stared stonily back at me in a finger-pointing silence. The shearer released the sheep he had been working on, and it scuttled off, looking embarrassed.

The boy pushed another sheep towards the shearer, who dextrously sliced into the fleece. "He's very good, isn't he?" I said to the boy. No reply. "Will he do me next?" I quipped. No reaction. "Well, 'bye then! I'll be off." He lowered his eyes, as he lined up the next victim, so I decided not to move. We kept this up for 5 more minutes, with me trying to catch their attention and start a conversation, and they succeeding in keeping themselves to themselves. In desperation, I resorted to the subject of the weather. "They say it could rain. What do you think?" It worked.

The shearer released his shorn sheep, and wiped his mouth with the back of his hand. The electric shears stopped momentarily, and the boy looked very nervous, as if expecting to have his ears boxed. "What do I think, you say? I think it'll rain sooner or later, mate, in this bleedin' country." Then he grasped the next sheep being offered by the boy, and started clipping again. His accent was definitely not Donegal, unless there is a Donegal in Australia. But what was an Australian doing in the West of Ireland? I was clearly going to get no answer from him, or from the boy (he at least must be local, surely?). The answer was obvious. This was a professional shearer, perhaps a champion, working his way around the globe. With a "G'day!" I gave a big wave, and went back to Ernest. Should we chase the fire engine? Ernest showed no enthusiasm, so I dropped the idea. He was quite correct in suggesting that there was no dignity in such a proposal.

We carried on to Dunfanaghy. In the centre of town is a building erected by "Alexander Robert Stewart Esq. of Ards House AD 1845", and another plaque was to the memory of his agent Edmund Murphy Esq. JP, who had occupied the post of Government Arbitrator and

Chief Receiver for Ireland. Unless they were among the handful of caring landowners and agents who looked after their tenants during the years of the Famine when the potato crop failed, it is unlikely they were much loved thereabouts.

In the hotel bar over a cup of coffee, the barman confessed he couldn't tell me anything about Messrs Stewart and Murphy. He was a stranger in town, himself. He didn't know where the fiddler O'Rahilly lived either, but suggested I try the Oyster Bar over the road. That looked a bit more like the sort of establishment a fiddler might frequent, in his experience. In the Oyster Bar they said it was a bit early for O'Rahilly, but I could try one or two other pubs a bit later on, around nine o'clock.

The barman was much more interested in the election news on television. The Government was being knocked out of a ruling coalition onto the benches of the opposition. The next item was a news report about a kneecapping in Belfast. The camera showed the location where a young man had been seized on the street and dragged into this smart new council estate of redbrick houses by three balaclava-hooded gunmen. They had made him lie face down on the ground just here by this child's bicycle, placed the muzzle of a sawn-off shotgun against the back of his knee, and then shot him through both legs. The camera pointed out the dark red bloodstain marking the spot. The studio newscaster added that one of the victim's legs had been partially amputated in a six-hour surgical operation, and he was still in intensive care.

I was horrified and transfixed by the images on the screen. It somehow seemed so much worse that it had happened in a bright, clean, litter-free modern housing estate. The Oyster Bar barman and the other customers had turned away from the television screen, and were discussing the local election results. Violence was not news to them: they had seen it all before.

~☆~

I finished my drink thoughtfully. With thirty miles to ride back to Letterkenny, I didn't fancy the idea of hanging around the pubs of

Dunfanaghy for the next three hours, and driving back in the dark. It was beginning to look as if I wasn't going to find the fiddler O'Rahilly, cousin of my London friend and confidant of my new friend from Ohio. I toyed with the thought of coming back another time, but once again I felt driven to keep going forward, according to my timetable. It is difficult to remain resolute when you're tired and hungry – which I suddenly realised I was – so I turned my back on The Oyster Bar, and started to think about dinner, as we pootled back along the road to Letterkenny.

At my request, Majella had taken my dirty washing to her laundry – sure it was her day to be going anyway – and when I arrived back home, there was a neat pile of shirts and underwear on my bed. For some reason I found this very exciting, and I thanked Majella profusely, going well over the top in my praise for her laundry arrangements. When you are on the road, considerations such as laundry take on a greater significance than normal. You make a mental note of the location of dry cleaners, and are always unconsciously searching for a wash and iron service. Majella's people did a great job at what seemed to me a very reasonable price.

That evening I walked into Letterkenny town centre. It was a long walk, and there was a drizzle of rain falling, but I thought Ernest deserved a break, and anyway, if I didn't have to ride back, I could have a drink or two. I had already checked out a pub with a restaurant on the first floor for dinner. On the way, I called into a promising-looking bar, with etched glass windows and a well-worn brass handle on the door, which suggested an interior with bags of character.

Most of the customers were seated at the bar, and I joined them, while I thought about what to drink. There were strange names to come to terms with, but they broadly fell into the categories of ale, stout, lager or flashy-sounding new-label wonder drinks dreamed up by the marketing men. The youthful barman was languidly discussing the state of the world with a disinterested customer at the other end of the bar. He lit a cigarette. He said he sympathised with the customer's point of view. He wiped a glass with a crumpled cloth.

At first I thought he was following the company line by allowing new customers time to think through the entire range of flashy-sounding new-label wonder drinks, before making up their minds. But after five minutes of being ignored, it occurred to me there might be another reason. Was I being cold-shouldered because of my sensible walking-in-wet-weather clothing? It was either that or incompetence on the part of the barman, or what my old existentialist pal Jean-Paul Sartre would have called "mauvaise foi". After seven and a half minutes I decided I didn't really care to find out which it was, and left the building. I was not missed, and neither barman nor customer acknowledged my leaving as I squeezed past.

I checked out another bar a few doors down, but it was full of smoke and chattering students, so I went straight on to where I had already decided to have dinner. The bar was one of those fashionable modern mock-ups, all brand-new old-fashioned brass and stained wood, but tastefully done, for all that. I went upstairs to the restaurant and after studying the menu, I confidently ordered the Chef's Special.

There was a young Italian couple at the next table. They read the menu with a mixture of disbelief and incomprehension, and wondered what the little plastic sachets in a bowl on the table were for, nestling among packets of Demerara sugar and saccharine. "What is this?" asked the Italian girl, holding up a sachet of brown sauce fearfully between her finger and thumb. "On no account should you eat that", I counselled. "It is a spicy brown sauce, which some people like to put on tasteless breakfast sausages, or burnt bacon. The other one is even worse" I added, pointing out the tomato ketchup sachet. "It is sweet!" They were both horrified, and she dropped the sachet quickly back into the bowl, as if it had burned her fingers. "Sweet? Really?" the boy said with disbelief.

Some elements of eating in modern restaurants in the British Isles are impossible to explain to visitors from another culture, where – unlike in these parts – the taste of food is considered important. "And please, what is the difference between a fillet steak and a sirloin steak?" said the boy. This one was easy: "I believe fillet steak is more tender, but sirloin has more flavour, and is cheaper." They decided to have one of each.

I was brought back to earth as my Chef's Special was bumped on the table in front of me. It was very enjoyable, and well presented. Catering colleges are now producing large numbers of good chefs, and this meal was the proof of it. I could scoff at the roadhouse presentation of tabletop sachets of sauce, but there was nothing wrong with the quality and appearance of the food. A sour note was struck by the in-house background music.

A boring country and western singer droned and plodded his way through an album of Elvis all-time hits. A waitress with a "Maggie" badge told me proudly it was Willy Nelson. Not the Willy Nelson I knew, so perhaps it was me that was out of sorts. Someone said that country and western songs fall into three categories: songs are either about Before Divorce, During Divorce, or After Divorce. This doesn't explain why Country music is so popular in a Catholic country like Ireland, where divorce is uncommon. Despite the competition from international pop rock, Country is the most popular music because it is sentimental, and generally tuneful. On the walk home, the drizzle had eased off a little, but the street lamps still bleached out the wet pavements.

The late night news told me that there had been three more kneecappings in Belfast. The tones of the newsreader were very matter-of-fact. This was just another news story. It is generally accepted that kneecapping is more often than not the punishment given to a drugs dealer or minor informer, and so nobody minds too much. It is the sort of flawed rough justice which is tainted by personal grudges and prejudices. It is third world stuff, and there is no other way of looking at it. A more cynical commentator would point out that the executioners are often drug dealers themselves, and this is their way of dealing with the competition.

We have mistakenly come to accept the term "kneecapping" as a sort of mild admonishment for someone stepping out of line, almost a slap on the wrist, or a warning razor-cut across the cheek. When kneecapping is carried out with a large-calibre bullet, or a shotgun, the damage caused is unthinkable. It doesn't just leave the victim with a limp to identify him as a wrongdoer for the rest of his life: even with modern surgery techniques, the wound cannot be repaired, and the only solution is to amputate the leg. The victim becomes a burden on society for the rest of his unhappy life.

Chapter 20
Rendezvous with a saint,

The next morning, I headed for the coast, passing through the Glenveagh National Park. This is a landscape of forests and lakes, but is not as special as I had been led to believe. Perhaps I was comparing it to the English Lake District, which strikes a more operatic note. A signpost led me to the birthplace of Saint Columba in 597 AD, who founded a few abbeys, and took Christianity to Scotland via the Isle of Iona. Beside a monstrous Victorian cross is a modest stone ruin, overgrown with grass and mosses. This is said to be the remains of the house in which Saint Columba was born, and it was attractively and even romantically evocative. I noticed a strange deposit on the grass, and when I knelt down I discovered it was melted candle wax. Odd. Even odder was the spectacle of me on my hands and knees in an attitude of prayer at the birthplace of a saint, so I hastily struggled to my feet, and looked around in case I should have been seen.

As an active member of the Church of Atheists for Christ, I was in danger of blowing my street cred. But I was quite alone. There were fresh cut flowers lying on a flat stone at the base of the cottage ruin. When I bought a newspaper later, I learned that by coincidence the day before my visit was the 1400th anniversary of the saint's birth, and that a small religious ceremony had taken place at the site, in the presence of no less than the then Irish President, Mrs. Mary Robinson. This explained the candle wax on the grass. The Roman Catholic Church is big on candles.

I pressed on through a valley floored with peat bog, a long road described as a "scenic route", which slipped spectacularly between high mountain peaks, and skirted a bleak, narrow lake and silent forestry plantations. As far as Ernest and I were concerned, it was just a very uneven, lumpy bog road, full of sudden potholes, lurking to catch you by surprise, and unexpected humps and bumps. It made the life of a scooterist very uncomfortable, and detracted my attention from what the guidebook describes as the "magnificent landscape". I was pleased and relieved when it delivered me safely to the village of Bunbeg.

The harbour at Bunbeg was more like Cornwall than Ireland, very cove-like and quaint, surrounded by rocks which gave it a hidden, enclosed, intimate feeling. To complete the illusion of a Cornish hideaway, there was even an artist, labouring over her easel in the struggle to get down her impressions of the landscape onto the canvas. And over there was another artist, and another. Altogether there were 14 elderly artists working on the quayside. I had unwittingly stepped into an art class, and I quietly stepped out again, and carried on my way.

I rode on through a day that was rapidly improving to display a blue sky and bright white cumulus clouds. This was a landscape of small lakes, well known to generations of salmon and trout fishermen as the Rosses. The centre of this fishing paradise is the town of Dungloe, and I had read about the delights of Sweeney's Hotel as a base of many memorable fishing trips. Across the road from Sweeney's was a Bank of Ireland, with a roadside hole-in-the-wall machine, to pay for my lunch.

The first time it rejected my card, I put it down to a simple mistake. When it presumed to reject my card a second time, I confess I became impatient. The bank was open to the public, so I stomped in and approached the counter. "Is there something wrong with your machine?" I angrily accused a rosy-cheeked teenaged teller. "I don't think so, Sir. Why, what's the matter?" "Well, it has just rejected my card twice", waving my card as I spoke. "Was it that card, Sir?" she asked sweetly, and I looked at the card. It was a phone card. "Ah! Yes. I see what you mean. Thank you, that must be it; I'll try again." and I backed out through the door, keeping flat against the wall like a cartoon cat, and guiltily sidled up to the machine. It clearly preferred my bank card over a phone card, and immediately gave me the money, without further ado. I gave a wave through the bank doorway to the perplexed teller as I passed.

Sweeney's isn't what it used to be. In place of a jolly riot of excited fishermen, the interior was deserted apart from a nervous travelling salesman hurriedly finishing a sandwich between calls. Perhaps it was the wrong time of day, and all the fishermen were hard at work at the waterside, lashing the water with their flylines and decimating the fish population. I had heard many stories of the mysterious failure of the runs of sea trout in the West of Ireland. This area was once world-famous for its prolific runs of sea trout, and this reputation sustained a healthy tourist industry. Some put the blame for the decline in the numbers of sea trout on diseases caused by the salmon farms. Others say it is just part of the natural cycle of rises and falls in the fortunes of sea trout over the centuries they have been running up Irish rivers.

There was a feeling of mute emptiness in Sweeney's, and after making short work of a passable cheese sandwich, I went out to buy a newspaper and read it at leisure in the bar across the road. By one of those Irish coincidences which I have now grown used to, the *Irish Times* chose that day to reprint an article written in the 1930s by the humorist Patrick Campbell about a riotous golfing weekend spent across the road, at Sweeney's Hotel.

I returned to Ernest, and was busy adjusting various items of my all-weather clothing, putting bits on and taking bits off, when a kindly-looking, elderly man approached. He was frail, and I judged he was in his late 70s; he seemed very interested in what I was doing. He spoke at once, and directly: "That's a fine machine you have there." His interest suggested he knew about these things. "Did you have one yourself?" I asked. "I do not, no. I never had one, but I can tell yours is a fine machine." And then, with one foot on the pavement and the other in the road he told me his life story.

He was born and bred in Dungloe, but he had been away for a long time. During the last war he served in the British Merchant Navy. He was on a coaster on the regular run between London and Glasgow, coal and such. Then he was away for 27 years working in America and Canada. He didn't come back to Dungloe until his working days were over. There was no work for him here at the time he went away, and that's why he left, along with many others.

Yes, he had seen many changes in his time. Yes, Sweeney's used to be the one and only hotel, and a very lively place it was too. There's another fine new hotel now, just on the edge of town. He'd been in there for a family wedding, and it is a credit to the town. Very modern. Yes, there are a lot of banks in town now, not like before. He could remember when there was only the one, but it was for people in business. Nowadays there's all sorts of people go into the banks. He didn't have enough money to worry about that sort of thing himself though. But it was nice to know the banks were there for those who need them. There were shops of all kinds too now. The shop behind him used to be the main shop, selling everything. If you couldn't get what you wanted there, you had to get it from a catalogue. Nowadays there's very little that people want for. Not like the old days. They were hard times.

Would I excuse him now? He was going to have his lunch in the cafe opposite, as he did every day. They did a good lunch there if I was interested. No? Then he would be on his way, or they would start to worry if he was late. They'd be sending out a search party! He laughed. Did I like his town? It was a fine town. Was I touring around? It was a fine day for touring around. And he wished me good luck. I wished him the same.

My next target was Lough Rosmore Bay, which I knew to be the site of another Armada wreck, still unlocated. You may remember that this was the *Duquesa Santa Ana*, the ship taken over by Don Alonso de Leiva, the designated deputy of the Armada leader, the Duke of Medina Sidonia. When his own ship, the *Sancta Maria Encoronada* went down further south in Blacksod Bay, he moved the survivors of his ship's company onto the *Duquesa Santa Ana*, only to be shipwrecked a second time, in Lough Rosmore Bay. He re-grouped his ship's company, and fortified a ruined castle on nearby Kiltoorish Lake, before marching overland to join a third ship, the *Girona*, which as I had already seen, was subsequently wrecked at Lacada Point on the Giant's Causeway.

There is a small holiday-home caravan park now beside a tiny sandy beach in the sparsely populated hamlet of Trawmore, which gives a good view of Lough Rosmore Bay.

As I looked about me, I agreed it was the obvious landing spot for the crew of a stricken ship, anchorless and de-masted, its remaining sails in tatters, driven to land by northeasterly gales. They probably managed to nudge the ship up against the submerged rocks over there, so the crew could offload as much as possible of the arms and provisions, sheltered from the storm here in this quiet bay. A wall is still standing of the island fort where de Leiva and the survivors of the *Sancta Maria Encoronada* and the *Duquesa Santa Ana* held out. Until recently, a small cannon salvaged from his ship by de Leiva could still be seen here in the fort, but it was spirited away in the 1970s, and is now rumoured to lie in a private residence.

These vacant, deserted landscapes were very evocative in the bright weather, with clouds scudding dramatically across the scene at storm speed. The isolated cottages dotted around showed no signs of life, not even a sheep to break the enduring texture of rocks, grassy clumps and water.

At the small harbour of Rosbeg there was an empty but recently concreted pier, and I rode out to the end with Ernest, staring down into the water and daring a relic from the Armada wreck to show itself. Nothing happened. I rode back down the pier, past an abandoned caravan at the entrance, with one end smashed open to reveal a distressed interior, as in the wartime photographs of bombed houses with incongruously hanging picture-frames and peeling wallpaper. As I pop-popped past, a door in the partition wall crashed open and a wild-looking woman burst through, shaking her fist and screaming at the intruder who dared to disturb her peace. She wore ragged clothes and had dishevelled spiky hair, with the demented look of the deranged. She appeared to live in the unsmashed end of the caravan, haphazardly parked at the end of this deserted pier, as though it had been abandoned in haste, after a nasty accident. I nodded in her direction, and acknowledged her cries, but I thought it best not to stop, and enter in a conversation.

Ardara is a town to go back to. I entered down a steep hill with pretty buildings on each side. At first, everything was too pretty, and too clean, as if it was competing for the annual Cleanest Village Award.

My suspicions were deepened when I spotted a group of tourists cluttering up a souvenir shop, but I carried on across a bridge and into a sharp right-angled bend.

Suddenly the over-tidy main street became a real high street with a lived-in look. There were the shambolic remains of a small street market, and this contributed to the feeling of bustle. I've always been a sucker for markets, however modest, and as I came within its magnetic field, I felt myself being drawn towards it. I parked Ernest nearby, and was immediately surrounded by a noisy crowd of excited bodies, and a television news crew, who came pouring out of a shop, spilling onto the cobbles where I had parked. It was all so sudden, and quite alarming.

They were not mobbing me, however; the centre of attraction was a grey-haired man who emerged from behind the shop-front and I now noticed it was plastered with election posters. The excited group wore rosettes, armbands and tee shirts with the mysterious letters MMDS – NO!

A nervous and equally excited television reporter was lining up the next shot with his cameraman. "So, we'll have him come out of the shop and join the band of his supporters. How's that?" The cameraman peered into his viewfinder and backed into a market stall as he looked for his shot, uttering mild curses and the sighs of exasperation which camera crew always make to show their contempt for production personnel.

"Will it work?" asked the youthful interviewer anxiously. The question went unanswered, and the interviewer bit his lip. I was obviously in their way. "Shall I move my scooter?" I offered, "Or do you mind it being in your shot?" "Would you ever?" said a surprised interviewer, "That would be really kind!" As I wheeled Ernest back a few yards, I asked my new, nervous friend what MMDS stood for. The explanation was surprising.

The grey-haired gentleman was Thomas Gildea, who was the newly elected parliamentary representative for the constituency of Donegal South West. He had stood for election as an independent against candidates from the main parties. Being anti-MMDS was not just his main policy, it was his only policy.

My nervous informant could not tell me what the letters MMDS stood for, but he explained it is a tax dreamed up by the previous Irish government, to be levied on the receiving of television programmes which are from non-Irish broadcasters. This means not only the programmes carried by satellite and cable companies, but also broadcasts received free from neighbouring countries, such as BBC-TV and Ulster TV from Northern Ireland, and other signals from independent broadcasters which waft across the Irish Sea. To make sure the tax was effective, it was levied on the relay companies who provide these extra channels as part of a cable and satellite service. It is argued that the tax is justified because it corresponds to the television license required to receive the state television company, Telefis Eirann.

Programmes from overseas are very popular. Many Irish viewers do not bother to watch what they consider to be the inferior, parochial service offered by the Irish state broadcaster, RTE, and they are violently opposed to being taxed for viewing what has always been free before. The Irish Government is very conscious of the political undesirability of viewing television from a foreign power, which expresses views which are in many respects quite unacceptable to the Irish State and to the established Catholic Church.

They misjudged the intensity of feeling against the tax, which proved to be so strong that Tom Gildea was elected on little more than just an anti-MMDS ticket. Under the system of proportional representation used in Ireland, he polled 17% of the vote on the first count, but 25% on the sixth count, enough to take him into third place and guarantee him a seat in the Dail. The Press referred to him as the "television deflector" candidate, but I met no one who could explain this term to me either.

Ardara reminded me of one of the first small towns I ever knew in the West of Ireland, Enistymon, County Clare. Most towns of this size are just strips of ribbon development along the main street, but Enistymon is unusual in that it has a crossroads, and is a popular market town. It is bigger now, but when I first went there, it was famous for having a permanent population of about 270 souls and 67 pubs. And they were wonderful pubs! Typically, a conventional, traditional shop front would be distinguished by a discreet sign of a brewer or whiskey maker. For example, there was a saddler, with a counter on one side of the shop displaying all the accoutrements you would associate with leather goods, and the other side of the room was a bar. This struck me as a very civilised arrangement – you could have a drink while you shopped. There was a grocer-bar, a gents-outfitters-bar, a newsagent-bar, a hardware-shop-bar, and a baker-bar. My favourite was the sweetshop-bar. On one side a cheerful white-haired lady sold gobstoppers to boisterous children, before moving round to the other counter to pull a pint. There were ordinary pubs in Enistymon as well, but I always favoured the shop-pubs.

Ardara has a good number of small bars – I didn't count them, but in parts it seemed that every other shop was a bar. I called into a likely looking establishment, and asked for a coffee. It was a cosily sized bar, but through an archway it opened out into an enormous function room. The landlady told me this was the music room. The town is well known for its music, and they have live music every night.

My timing was wrong again. For a moment, I considered going to the concert that night, but live music without a drink loses half its effect, and there was no way I could risk a drink before a long ride back through unknown roads in the dark. It was not just the fear of being caught by the local constabulary. If you make a mistake driving a car, you might damage the paintwork. If you make the same mistake on two wheels, you could end up dead. So I decided to leave Ardara's musical hotspots for another occasion, and after a stroll around the town, I pointed Ernest towards the way home and kick-started his eager 125 ccs of throbbing power into life.

Chapter 21
South to Donegal

The following morning, I overestimated the distance to Donegal, my next stop. The weather was grey and miserable, but at least it made no pretence to be otherwise. I dressed sensibly for the rain I knew I would meet on the road, and when it came, I was already close to my destination. Shortly after I started out, I saw a roadside signpost to Lifford, which triggered something in my memory.

Lifford was the frontier crossing point from Donegal to the Hiring Fair in Strabane. Until as recently as the Second World War, impoverished Donegalers would walk long distances from their homes in the Republic to present themselves in the market place at Strabane. In this hangover from the Medieval Hiring Fairs, if they were lucky enough to be chosen, they would be taken on at slave wages by wealthy Protestant farmers in Northern Ireland. The contract was typically for six months, and the conditions were utterly miserable. Children were paid about £1 a month, which they didn't receive until the end of the contract. This relic of the Feudal System didn't disappear until the late 1940s. But the unfeeling exploitation of their wretched relatives, living on the verge of starvation, lives on in the folk-memory of modern citizens of the Republic, and it will be a long time before they can find forgiveness.

The directions I had been given for the house I was looking for didn't work out, until I realised they had assumed I would be coming into Donegal City from the opposite direction than the one my landlady had assumed I would be using; instead of the more usual clockwise circuit, I was on an anti-clockwise route. I mentally reversed the directions, and immediately found the house without difficulty. I was too early again, so I went for a ride around in the rain.

I had expected a town as old as Donegal to be quite traditional, but there were tourist coaches nosing around the central Diamond, and too many new buildings and too much fresh paintwork. One advantage as far as I was concerned was that the cluster of retail shops included a bookshop.

Most bookshops are designed for browsing, even when you're wearing wet-weather gear and carrying an orange bomb; I find it very easy to lose an hour even in the most modest bookshop. In the Donegal bookshop, the religious section was unusually large, but there was also a good selection of Irish books, literature as well as folklore. It used to be quite difficult to find a copy of such Irish literary classics as *Twenty Years A-Growing*, or John Millington Synge's *The Aran Islands*, but here were several editions of these titles and others, lined up on the shelves, waiting to waylay the unwary tourist browser. I like to think demand for these titles comes from the locals as well, but the most important fact is that the books are readily available to whoever passes by.

The house where I was staying was modern and rather grandly middle-class. I peeled off my several layers of waterproofs before announcing my arrival. The wet rubber overshoes were particularly difficult to roll back while standing on one leg, wobbling dangerously, leaning against the front door. I must have pushed against the doorbell without realising, because the door was opened by the lady of the house, who ignored the spectacle of what looked like a half-undressed motorcycle messenger hopping on one foot, and holding on to her porch. She smiled in welcome (I think) and showed me up to a small but over-furnished room under the eaves of the roof.

When I had satisfied her enquiry about the time of my breakfast for the next morning, I unloaded my travelling luggage, and took a hot shower to warm up. I took my leave of my new landlady, who advised me to wrap up well against the rain because "There'll be some more of it before long." Since it was still raining, as it had been doing all morning, I wondered if she meant it would rain more heavily, or for longer, but I didn't ask, and she went about her business.

I felt lightheaded without the burden of my extra luggage; I set out again with Ernest, singing loudly to myself – a strange acoustic effect in my crash helmet – as I headed westwards. My ultimate destination was to be the somewhat ominous-sounding Heritage Centre Village at

Glencolumbkillie. This tourist facility was dreamed up and put together by the local priest, one Father McDyer, to create employment for the inhabitants of this remote, under-resourced and impoverished parish, and put a stop to the emigration that was stealing the valley of its youth.

I had read that the main attractions were a folk museum and a group of vernacular cottages which had been restored with the interiors of earlier centuries, for the benefit of visitors, and that sounded like an interesting prospect. My visit would coincide with the tail end of the celebrations of the 1400th anniversary of St. Columba, who gave his name to the village by reason of some association he had with the glen, although I can't remember quite what it was. It seems to me that he was always founding monasteries wherever he could hang his hat. Even the awful weather could be looked on as a positive advantage: who else would be foolish enough to visit the remote Glencolumbkillie on a day such as this? Surely I should have the place to myself.

As I pressed on, the weather became more wet, and the road became more uneven, and the closer I got to the fishing port of Killybegs, the more juggernaut cold-store trucks I met on the way. I was quite looking forward to seeing Killybegs, not only because it was yet another location associated with the Armada, where the beleaguered Don Alonso de Leiva joined the *Girona*, his last ship, but because it was famous as a traditional fishing port. In recent years, it has flourished in the changed modern climate of big business deep-sea fishing, which is dominated by giant, but faceless European multinational corporations.

Perhaps it was the weather, but I couldn't find a place to park. Every inch of roadway was edged with the dreaded yellow lines, and even Ernest couldn't be fitted into the gaps. I pootled around, getting wetter, and grumpier. Somehow, it was more depressing driving slowly through the rain, than speeding along through open country. I rode down to the harbour, and drew close to the fishing boats. They were like monsters, absolutely huge, towering above the quayside, leering scornfully down at the miniature human figures who dared to approach them. These were modern factory ships, capable no doubt of netting, stripping, gutting, filleting, packaging and freezing every fish which came their way. They had nothing of the jaunty, jolly, bouncy little fishing boats of my youth. Not a salt-caked smokestack in sight! And no jolly fishermen, either.

I sought refuge from the weather in the Harbour View Bar overlooking the harbour. Once inside, I realised that there wasn't even a window, let alone a harbour view, but already things began looking better. There was hot homemade soup on the menu, and a group of young people at the far end of the bar was enjoying a laugh and a joke. If the youth of Killybegs could find something to laugh at on a cold, miserable June day, Killybegs couldn't be as bad as it seemed.

My mood improved as I removed layers of wet clothing and absorbed spoonfuls of steaming soup. My fingertips tingled as the blood found its way back into the extremities. A discreet puddle formed around my feet as water-droplets trickled their way down the folds of my over-trousers and plinked onto the lino. A distant television droned on comfortingly and anonymously. Such warm cosiness could not be allowed to last, however, and I pulled myself together. Ernest and I had a Heritage Centre to visit! The wind and the rain would not stop us. We shall overcome! The noisy group from the end of the bar passed by on their way to the street. Their accents told me they were not happy-go-lucky locals, but holidaying Americans.

The road out of town became even bumpier and pockmarked with puddles. These needed to be treated with respect by Ernest; there was no telling how deep the puddles were, and a scooter wheel could easily disappear in some of them. At least there was very little traffic, presumably because it was all heading eastwards from Killybegs towards Donegal City and beyond, while all there was in the direction I was heading was the west coast, and beyond that – America.

The road narrowed, and the hedgerows closed in to meet the edge of the tarmac, soggy fuchsia bells glistening as I passed by. Suddenly, as I rounded a bend on a dark section where the trees touched together overhead, I came upon a solitary bedraggled kitten, trotting down the middle of the road. There was no sign of a house, or even a gateway, and I could not imagine where the kitten could have appeared from.

As I slowed to wonder whether I should go back and at least guide the kitten back to the hedgerow, a giant timber lorry roared around the bend towards me, rattling and bouncing, well over the central line and forcing me across the roadway towards the verge and the ditch.

Ernest was startled, and he gave a definite lurch and a wobble. No sooner had we recovered control, than two more timber lorries cluttered around the bend in mad pursuit of their leader. If the kindly patron saint of kittens was on the job, the bedraggled kitten would be snatched up in the palm of a holy hand and held safe while the lorries rumbled past. If the saint was not paying attention, their charge would by now almost certainly be in Kitten Heaven. Either way, there seemed no point in me going back to pick up the pieces. This was the argument I had with myself as I continued guiltily along the wet, potholed road to Glencolumbkillie.

I felt somehow to blame, so to be on the safe side, as I rode along, I made up a story for myself about a certain naughty little kitten who went out to play in the rain. He was frightened by a big lorry, and ran back to his Mummy as fast as he could go. She was very pleased to see him, and licked him all over, and told him never to go off in the rain again. And they lived happily ever after, of course.

The Heritage Centre had better be worth all this, I added through gritted teeth, as I splashed and bounced ever westwards. But it didn't come up to expectations. My first discovery was that the three period cottages could only be visited as part of a guided tour, which had to be booked in advance. So they were off the agenda. The good news was that in the Heritage Café they served excellent mugs of something hot (it may or may not have been instant coffee, or perhaps tea – hard to say) and a very passable homemade fruitcake. The mugs were chunky and comfortable, fitting perfectly into my cold hands.

A small group of us visitors huddled together in what may have been a scout hut, travellers taking refuge from the storm, trapped by the elements after succumbing to the attractions of a visit to Glencolumbkillie in the rain, only to be disappointed by the non-availability of the cottages. We concentrated on making our mugs of hot liquid last as long as possible, searching out every last crumb of fruitcake from the folds of the paper doily, and then examining the parish notices on the wall with great interest. Anything to delay the moment when we would have to go back to the weather outside the hut, where drops of the Atlantic Ocean were travelling in level flight through the air.

This horizontal rain is a characteristic of storms in the West of Ireland. I was once making a call in a telephone box which had some of its windows broken. I stopped in mid-conversation when I realised that the rain was coming in horizontally through one broken windowpane, and exiting through another, on the other side. Back in the hut, I nonchalantly produced a map from my pocket, and realised that everyone else was doing the same. Wet walkers pored over large-scale survey maps, and blue-rinsed Americans tried to make sense of complimentary small-scale car-hire Motorist Maps of Ireland. We were all of us working on how to leave Glencolumbkille with the least fuss.

I opted for another route back to base which avoided the possible risk of finding the flattened remains of a bedraggled kitten upon the roadway. There was a network of minor roads inland, passing through mountains and running close to the town of Ardara. I liked the sound of that.

This road surface was much better, and even the rain seemed lighter and not so cold. The road dropped down between two mountain peaks in a twisting snake pass. This was the famous Glengesh Pass, and it was great! The silver strand of the asphalt track wound downwards through a widening valley of glistening, green grass, and Ernest swept into every hairpin bend with relish. It was typical of our trip through Ireland, these sudden changes through highs and lows, from discomfort to joy, from rain to sunshine. And so it proved. By the time I reached the bottom of the valley at the foot of Glengesh Pass, the sun burst through the clouds, and glinted welcomingly in the puddles, pointing out the way back to Donegal City.

Although it meant another long walk, again I opted to leave Ernest at the B & B, so I could have a few drinks in the town. The first pub had a nondescript decor which alone could have placed it anywhere. A bunched handful of locals were talking in hushed tones among themselves. The bar area was dominated by the volume of a boring, meaningless, so-called "friendly" international football match between France and Italy. In the way of the modern game, no player was stepping out of line to attack the opponent's goal, playing to instructions by keeping the ball in the centre of the field, with the occasional back-pass. To break the tedious monotony, the carefully choreographed players took it in turns to make "dives", rolling on the ground in operatic displays of agony. One of the Italians was awarded a yellow card for his dive.

I finished my drink, yawned and moved on. In the street outside I was handed a leaflet advertising another pub which boasted "live entertainment". What kind of a town was it that pubs needed to advertise for business? I eventually settled on a pub which bore the signs of recent heavy restoration. The plaster had been scraped back to the bare brick, glossy varnished pine was everywhere, and young waitresses bustled to and fro with bulging hamburgers for equally young customers. There was a knot of solitary male drinkers gathered at one section of the divided bar, and I joined them.

The football match was still on the television screens, but the solitary males seemed to share my lack of enthusiasm for a pointless game being played out in a far country. The conversation was about the cheapest way to fly to London. I was surprised that they were in favour of Belfast. "Isn't Knock Airport or Shannon nearer?" I asked. "There's not much difference, but you can get more deals from Belfast" explained the young barman. "And flying into Luton or Gatwick Airport is no use to me. My mates all live near Heathrow. And when you're only flying in for a drinking weekend, every hour counts." "How does it work with the car parking?" asked another. "Well it's about 2 hours from here" said the barman with an air of knowing every inch of dual carriageway between Donegal and Belfast. "You leave the car at the airport, and whoever picks it up pays for the parking."

This didn't make much sense to me and I felt sure I had missed something. It satisfied the questioner though, and he nodded wisely, and said conclusively "Ah!" Not so long ago this remote, old corner of the British Isles was so isolated that a journey to London took at least a week's travelling. Now London is just another place to go to for a few jars with the lads.

I had already picked out a likely looking restaurant from the selection of fast food takeaways and white-table-clothed hotel dining rooms on offer. When I went inside, I was surprised to discover that the steamed-up windows concealed a busy restaurant with full tables, but the owner was quick to reassure me that there would be a table ready for me in a few moments.

The jolly atmosphere was generated by large numbers of overweight American tourists. I overheard one say to another: "Exercise? Oh sure, but I have to be careful with my catheter!" I wasn't absolutely sure if she was joking, but she was laughing. They were all laughing a lot. I became somehow included in their conversation as they made their arrangements to leave, gathering up armfuls of anoraks and plastic shopping bags stuffed with souvenirs. They told me they were from the Bay Area, which is a suburb of San Francisco. I heard myself saying "I confess I am a great admirer of your BART subway train system in San Francisco."

Why does one speak a more stilted form of English to Americans than to anyone else? I was playing out the stereotype of a tight-arsed Englishman. They told me they were real pleased that I liked their BART, and that they liked my Donegal. I was about to explain their mistake in taking me for a local, but I left it alone, and waved them on their way.

Dinner was very good, and I rolled up the hill towards home, glowing slightly despite the light drizzle which was still falling.

Chapter 22
A Distant Encounter with Ecstasy

At breakfast, I met an elderly couple from Arizona. They liked the damp grey weather, because for the rest of the year they experienced nothing but boring desert sunshine. She was big and bubbly, and her strangely mixed accent was revealed to be a blend of Arizona and Belfast. She loved Ireland, and had been back many times. No, she had never been back to the North since she left. It was too dangerous. Had I really had no problems in the North? Had I really seen nothing, seen no signs of violence? They were amazed.

Most Americans have a strange sense of world geography, and it was not surprising that their impression was that the North was a warzone, comparable to Beirut. She liked shopping, and elevated it to the status of a serious hobby. If it was available as a University subject, she told me, she would have taken a Masters degree in Shopping. Currently, she was determined to find an old-fashioned chamber pot. Did I know of any suitable antique shops?

He was very interested in my scooter. Had I really come all that way on such a small motorcycle? He used to have a Harley Davidson, but that was a long time ago. I suggested that now he was retired would be a good time to take up motorcycling again. He wasn't convinced. Where was I going today? They were going further into Donegal. They had been there before, and they liked it. While I was heading South, they were going North, in search of the definitive chamber pot.

In fact, I was the one who went North, into Northern Ireland that is. I crossed the border on a planned loop around part of Lower Lough Erne. In the border town of Pettigo I stopped to admire an impressive memorial at the crossroads. It is a statue of a Republican Volunteer, striding purposefully forward, wearing the early IRA uniform of a gabardine raincoat and trilby hat. The figure was also shouldering a British Lee Enfield .303 rifle; or perhaps it was a Mauser. The imposing statue had something of the romantic grandeur of between-the-wars Soviet poster art. It commemorates the deaths of three IRA men on 4th June 1922, killed by British forces.

Until recently this area used to be serious bandit territory, but now the signs just say "Come back again to Donegal" and "Welcome to Tyrone". As before, there is no frontier post. I momentarily confused the massive Lough Erne with the diminutive Lough Derg, which lies to the north of Pettigo, and I took a wrong turning. Lough Derg is home to the island shrine known as St. Patrick's Purgatory, which has been a centre of pilgrimage since the 5th Century – quite a long time for a tourist attraction.

In medieval times, the pilgrimage involved a fifteen-day fast before even beginning a solitary vigil locked in a damp cave on the island. The original church became one of the many buildings in this part of the world which didn't survive the upheavals of the 17th Century, but it has been rebuilt since then as a gloomy basilica, moodily rooted in the remains of the foundations of the earlier building. In keeping with the progressive image of the Catholic Church, the website gaily advertises options of a three-day pilgrimage or a one-day retreat for the hardy and devout.

There have been a number of well-written accounts of this experience, for we are talking here about a tradition deeply embedded in the Irish psyche, which has never failed to fascinate generations of Irish writers in search of an answer to life's many mysteries. Nevertheless, outsiders like me find it hard to understand why in modern times it still attracts a constant stream of loyal Catholic pilgrims to suffer in deprived devotion, prayer sequences and fasting over selected periods in the summer months. 30,000 visitors is the oft-quoted figure, and I have no reason to dispute it.

According to reports, the greatest discomfort is caused by the complete deprivation of sleep, although I imagine the fasting plays an important part too. Hallucination is only a step away from religious ecstasy, and there are important precedents in the Bible which run parallel with this experience: Jesus of Nazareth's forty days in the wilderness is only one example. Intense cold is often endured in the course of the vigil in St. Patrick's Purgatory, and this is exaggerated by the obligation upon all pilgrims to go barefoot, whatever the Irish weather throws at them. Most descriptions agree on the state of near ecstasy that many pilgrims discover on the island by this ancient process.

The website makes it clear that the admission fee includes the boat fare to and from the island, which is set in the picturesque waters of little Lough Derg, so no one has to worry about swimming back. I was not tempted to join the pilgrims, but stood scowling moodily from the shore, while Ernest kept an eye on me from the large car park, in case I got carried away. I have to report that I saw nothing of this medieval entertainment from close up.

Lower Lough Erne is very big indeed, and is set in a wide-open but deserted landscape. The tarmac surfaces of the roads of Tyrone and Fermanagh are beautifully maintained yet carry hardly any traffic. I saw no more than half a dozen cars in the first fifteen miles or so, and then suddenly a high-powered family saloon came towards me being driven at speed. As it passed me at about 100 miles per hour, I saw inside four young British soldiers, not in uniform but recognisable by their standard issue short haircuts and thick necks. Were they on a mission? Were they on a pub-crawl?

Riding along on roads as empty as this was a strange experience to me. There was little to worry about in the form of bends to negotiate, or crossroads to watch out for. I relaxed, and took up a more central position in the roadway. I toyed with the idea of driving on the wrong side of the road, continental style, but my light-headedness didn't extend that far.

Without the need to keep my eyes glued to the road ahead, watching out for potholes, I was more free to take in my surroundings, and they were very attractive indeed. It isn't only the special quality of light associated with large expanses of water at certain times of the day that is so magical. The lakeshore, and the well-watered landscape produce a variety of greens which the most talented of water-colourists would find it a challenge to capture. My reverie came to an end as I arrived at the outskirts of a small town, and my attention to the road conditions returned to normal.

I stopped in what turned out to be the border town of Belleek. It wasn't until I bought a newspaper, that I realised I was back in the United Kingdom again. But like frontier towns all over the world, they accepted Irish coins and there was no problem. I tried my mobile phone and discovered I couldn't get a UK signal, but it did pick up an Irish station. I found a phone box, and noticed it was painted red, like all British phone boxes. It accepted my BT card, to my great delight. I noted at least one cultural advantage in the British phone system; a phone box in Belleek would accept either coins or cards. In the South, there is one phone box for coins and another for cards. Ominously, the two different types are kept strictly segregated.

Belleek is at the narrow neck in County Donegal where Northern Ireland sticks out in a beak-like salient, as if straining to reach the Atlantic Ocean. Only five miles downstream from the town of Belleek, the River Erne meets the sea at Ballyshannon, and as if to celebrate this happy event, an unsightly Power Station has been thrown up to mark the spot. Ballyshannon is also famous as the birthplace of Henry Allingham, the Victorian poet who wrote "Up the fairy mountain, down the rushy glen." He was married to the Victorian painter, Helen Allingham, who devoted her life to painting exquisite watercolours of bucolic English country cottages in the Home Counties, before they vanished from the landscape. I don't think that Mr. and Mrs. Allingham would have liked Ballyshannon Power Station much.

Shortly after Belleek, I got lost again. I remember going through a rundown town with the unpromising name of Garrison, near a pretty lake called Lough Melvin, and the next thing I saw was a sign saying Manorhamilton. In the absence of border signs, I had no idea whether I was in the North or the South, so I pulled up at the Heritage Centre Teashop next to a massive ruined castle.

The place was deserted except for a very young, bright-eyed girl behind the counter. I asked for a coffee and let her talk me into having a piece of cake. I read in the leaflet provided how the castle was built in 1638 by a particularly unpleasant Scottish planter laird called Sir Frederick Hamilton, who torched the surrounding countryside and put its inhabitants to the sword. Why did people always do that? Was it due perhaps to a lack of any suitable alternative entertainment? Hamilton was defeated and driven out in the 1641 uprising led by local warrior chiefs O'Rourke, O'Connor and Maguire. Hamilton returned to Scotland, and died soon after, and no doubt O'Rourke, O'Connor and Maguire danced a jig at his memorial wake. "Rather than keep alive the memory of such an evil man," I asked, "why didn't they change the name of the town?" "It's not really important," she said. "The town already has an Irish name." With such impeccable logic, I could only be in the South again.

I have read books which told me that only a few years earlier, the deserted area where I had been carelessly threading my way backwards and forwards across the border was a war zone. Crossing points like bridges were blown up and barbwired, so access was limited to those crossing points where army checkpoints were set up.

Of course, the real villains crossed backwards and forwards without much difficulty, and the only ones to be inconvenienced – 'suffer' isn't too strong a word – were the innocent locals. 'Innocent' is probably not the right word either, because under such a regime, it is almost impossible not to infringe the law in some way, however minor. Fortunes were made and lost, but so were decent livings. A modest shop serving a community could be physically destroyed, or just isolated and bankrupted by an arbitrary military decision to site a checkpoint or a barrier in one place rather than another. I saw not a trace of all this, but the very emptiness was the only obvious sign of what had gone before.

I entered the seaside town of Bundoran by a back road, crossing a bridge by a pub cleverly called the "Bridge Inn". Cruising the main drag, I was mildly horrified to discover the jumble of fast food joints, garish pubs, entertainment arcades and cheap holiday hotels that one associates with a run-down English seaside resort. I turned Ernest round, retraced our route, parked by the bridge, and went into the more modest bar of the Bridge Inn.

Okay, so the interior was disappointing, all fishing nets and plastic crabs, but there was soup and a chunky cheese sandwich for lunch. Having dealt with the exacting business of ordering lunch, I relaxed into the warm atmosphere, and was pleased to notice I was the only tourist. The other customers were real people on their actual lunch breaks: building workers hurried their food to get back to the job while the weather stayed fine. I read my newspaper, and then fell into conversation with an elderly man at the bar.

He had one of the most outrageous noses I have ever seen. It wasn't just big, it was extraordinarily distorted in great red lumps, witness to a lifetime's dedication to drinking. He told me he was retired from the Irish Army, having served for 18 years in the Artillery. He was in the process of claiming compensation from them for ear-damage from the guns. His father had been a professional soldier before him, serving in the Connaught Rangers during the Second World War.

My ears pricked up at this, because I knew the Connaught Rangers were dissolved at the time of Irish Independence in July 1922. I worked out that if my friend with the nose was 70 or so now, and if his father was 30 or 40 when my friend was born, he just might have served in the Connaught Rangers in the 1st World War. "Was that the 1st World War or the 2nd World War?" I asked. My informant was no longer sure. He was confused. He was waiting to pick up his grandson from the school down the road. With his daughter and son-in-law both working, that was his job now – to pick up the kids from school. Did I have the time? He'd best be off, he mustn't be late. Had I finished with my newspaper? He would read it later. Thank you so. Goodbye now!

Chapter 23
Three Wrecks,
in the footsteps of Captain Cuellar

The authorities have built a viewing platform in wood and stone.

Just South of Bundoran I met my first and only roadblock. Disappointingly, the Garda took one look at the wally with the orange bomb, and waved me through. He was clearly of the opinion that terrorists look like terrorists. I would have liked to discuss the point with him for a while, but he would have none of it and waved me all the more vigorously through. I wondered idly if they picked up many common criminals in these roadblocks. Were they trained to distinguish between criminals, terrorists and wallies?

Before me now stretched a long wide straight road following the line of the coast, and Ernest sang as he gobbled up the miles. I joined in with a few choruses of *The Rose of Tralee*, and we all too soon arrived in the village of Grange, our destination. My B & B just outside the village was promisingly called "Armada Lodge". It lay set back from and overlooking the shallow, sandy bay of Streedagh Strand, where the wrecks of the *Juliana*, the *La Lavia*, and the *Santa Maria de Vision* have been discovered. A fourth ship from the Indies Treasure fleet, *San Juan el Menor*, also went down in this bay, but the wreck has still to be found.

The Spanish kept meticulous records of all their military exploits and colonial activities, and the naval records are of special interest. These records are still preserved in the Archive of the Indies in Seville, and are a popular source of study for historians and treasure-seekers alike.

It is known that the *Juliana* was a converted merchantman from Naples, and carried a contingent of 70 sailors and no fewer than 325 soldiers. The *Lavia*, from Venice, carried 71 sailors and 203 soldiers. The *Santa Maria de la Vision* was similarly equipped with 71 sailors and 236 soldiers. *San Juan el Menor* was a fighting ship, and carried 113 sailors and 163 soldiers. This was a considerable force of men coming ashore in a small area, but those who were lucky enough not to be drowned were half-drowned and sick from days on a stormy sea. They were no match for the hordes of locals awaiting them on the beach, who slit their throats as effortlessly as they slit their purses; only a handful survived and made it off the beach.

I studied the landscape from the window of my room, where I looked down to what must have been the point where Captain Francisco Cuellar had scrambled ashore. On my right were the mountains he described in his account, where he sought sanctuary to escape from the many gangs of marauding robbers patrolling the shore.

The sandy bay area was very flat, and I narrowed my eyes and pictured how it must have appeared when Cuellar scrambled ashore. The beach merged into a series of sea-lagoons, exposed sandbanks, tufts of grass and rolling dunes. Further back, the fields continued the flat profile, with no trees and only the remains of earlier stone dividing walls. This was rabbit country. A clumpy hedgerow screened the next group of houses; I tried to imagine how the terrain might have altered in 400 years: a drifting, sandy landscape like this is constantly on the move. Had the shoreline originally been closer to the small island known as Spaniards Rock, or was it further back?

According to my large scale map, the hamlet of houses next to Armada Lodge is called Moneygold. Was this the name given to the spot where a fortune in gold coins and jewellery was brought ashore by the Spanish survivors 400 years ago? Had the English mapmakers translated an ancient local name?

I left my luggage in the room, and hurried off out again to drive out to the spit of sand shown on my map, overlooking the bay, for another viewpoint. I followed newly painted signposts to the "Spanish Armada Memorial" and came upon a viewing space, a tiny memorial park constructed to commemorate the 400th anniversary of the Armada. A handsome plaque describes how on 6th September 1588 the three ships were wrecked in a storm with a loss of over 1200 lives. They say only 300 survivors came ashore, by a rock still known as Spaniards Rock, but that statistic must be impossible to prove either way.

The authorities have built a viewing platform in wood and stone, evocative of a ship's prow, complete with mast, and there is a picnic table for visitors. The view from the platform across the bay is unobstructed onto the dunes, but I wanted to be higher up to see better. I rode down to the beach past grazing cattle, and watched the breakers fall onto the crescent of sand. I could clearly make out the Spaniards Rock and some other rocks out in the bay. Behind me the sand disappeared into dunes and shallow lagoons, but looking across the bay I could see in the distance where a promontory rose up from grass-topped cliffs.

The only other building in sight was an over-sized Gothic heap on the top of the far-side cliffs, which I took to be an hotel. It stood there with a sinister air of sullen arrogance, refusing to fit in with the landscape. I concluded that the view of the bay from there must be perfect for a photograph, and decided to check it out.

The gloomy Gothic castle was at the entrance to the port of Mullaghmore. It was not a hotel at all, but a private residence, as the unfriendly notice on the padlocked gates to the estate made clear. There was a white poodle observing me curiously from the window of the lodge house, and I knocked at the door, but there was no reply.

I followed the coast road around the point, hoping for a glimpsed view of the bay, but barbed wire fences protected the Gothic castle's fields, and the first viewing point was too far round the promontory to see the bay. The dangers of the coastline were underlined by two private memorials on the cliff path to seamen who had died on the rocks below. One was a twenty-three-year-old from Moycullen "taken by the sea".

The harbour at Mullaghmore was surprisingly extensive and busy: hundreds of small boats bobbed shoulder to shoulder. A regatta of sea scouts criss-crossed each other in tiny sailing dinghies. After a final rattle at the locked gates of the castle, I decided to head for the city of Sligo instead.

Chapter 24
Yeats Country

Benbulbin dominates Streedagh Strand, where Captain Cuellar came ashore.

Near the village of Kiltartan, somewhere in the countryside near here, used to stand Lady Gregory's Coole House, where Irish nationalist intellectuals gathered for house parties to revive disregarded aspects of Irish culture. In an act of vandalism, it was sold off for scrap by De Valera's government in 1941 and subsequently demolished.

I knew that I was entering the region known as Yeats Country, when the mountain range where Captain Cuellar sought refuge turned into the mystical mountain of Benbulbin. This smooth-sided mountain rises up steeply to almost 2000 feet (526 metres), to look down on Drumcliff Churchyard, and the grave of William Butler Yeats himself. The peak of the mountain was hidden in low clouds, which it wore like a floppy, wide-brimmed hat.

The land to the west of the main road is crisscrossed by very narrow country lanes, intimidatingly enclosed by an edging of dense trees. According to the area map, it is rich in megalithic burial sites, ancient forts and Early Christian churches. The Warrior Queen Maeve of legend is believed to be buried in a megalithic tomb on the other side of Sligo Bay.

The atmosphere in this landscape is magical, and it is easy to understand why Yeats was repeatedly drawn back here, and chose to be buried here. His epitaph is well known to every Irish schoolchild: *"Cast a cold eye/On life, on death. /Horseman, pass by"*. As a modern version of his Horseman, astride Ernest, and an admirer of his work, I hoped to do more than pass by. A few moments at the great man's grave in the shadow of his beloved Benbulbin mountain should be one of the highlights of the trip.

As I drew near, the parked tourist coaches pointed out the way to the church. I rode up to the churchyard, ignored the yellow lines, and parked right outside the gate. Monster coaches were navigating in and out of the official car park; brightly clothed American tourists squeezed themselves back into their buses, just as uniformed Irish schoolchildren were discharged from theirs. I reluctantly allowed myself to be swept up in the rush of dutiful Irish youth, and waited patiently while the camera flashes popped, and the schoolgirls mentally ticked Yeats's Grave off their to-do list.

When they had dissolved away, and returned to their coach, I approached the graveside alone. What I saw didn't seem right! The headstone, the marble chips, the stone surround, all looked brand new, as if fresh from the monumental mason's shop window. There were no signs of weathering, no romantic lichen, no patina of age. I concluded the original grave must have been replaced, not just restored. Perhaps the non-stop waves of tourists and schoolchildren were considered too much for it. Had visitors broken off bits of the original grave for souvenirs? I felt strangely unmoved by the thought of being so close to the grave of one of the finest poets of the 20th Century. Disappointed, I took his advice, and passed by.

I had a drink in the village of Grange on my way to look for some dinner. It was a pleasant, old-fashioned bar in a grocer's shop, with a young mum behind the bar. I read the latest news in the local paper. It was all about the local election results. A farmer looked in for a pint. He enjoyed some village gossip with the young mum, about the occupant of one of the cottages across the way. I idly read the village notices pinned to the wall, about choir practice, a one-day shopping trip to Dublin, a fixture list for the village Gaelic football team.

When a third customer joined us in the bar, I noticed that the farmer became visibly agitated. He gulped down the pint which he had been drinking so leisurely before, made his excuses and beat a retreat. The new customer had a strange look; he had wispy, bright red hair, almost orange, and protruding eyes. His tightly buttoned tweed jacket didn't quite fit. His shirt collar showed the grime of several days. His appearance was eccentric, rather than ragged.

The young mum asked if he wanted "the usual", and the newcomer mumbled a reply. After a sip, he spoke a line which was completely incomprehensible to me. He spoke with the slur of a heavy drinker, combined with an impenetrable accent. I asked the young mum if she knew anything about the Gothic castle at Mullaghmore. She wasn't sure who had it now, but she believed it had finally been rented out only recently, to a wealthy, elderly businessman from Dublin, and his middle-aged son. It had been empty for a long time. The redheaded man added some words, but I couldn't understand him. Was he speaking in Irish, I wondered? "It's been empty since Mountbatten," said the mum.

And suddenly it clicked. This must have been Lord Mountbatten's place – I knew it was somewhere along this coast. A rogue faction of the IRA killed him when they blew up his boat in the harbour in a massive explosion. A bad business in which Mountbatten's innocent grandchildren who were with him on the boat were killed and others were severely injured. Mountbatten wasn't an obvious political target, so I imagine there must have been some local resentment by a few hotheads.

The red-headed bar customer began to tell me what had happened, and although he was still incomprehensible, I could somehow follow bits of it. Intelligible words surfaced from time to time in the rise and fall of his voice. In this way he told me he had acted as a local guide and helper to the circus of journalists and television crews who descended on the place at that time. He described himself as their secretary. He had enjoyed that. They had a fine old time while Grange was at the centre of things, and everything revolved around my informant. And then the "media people" went away again, and things slowly got back to normal.

He was sorry about the children. That wasn't right, and he didn't mind who heard him say so, he said defiantly. He looked at me expectantly, as he finished his drink, and smacked his lips. It wasn't hard to realise that he was asking for another, but I was not about to buy him one, so after a few more words about the state of the nation, I followed the example of the farmer, and left.

It was near closing time when I sat down to a colourless meal in an almost empty truck-drivers' restaurant. The best feature of the place was the collection of pictures on the walls. Grouped together were examples of every type of competitive motorsport. Racing trucks, Formula One racing-cars, sports cars, stock cars, rally cars, Grand Prix motorcycles, motocross, speedway bikes. I stared at them all as I munched my way through defrosted haddock in batter and a plateful of giant chips piled high. I should have ordered a fry-up, a later than late breakfast with fried eggs and bacon, which was certain to be their speciality. Out of their line of vision, above the heads of the all-female staff behind the counter was a collection of topless model pin-ups and car numberplates.

Almost everywhere in Ireland, chips are given pride of place on the dinner plate. They are normally considered the most important element in any meal, and there is probably a star system to recognise the degree of excellence of an establishment's chips - a sort of Good Chip Guide. Experienced travellers know that the best chips are made in France. Long, thin delicately browned *frites* are a gourmet delight. The Belgian ones are not bad either.

CHAPTER 25
SLIGO

Mullaghmore Harbour

At breakfast I met a newlywed Italian couple from Milan. I told them Milan was not far from where Ernest came from, and they were impressed, – either impressed or puzzled, it was hard to say. They gingerly tried some brown sauce on one of their sausages.

A middle-aged couple from Düsseldorf was concerned for my safety, travelling so far on a Vespa. He used to have a Lambretta, but that was a very long time ago.

An eighty-one-year-old lady named Kavanagh from Pittsburgh, Pennsylvania, was travelling round Ireland with her daughter. I told her we were probably related, because my great-grandmother was a Cavanagh: the difference in spelling is of no importance. "Wasn't Pittsburgh famous for the Molly Maguires?" I asked Miss Kavanagh.

In the late 19th Century striking miners fighting the strikebreaking bully-boys employed by the coalmine bosses, disguised themselves as women so they couldn't be identified and victimised. They took their methods and their title from the West of Ireland Molly Maguires, who employed the same tactics against the eviction agents during the Irish Famine.

Miss Kavanagh said the coal industry had changed completely in Pittsburgh in recent years. Sales of coal had dried up due to lack of demand, the coalmines had been closed down and the miners had moved away. Just a few small groups were left, living in "ghettos" - her word. As a result, new electronic industry employers have moved in to fill the vacuum left by the coalmines, and a former staunchly working-class town has now become middle-class. It was a familiar story. "The coal we use in Britain now is mined in Colombia by eight-year old children" I explained, simplifying the facts only a little, to aid understanding. "The Conservative Government told us it's cheaper!"

I went back to Mullaghmore to take some pictures and check out the lodge house again. Still no answer to my knocking, but the implacable white poodle was still there. So I rode back into Sligo Town, and tackled the one-way system. William Butler's painter brother, Jack B. Yeats, famously said he learned to paint at the Garravogue Bridge over the river in Sligo.

They were fishing for salmon from the road bridge when I passed by. All real fishermen feel compelled to look down into the water from any bridge they cross, and I am no exception. As the heavy flow of traffic rumbled past a yard or so behind them, two or three anglers fished bunches of worms down into the peat-coloured water. One even tried a fly. The river was shallow, and you could see the inevitable signs of civilisation on the riverbed - an abandoned pram, plastic bags, a traffic cone.

"What do you catch here? Just small stuff?" I asked one of them. His reply was surprising: "I had a 10 pound salmon yesterday!" Even at today's low prices, a wild 10 lb. Salmon was worth a lot of money. The fishermen caught nothing while I watched, and eventually I left them to it.

The town of Sligo has found an interesting solution to the modern demands for shopping centres and car parking. They have built a quadrangle to provide parking spaces for the shoppers, in the area previously occupied by gardens and work yards, in the centre of each block of terraced houses. Cars drive from the one-way system straight into the central quadrangle, which provides parking and access to the nearby shops. Sligo is a busy, bustling town with a good selection of real shops, keeping their ends up in spite of the competition from the chain stores commonly confined to a shopping centre.

I sought out a laundry to clean my off-white sweater, which had begun to look decidedly grubby. I am not very good at noticing when items of clothing are dirty, so if I thought it was grubby, it was probably filthy. I queued up with a mixed group of customers in the laundry. I needed advice. Should I go for a wash or dry-clean? The technicalities were explained to me with the patience reserved for school infants, and I took their advice that a good wash was what was called for. Could I come back in one hour?

It wasn't easy squeezing into a crowded small town pub to have an early lunch while I waited for my sweater to be laundered. I swung my orange bomb onto the floor, and looked around at the other customers, who were all either old age pensioners, or unemployed punks.

My newspaper was full of arguments for controlling the Orange marches in the North: attention was being focussed on the town of Drumcree. It was a typical situation, where the traditional route of a Protestant parade lies through streets which used to be occupied by Protestants, but are now 100% Catholic.

When I collected my sweater it was only a shade of its former self. More accurately, it was a new shade of bluish-grey. Still, the more I looked at it, the more acceptable it became: it was certainly clean! After a few minutes, I was already thinking how nice it would be to be wearing a bluish-grey sweater, if only for a change.

I asked Ernest which route he would like to take to Ballina, and we decided on the coast road. If Ernest had been as great a lover of Irish music as I am, he might have been tempted to suggest travelling southwards, keeping to the East of the Ox Mountains. This is the country of Michael Coleman, who was to the Irish fiddle as Charlie

Parker was to the saxophone. The influence of Coleman's early American recordings was so great, that to listen to his music now, it sounds like a series of perfectly executed fiddle clichés. At the time, every piece of phrasing was original, but almost every fiddle player since has reproduced them faithfully. For this reason, just like Charlie Parker, his originality is hard to judge, so his genius is evident in his freshness and fluidity, rather than in the musical phrasing. His old 78 rpm recordings made in the 1920s and 30s, are now available on a digital compact disc, which is where I heard them.

The prospect of tackling the small road over the Ox Mountains looked too much of an adventure on a damp, windy day, so I was quite happy to let Ernest have his head, charging across a long East-West bog road towards Ballina.

The wind grew stronger, and was sweeping in from the North, unobstructed, across Sligo Bay. It was hitting us at an angle three-quarters head-on, and I felt we were leaning over increasingly into that direction. I could see a cement lorry heading towards us, the type that has a constantly revolving drum on the back. The driver must have had his foot on the floor, because when the cement lorry passed me at high speed, the air turbulence created behind the massive drum lifted us into the air.

On reflection, we were probably going too fast, but after an impressive wobble, we shrugged off the worst of the effects, and carried on our way, more than a little elated. Good sense took over though, and at the first opportunity, we turned off the main road to explore the loop of byroads between the main trunk road and the sea.

Chapter 26
Fishing the Moy

...rows of salmon fishermen hard at work...

My B & B in Ballina was next to the Cathedral, situated in the very middle-class looking Cathedral Close. My landlady did not seem fazed by the sight of a motor scooter in the parking space in front of her smart, detached house, but she suggested it might be safer to leave it "round the side". Would I like to put it there? Now, what would I like for breakfast in the morning? And at what time?

In front of the Cathedral flows a serious-looking river, lined with rows of salmon fishermen hard at work, caning the waters. My landlady informed me, proudly and in a confidential tone, as if I was being invited to share an exciting secret, that: "The house of our President is the one with the red door on the other side of the river, directly opposite the main door of the Cathedral".

President Mary Robinson, who I had missed by a day at the birthplace of Saint Columba, resigned from office in order to accept the offer of the job of High Commissioner for Human Rights at the United Nations. We chatted about this aspect of her career, and I like to think my landlady felt reassured that I was so well informed.

After a hot shower, I walked across the bridge into the main part of the town. A sign told me that the river I was crossing was the River Moy, the most famous salmon-fishing river in Ireland. I watched the fishermen for a while, concentrating intently upon the task in hand, before the cold wind drove me to seek refuge in the crowded streets of the town.

There are an awful lot of pubs in Ballina. It is in many respects, a wild, lively town. Salmon fishing is clearly an important activity, and fishing tackle and permits were offered in shop windows all the way up the hill from the bridge. Some of this tackle was very expensive American imported tackle, aimed at experienced, well-heeled anglers who know the ultimate value of superior handcrafted rods and reels. The first pub was mysteriously called a "Treffpunkt", and it advertised its wares in German. German anglers visit Ireland in great numbers, but I had never before seen such evidence of their colonisation of the West.

Early on, Germans discovered Ireland as an outpost of unpolluted landscape in Europe, and many take their holidays here. Some are lucky enough to have houses in the Republic; the really lucky ones have business interests too. A friend from Hamburg bought a small house by a lake in County Clare. He restored it beautifully and faithfully, using local workmen, and over the years he became a familiar sight, peddling around the country lanes on his ancient, upright roadster bicycle. He drank in the local pub, the Black Sticks, but was unhappy that he was never really accepted by the locals. He felt he was looked on with suspicion, as a source of occasional employment and little more.

He normally left the pub obediently at closing time, but on one visit, he was deep in conversation and didn't realise that the official closing time was long past. No one showed any sign of leaving, so he stayed on too, and was finally shown the door - much the worse for wear, he admits - with the other diehards in the early hours of the morning. His high spirits were not solely alcohol led. He was elated to discover that the more he drank, the more friendly his Irish neighbours became. The Irish have a good reputation for benign tolerance of drunks. They are quite uncritical of someone who is "in their cups", because they know that it can happen to everyone - well, almost anyone. My friend felt he had at last arrived in the community; he mounted his bicycle, waved his new friends goodbye, and pedalled off down the road.

Now this was a country road, with no street lighting, and it was a dark, moonless night. When he reached the T junction at the bottom of the road, he just kept going, and crashed into the hedge on the far side. He struggled weakly to free himself, but was held fast by the brambles. Hours later, he woke up in the morning light with a sore head, still hanging in the bushes at the side of the road, his bicycle in a twisted heap underneath him. A passing farmer, on his way to work, helped him down, and from that time on, my friend was always warmly greeted wherever he was seen going about his business in the district.

I had a sandwich in Ballina High Street, and then found a wonderful pub cum tobacconist. At first I thought it was all just superficial decor, perhaps the origin of the sort of "theme" Irish pubs which interior decorators are putting up all over the globe. But this pub was authentic; I saw the barman make up a blend of different loose tobaccos, weigh handfuls carefully on a set of old-fashioned scales, and package it up ready for customers.

There were engaging posters, mixed in with all the fading paraphernalia of pipe adverts, Sherlock Holmes pictures, Toby jugs and mysterious jars and enamelled cans. The local theatre company was looking for a cast for its latest production; entries were invited for the Chess Championship; Gaelic football fixtures were on display. The clientele were well looked after, whatever their interests. The pub was full without being uncomfortably so, and the atmosphere was superb.

I reluctantly left to find a public telephone, and was caught in a short, cold shower of rain. I was shivering, and took shelter in another bar, and ordered a half-pint. As an afterthought, I asked for a glass of Irish whiskey to warm me up. I had remembered that in Ireland, a "glass" of beer means a half-pint, but I had forgotten that a "glass" of whiskey means a large one. And an Irish large one is a very large one indeed. I was absentmindedly looking around the bar. It was vaguely Edwardian. It was only when the barman failed to bring me any change, that I realised I had ordered a large whiskey by mistake. Still, by the time I had finished my drinks, the cold rain had stopped, and the day already felt much warmer.

I went down to the river to watch the salmon fishermen. There was a well-ordered group of six pals from the Manchester area; they told me they booked the same week every year. In the morning, they fished the lower beat, and in the evening they fished the preferred higher beat. A local ghillie assisted them with advice and baits. They hadn't caught a fish today between them, but they had seen signs of salmon running upstream, and they assured me it was only a matter of time. They were using a variety of different baits between them, spinners, flies and even worms.

In answer to my question, I was told that indeed there most certainly were rules and regulations to be observed in the permitted fishing methods, but the fisherman wouldn't go into any more detail than that. My informant had just emerged from the river after a spell wading in the shallows, and I imagine he was feeling the cold. He had had a fishless day, and he was irritable.

As we spoke, there was a shout, and a tubby angler fishing worms at the far end of the string of privileged anglers on this stretch, had obviously hooked a fish. As we watched, it leapt clear of the water, a fresh-run salmon of about five pounds. It leapt twice more, and then was gone. The rod straightened. I couldn't hear what the tubby man said, but his friends near me were cursing as hard as if they had lost the fish themselves. Those already in the water began fishing again with a new intensity, encouraged by the knowledge that there were fish in the vicinity. I slipped away. It was time for dinner.

Once again, I was wrong in my choice of restaurant. There was nothing wrong with the ingredients, it was just the way they were overcooked and re-heated. It is true to say it is just as easy to cook food well as it is to cook food badly. There was nothing wrong with the decor or the service. It was just that there was no respect for the quality of the food as presented. This is still a common failing in the British Isles – with notable exceptions. But things are getting better, and customers are becoming more demanding.

It was hard to resist the attractive-looking pubs dotted all over Ballina, and to be honest I wasn't trying very hard to resist them. On my way back to the Cathedral, I dropped into another likely looking pub. At the counter, I fell into conversation with a man who had spent a long time out of the country, and confessed he was a bit out of touch. He had been away a long time, working in Yorkshire for many years for a Sheffield firm, installing double-glazing windows. I was watching a soap opera with English subtitles on the bar television set. "Why are there subtitles?" I asked, thinking it might be a cheap foreign import; Spanish television has been flooded with low budget South American soap operas. The acting is embarrassingly melodramatic, the scripting is laughable, and the production costs are basic. But they are hugely popular in Spain, and their stars fill the ever-hungry pages of the gossip magazines.

Even as I asked the question, I realised that this was not a Latin soap opera, but an Irish one. The actors were speaking Irish, and the subtitles were for non-Irish speakers. My new Irish friend was not happy about being spoken to with a direct question. He kept his eyes low, and mumbled that he didn't know what the subtitles were for. Sensing that I had somehow said something to cause this embarrassment, I asked "Is this language Irish?" Well now, he couldn't rightly say, it was a show he'd never seen before. He was sorry he couldn't help me.

I crossed back over the bridge, and peered again into the murky waters, now twinkling back the reflections of the street lamps.

Chapter 27
Return to Mayo

A Mayo bog road.

Shortly after leaving town the next morning, on an empty road across the bogs, I crossed with a convoy coming in the opposite direction. An escort of Irish Army soldiers and Gardai were accompanying a Securicor armoured car shipment between banks. I had often come across similar groups standing guard in town streets, as cash takings were moved around under the protection of heavily armed soldiers and police.

We were now in County Mayo, but this part of Mayo was further North than the Mayo I had visited before. Unexpectedly, somewhere along the coast road, I came upon two memorial busts, side by side, both to one General Humbert; I didn't know who he was, so I stopped to read more. Humbert led an unsuccessful invasion force of French revolutionaries in 1798, sent by Napoleon to sow the seeds of revolution among the Irish, and to break off the island of Ireland from the rest of the British Isles.

Further along I came upon a memorial to one of the French soldiers who had been killed on this spot. Napoleon had been impressed by the personal appeals of the Irish patriot Wolfe Tone, who united fellow Protestants and Catholics alike in the struggle for Irish independence. Wolfe Tone was captured higher up the coast, still wearing his uniform as a French officer. Because the English didn't give a fig for such niceties, they sentenced him to death by hanging for treason, but he cheated them and took his own life.

The countryside around Killala is full of scattered ruins, and it reminded me of the deserted landscape of what was known as the Congested Districts of Connemara. The ruined villages, lone houses and small farms were evidence of the wholesale emigration from these parts when the land could no longer support the population in the 19th Century. It was the beginning of the Irish diaspora, and Irishmen were subsequently dispersed all over the globe; it is said that there are more Irish living in Boston, USA, than in Ireland.

I was heading for the town of Belmullet, in the far west. My reasons for going to this remote spot were largely sentimental. One time I was changing trains at the London Underground station of Camden Town, some years ago now. Along with the London districts of Kilburn and Finsbury Park, Camden Town was traditionally home to thousands of Irish migrant workers, chancing their luck in London Town, where the streets were said to be paved with gold.

On the Northern Line, Barnet Branch platform, there was a very drunk Irishman – an unfortunate soul, down on his luck, and deep in his cups. His case was another statistic in the sad story of millions of migrants all over the world who are driven into lonely exile because there is no work for them back home. They are typically exploited and underpaid by unscrupulous employers, with no security. They suffer poor living conditions and a crippling lifestyle, all the while remembering their carefree days of a childhood in a happier place.

The Camden Town drunk was smelly and staggering, as he greeted me, and when I heard his West Coast accent, I asked where he came from. He concentrated his energies long enough to say "Belmullet, County Mayo" and then, brightening up he said, "Do you know it?" I didn't want to disappoint him so I said I had been there, but that I was only passing through. "Well you must go back one day then. It's a fine town! A great place!" So, I always felt I should make an effort to visit his hometown someday, and this was my first opportunity.

Belmullet used to be an important seaport. For centuries there was a constant coastal trade between Belmullet and Scotland, trading cattle and peat for grain and vegetables. Migrant workers shipped out from here to work on the harvest in Scotland every year; some went further, and took ship from Liverpool to America and Australia.

From the map, I realised that I would arrive in Belmullet by a long, featureless road across bogland. It was a dead end, because this was a road which didn't go anywhere, except to Belmullet. Belmullet was the end of the line: the next parish was America. You only arrived in Belmullet if you were going to Belmullet. I realised that there was no way that a traveller could be "passing through" on his way to somewhere else, as I had claimed. The town sits at the narrowest point on a peninsula which separates the Atlantic Ocean west of Donegal Bay from Blacksod Bay to the South.

On my way to Belmullet, I rounded a bend on a headland overlooking a steep descent down overgrown cliffs to the deep blue sea of Sligo Bay. The German writer Heinrich Böll referred constantly to the Atlantic being green in colour, as it crashed against the shores of Connemara, but the sea is so clean here that as soon as the sun shines out in a blue sky, it rivals the blueness of the Mediterranean.

At the side of the road, hunched up on the grass verge, I came upon a couple of cyclists. It seemed to me they were clearly in distress, and passing traffic on this remote coast road was few and far between. I pulled across and removed my helmet. Two mountain bikes, the wheel of one of them removed; a boy and a girl wearing designer cycling clothes. I was in no hurry; what could I do to help? They were North Americans.

He was cursing over the puncture he had just finished repairing. The seventh puncture in as many days, he hissed. "Crap British bikes!" He spat. I asked him where they had got the bikes from? I wondered why one bike should be more susceptible to punctures than another? They had rented the bikes in Dublin, and were riding them around Ireland. Everyone else seemed to be travelling in a clockwise direction.

The North American bikes back home were far superior to this crap, the American cyclist told the landscape venomously. "Why didn't you bring your own bikes on the 'plane?" I asked innocently. North American Man was mad. He angrily kicked the wheel back into the bike frame, and gave it another kick for good luck. "We were going to; but two weeks before we were due to leave, we got a call from the airline. They had just decided to change the rules, to introduce charges for carrying bikes as luggage. To carry their two bikes, the airline now wanted to charge a sum equal to more than the price of an extra ticket.

In haste, they arranged to hire bikes locally in Ireland, which was very expensive, but less than the cost of shipping their own bikes. But they wouldn't have had so many punctures, and they would have travelled further. These British bikes were crap. The girl didn't say anything, just nodded and said "Crap!" in a soothing tone. No, they didn't need anything. No, I couldn't be any help. He started to kick the bags as he loaded them back onto the stricken bike, and I saw a cue to leave. "Nice meeting you!" I called back from the safety of the inside of my helmet, over the roar of Ernest's exhaust, as I accelerated away from the Bad Tempered North American. He was beyond irony.

I was now entering the Mullet Peninsula. At Annagh Head there are rocks believed to be about 2000 million years old, give or take a 100 million years. As well as being the oldest rocks yet recorded by geologists in Ireland, they are of interest because they more or less match up with similar rocks in North America and Greenland. This leads the boldest of the geologists to suggest that about 200 million years ago, broadly speaking, these shores were all joined together, before they were rent asunder by great forces and pushed back to their present positions, as the plates of the Earth's crust shifted to a more comfortable position. The gap between the rocks was thoughtfully filled by the Atlantic Ocean, and the Earth then settled down to work out more important things over the next 200 million years, such as inventing life, and then putting a full stop to the dinosaur experiment.

As if all these historical thoughts weren't enough, I was also reminded that this obtrusive peninsula, jutting out into the inaccurately charted Atlantic Ocean west of Ireland, had proved a severe obstacle to the ships of the Armada. The *Santiago* was wrecked in Broad Haven Bay. She was a relatively small craft with only 19 guns, carrying just 30 sailors and 56 soldiers, lost with all hands, including Captain de Luna on 21st September 1588.

I already knew Blacksod Bay to the south was another Armada wrecksite. Don Alonso de Leiva lost his first ship here, when he ran aground in the *Sancta Maria Encoronada* (some records describe this ship as the *Rata Encoronada*). Unable to free his ship, he decided to remove the crew to safety, before scuttling the vessel and setting it on fire. He survived the experience, and transferred to the *Duquesa Santa Ana*, but was eventually drowned in the *Girona* at the Giant's Causeway. Having started by seeing his Order of Santiago medal in Belfast Museum, I was now retracing his final days

Chapter 28
Back to Belmullet

On arrival in Belmullet I rode straight through the main street and down to a massive quay. I could imagine a quay this size must have been a bustling hot spot of activity in the heyday of the port, but it was now deserted. Where was the famous fishing fleet of Belmullet? This was the question I asked the man sitting on the wall by the bank. He happily explained that the fishing fleet used the other pier, the one at the other end of town, which opened directly onto Donegal Bay. He was keen to show me the way, and he almost took me by the arm to lead me down to the other pier.

On the way he engaged me in conversation. Where was I from? Well now he had been to North London too. Did I know Camden Town? I took a long look and searched my memory bank. Was this my Belmullet man from Camden Town Underground station? He showed me where the fishing boats would have been, if it weren't for the fact that they were all away at sea, fishing. There was only one fishing boat in its place, left behind for repairs. He said Belmullet was a fine town. Had I been there before? Where was I going next? Wasn't it a fine day? He didn't think it would rain, so. Goodbye, now! And good luck! And he went back to sit on his wall by the bank, waiting for the next tourist to entertain.

I sought out a bar, where I asked for a sandwich and a cup of tea. The barman couldn't have been more apologetic. He was sorry, but he didn't do sandwiches any more, but he could certainly make me a cup of tea. Would I just sit down? I said not to worry; considering the hour, I would have a glass of Guinness instead, with a packet of crisps, and I made myself comfortable in a corner.

He introduced himself as James Lenehan, and I told him my name. The sun was streaming in at the top of the window, and it was all very pleasant. After no more than ten minutes, James re-appeared from upstairs with a tower of ham sandwiches and a pot of tea, which he arranged next to my glass of Guinness.

He had been thinking about my name. Perhaps he ought to have recognised me? Was I famous? He wouldn't take any money for the tea and sandwiches, no: that was a gift, because he was embarrassed that he didn't do sandwiches any more.

We had a long rambling conversation about all sorts of things. Sea angling was very popular hereabouts. They took great pride in the numbers of different species of fish which could be caught locally. There was always a special prize for the most species in every angling competition.

And Championship Darts. He was personally very keen on that, and his pub team was one of the best for miles around. Earlier in the year, they had travelled to a competition in Galway. They did very well, but they didn't win. He said I reminded him of a certain champion darts player. He couldn't remember his name. Was that me? Anxious to offer him some consolation for my lack of fame, I told him that Eric Bristow, the World Champion Darts player, used to go to my old school. He seemed satisfied. That was fame indeed. Same school, eh? That's something.

Were my sandwiches ok? It was marvellous what the food companies were doing nowadays. Packets of sliced cheese had been out for a long time now, so convenient because the slices stayed fresh for weeks on end. And now they do packets of sliced ham the same. Some people didn't even keep them in the cool, but I shouldn't worry - he always kept his packet of ham slices in the fridge. I looked at the remaining crumbs of my half-devoured sliced ham sandwiches with some apprehension, hoping the packet hadn't been open for too long.

While he attended to a new customer, I spoke to another man at the bar, waiting for his wife to finish the shopping. He used to be a plasterer, and had lived for twelve years in Southend-on-Sea in Essex pursuing his trade. Before cheap holiday packages to Spain, Southend used to be the seaside playground for millions of East End Londoners - all fish and chips and funfairs. He was well paid as a plasterer, but he was young, and he spent all his money in the Kursaal, the local Southend fairground.

He couldn't have spent all his money though, because he came back home to Belmullet, married his childhood sweetheart, and bought a small farm of 40 acres. "Plastering is a young man's business, very physical" he explained. All through our conversation, he avoided my direct gaze, common in many shy Irishmen. He turned his face away and addressed me in profile, offering me his ear rather than his eyes, and speaking in quiet tones. His wife returned with the shopping, and he made his farewells and left.

I asked James if he had ever been to England, and his tone changed as he replied that he had not, he had never been away from Ireland, and Dublin "was quite far enough". His own father had done enough of the travelling, he added sadly, and he told me his story as he wiped down the counter and tidied up the bar. He heard this story from his mother.

"When he was still a young man, my father had a good job, but it took him away from home a lot. There was no work at all round here in those days. He was the foreman of an asphalting gang working in England, a team of specialists who were paid by the job, not by the day or the week. The five of them always worked together, and they soon earned a reputation for working fast and doing a good job. In the post-war boom, they could have as much work as they wanted, and they were well paid, and always got their early finish bonus.

"They won a really big job for a residential council estate in a new town in the North East of England. They were given the choice of a weekly wage, or being paid at the end of the job, and they would get an extra bonus. They all got together and agreed to take the lump sum. It would meaning living poorly for the three months or so they would be on the job, but they would get a fine pot of money at the end of the job, enough to send them all back to their homes with a nest egg to spend on a little business, that would set them up for life. They were all up for it.

"Well, it was a long hard job, but they were up to the task, and they worked together and looked after one another. They kept their own company, and they grew very close. And it wasn't easy, because they were young men with normal needs and desires, but they wouldn't go out drinking their money away. One drink on a Friday night was about all they allowed themselves.

"To cut a long story short, they finished the job ahead of time, and they were paid their money. They could scarcely believe it. These were ordinary working men, and they'd never seen so much money in their lives before. My father had almost £8000 in his hand, eight thousand English pounds, and a fortune in those days, that would buy you a small farm and see you married to the girl of your dreams!

"Of course, they allowed themselves a little drink before they all went their separate ways; not all the boys were Irish, and they knew they would probably never see one another again. It was an emotional time, and the ale was flowing. After a while they realised they were the only people left in the pub, and the landlady was staying on just to serve them. At closing time, she locked the doors and let them go on drinking "after hours" - she even bought them a round of drinks on the house, and made them sandwiches.

"At about midnight, they said it was time to go home, because they all had a long way to go early in the morning. My Dad was caught short - you know - he had to go to the toilet, so he went and did his business, if you'll excuse the expression. He took down his trousers, and remembered his fat wad of money that he had stuffed down his underpants for safety. He took it out, and laid it carefully on the floor in front of him. Then he finished his business and went back to the bar to join the others. They had one more round "for old times sake", and finally left the pub at about half past 12.

"My Dad stood there on the street, saying goodbye to everyone as they went their separate ways, and he was the last to go. Suddenly, he felt for his wad, and it wasn't there! He remembered taking it out when he went to the Gents, and he turned round and banged on the pub door.

"The landlady opened up right away; she had just cashed up and was about to start her rounds. He went straight to the toilet, but there was no sign of his packet of money. He looked everywhere, all the time more and more desperate. Here, there and everywhere. The landlady swore she hadn't checked the toilets yet. The only people who could have been anywhere near the money were his own mates. One of them must have picked up the wad and held on to it; there was no other explanation. My Dad couldn't believe it. He knew them all like his own brothers. But one of them had stolen his wad. His heart was broken, and his pockets were empty.

"What could he do? He wrote a letter home saying he wasn't coming because he had another job to do, and he spent a few more months trying hard to scrape together some money. He was a changed man – he never had another drink as long as he lived. He never saw any of his team again, and he went back to Ireland a broken man. His health had gone, and he had just enough money to put down a deposit on this pub. He came back to his young family, but he died before I was born. He was only 24 years old. The doctor said he could find nothing wrong with him. He died of a broken heart."

I listened to his sorry tale in silence. After a respectful period, I left. There is nothing in life so hurtful as a trust betrayed, and I was left very sad by the story of his father's betrayal. Was there any other explanation possible? It was hard to imagine one. He had been robbed by one of his closest workmates, and that's all there was to it. In one way, James was still paying the cost. Where would he have been now if his father had returned with enough money for a farm or a small business?

Belmullet was a town I enjoyed very much. It sits in such an extraordinarily remote position that one would expect it to have a run-down economy and a despondent community, but I found none of this. On the contrary, there were signs of new building, and even the restoration of dilapidated older buildings. Perhaps this is EEC money at work, giving aid to depressed areas. Perhaps I was just fortunate in meeting up with only friendly, optimistic souls. The Camden Town drunk was right in saying Belmullet is a fine town, and I hope to go back when I've more time to spare, not just "passing through".

Despite the vehement protests of ecologists and others, the Irish authorities have seen fit to allow Shell to bring a pipeline with untreated natural gas ashore here, across the virgin bog. Despite a Public Enquiry, a refinery terminal is due to be opened in 2010. I fear the effect on sleepy Belmullet will be colossal.

Chapter 29
Tina – Way out West

After leaving Belmullet, as we curled our way across the Mayo bogland to the South, I sighted another cyclist in distress, standing at the roadside as she worked on her upside-down bicycle. Now wary of grumpy cyclists struggling with sick machines, I didn't pull up with quite the same flourish as before. Better to assume she had the situation under control, I reasoned, and threw the cyclist an "OK?" as we cruised slowly past, without stopping. A cheerful wave was suddenly turned into a "Perhaps you can help!" so I stopped and walked warily back.

Tina was from Berlin, and had been touring Ireland for the last six weeks. She was rather proud that she had managed to replace a wheel-spoke without assistance, because she had never tried it before. She spoke excellent English – she even had the word "wheel-spoke" in her vocabulary. I think she asked me to stop so she could show someone how clever she had been in tackling the wheel-spoke. Thinking back to the last time I tried to adjust a wheel-spoke, and was driven to attack the bike in frustration and adolescent anger, I warned her that "Spokes are tricky things" and helped her fit the rear wheel back in the forks. It looked a bit bent to me. It was in fact horribly bent, and the more Tina tried to correct it, the worse it got. This was all looking horribly familiar.

She tightened one side and the other side banged against the brake-blocks when she gave the wheel a test spin. "You need an expert to put this on a bench. Someone who knows exactly what they're doing could fix it easily, but you and I could struggle for the rest of the day. You might even do more damage. Where are you going?"

The time was almost four o'clock. The nearest bicycle shop was probably in Westport, a distance of about 20 miles. The shop, if there were one, would shut soon. We worked out that if we removed the back brake-blocks, the bent wheel would probably rotate without hitting the forks, enough to get her there, anyway. Tina took out her map and agreed to scrap her plan to travel to Achill Island, which is probably too remote to boast a bicycle shop.

There was a youth hostel listed in Westport, but she couldn't trust her limping bike to take her all the way to Westport with all her luggage. Could I take her bags and leave them at the hostel in Westport? Here at last was a chance for me to play Sir Galahad. I produced my mobile phone and called the hostel. Yes, they had a bed available. Yes, there were two bike shops in town. They thought the bike shops probably closed at about five thirty.

I gave Tina the phone number of my own Bed & Breakfast in Leenane, in case anything went wrong, advised her to hitch a lift if the wheel let her down, and watched her wobble off down the road. Then I loaded up her side-bags onto Ernest. His happy roar as we set off on our first errand of mercy suggested that Ernest too thought we had done the right thing. Tina was very trusting, somehow sensing that a wally on a scooter is not only not a terrorist, but also not a thief. I gave her a reassuring toot as we passed her progressing unsteadily down the road to Westport.

We hadn't gone far down the road across the bogs when I spotted an unusual sight. In a landscape empty of signs of habitation, I made out a brightly-coloured object flying in the sky, an unidentified flying object. As I slowed to take a better look, I made out the silhouette of a figure beneath the coloured UFO on a low rocky bluff in the green bog. It took shape as a person flying a kite, but why here? The kite was making good use of the light breeze that was blowing, and responded readily to the tugs of the flier below.

It is fascinating to watch a well-flown kite, and I know myself that it can be great fun to take part. The flier was completely absorbed in the antics of the kite, and didn't notice me stopped at the side of the road, watching every dip and swirl as the kite soared and fell. I could see no parked car, or even a bicycle, so how the kite-flier got there was a mystery. But my delivery mission called, and so I reluctantly kicked Ernest into life and we carried on down the road.

The ancient port of Westport has become a one-way system gridlocked with stationary tourist traffic. I was last in the town about fifteen years before on a sea-fishing trip. Our skipper was a Welshman called Reg, and what I remembered most about him was that although we caught next to nothing on a dire day, he refused our request to call in at Clare Island in the middle of Clew Bay.

In those days, Clare Island had a rascally reputation as a place where the pubs stayed open all day, in defiance of the licensing laws, and we four empty-handed anglers thought that was a pretty neat idea to brighten up a dull day. But Reg was in charge, and Reg didn't want to know. He wasn't too worried about the fact that we caught no fish either. He just munched his sandwiches and every hour or so announced his intention to move on to a new mark. In fact, I think he wasn't too pleased really by the idea of having us on his boat, making it look untidy. We weren't too pleased to have found the only unhelpful Welsh skipper in Ireland either.

After negotiating the one-way system, and allowing a helpful passerby to give me the wrong directions, I eventually found the hostel in a handsome converted 300-year-old water mill. I deposited Tina's bags with reception and left her a note. They didn't seem at all concerned about having a pair of Berlin bombs left with them. What's really strange is how the rest of us have all become conditioned by the over-elaborate security measures introduced in the post-terrorism years, to be suspicious of everything.

I crossed the road to an unassuming pub, and slipped into conversational patter: "There've been a few changes since I was last in these parts!" (This can generally be relied upon to provoke a sympathetic response from the publican and customers alike, and it didn't let me down this time.) When was I last here? So I wouldn't have seen the one-way system before? And there were quite a few new buildings on the edge of town now. And some of the older ones had been slicked up too.

Where did I stay before? That particular hotel has been bought and sold three or four times since I last stayed there. They blamed the changes on the Common Market, although they really mustn't complain. They all agreed, the old days were very hard. I asked after Skipper Reg, and they knew him. The barman adopted a solemn tone and regretfully informed me that Reg had "passed away" just a couple of years back. He was quite a character. "Oh yes!" I agreed, remembering Clare Island.

In a corner of the bar sat a young lad with a guitar case. I sat at the table next to his, and he immediately started talking, telling me about himself with infectious enthusiasm. He was going to play in the bar tonight; he would sing his own compositions; he wrote all his own stuff, which he called his "material"; he was going to be big, he was going to be famous; this was just the beginning of a fabulous career; he was going to be bigger than the Beatles; was I going to stay and hear him? He was due to go on at 8 and then again at 10.

I explained I had to move on if I was to reach my digs before dinner, and would need to be leaving soon. "I could play you something now, if you like" he offered eagerly, but I was already on the back foot. "That wouldn't be fair on the others coming later" I ventured, unconvincingly, but the lack of logic went unnoticed.

"This gig is all about getting me more experience, y'know? My agent told me to get some on-the-road touring experience. Well, he's not my agent yet, y'know, but he'll take me on when I've got more experience. He says it'll round off the edges, y'know? But I'm really a writer first, a writer that sings, you know, people really like my songs. They're sort of rock with a folk edge, y'know? Can't you come back tonight then? You'll kick yourself for missing it."

He ended all his sentences with a question, going up at the end of each phrase. His generation has learned this affectation from Australian tv soap operas, and it can be very annoying, y'know?

I asked him about his influences, who were the singers that he liked? "Well, there's Dylan of course, and the blues, but there's a lot to be said for the modern poets, like Blur, Oasis, for example. But they are only some people whose music I like. I don't imitate anyone; I'm my own man, you know? That's why I'm going to be so big, you wait and see."

The enthusiasm and self-confidence of the young is refreshing and contagious, but it's very tiring after a day of adventures on the road. In case he's right about his prospects, look out for my young friend on the way to the top. His name is – now what was his name again?

CHAPTER 30
LEENANE – HAMILTON'S AND DELPHI

Hamiltonville

As a special treat for myself, I had booked a room for the night in an up-market game-fishing hotel near the village of Leenane. I have known Leenane, in the main, from earlier fishing trips, and it holds a special place in my sentimental old heart. It is situated on a spectacular fjord-like inlet, known as Killary Harbour. At the toe-end of the inlet is a waterfall where a salmon river meets the sea.

The first time I came to Leenane, the water was low, and the salmon couldn't get up the falls. They were packed shoulder to shoulder in Killary Harbour, waiting for the tide to rise to meet the level of the low river. While they waited, they periodically leapt out of the water, like the fish in a Walt Disney cartoon. No one knows why they do this, although there are many theories. My own theory is that they jump out of the water to cock a snoot at the fishermen, and so it proved. I hurriedly assembled my spinning tackle, and cast into the middle of them, confidently expecting a take. After an hour or so with no result, I realised something was wrong. I fumbled as I changed my spinners too hastily, trying to find a lure the salmon would find irresistible. All the while, the salmon leapt out of the water with a "plip" and landed back in the same hole in the surface with a "plop". If you looked closely, you could see them wink.

I was driven to distraction, but I wouldn't leave the waterside even when it was too dark to see. My companions had to drag me away, babbling oaths about the stupidity of those migratory fish. They took me to Hamilton's, which was the pub, general store and Post Office, the only shop in the village. One side of the room was a bar; the other side was a grocery shop, with a door through to the Post Office. At the back was a pool table. Everyone came to Hamilton's because there wasn't anywhere else to go. Mr. Hamilton could sometimes provide a plate of hot soup and a wedge of soda bread. It was a fine place, and the longer you stayed, the finer it became.

Since those days, the village has hosted a couple of film shoots. The film company making *"The Field"* built a bar at the side of the original Hamilton's, for filming interiors. Mr. Hamilton was always quietly well-off, rumoured to own considerable amounts of property in the village and in the neighbourhood. There was a small garage, a boat yard, a Bed & Breakfast. I had already been back to Leenane since the coming of *"The Field"*, so I was prepared for the alarming spectacle of the Field Bar, and the Field Stores, but I was surprised to discover the Field Grill and the Field Restaurant. Did I imagine I saw the Field Holiday Launderette?

The impact of tourism is particularly marked in this small village, with its Heritage Centre and Museum, and Craft Shop. Tourist coaches doing the circuit of Connemara pass through constantly, and some of them even stop to unload their passengers for a ten-minute tour. Some coaches only slow down to a walking pace, and open-mouthed faces press against the windows to gawp at the passing splendours of the Leenane film set.

Inside Hamilton's, the bar had now expanded, pushing its grocery arm back to join a bigger, brighter sub-Post Office in what had been the house next door. The bar tables around the peat fire were full of tourists, less blue-rinse brigade but more bright-anoraked and activity-seeking souls. Even vegetarian dishes were available from the bar. Rucksacks cluttered the floor. Serious-looking bicycles were stacked neatly outside the door.

A tall Dutch hiker ordered eight pints of Smithwicks, carefully pronouncing each syllable of the name of the beer known to the Irish as "Smiddix". He carried the dripping tray of drinks over to the peat fire, where they were received with whoops of Dutch delight. The barman was prepared for big orders of this size; someone had thoughtfully placed the taps for pouring Smithwicks and Guinness doubled up in twos. He placed two glasses beneath each two-tap set, and flicked all on together, thus pouring four pints at the same time. He was a hardworking barman, serving tourists and locals with the same energy, and delivering plates of hot bar food to the waiting tables singlehanded.

In the old days, Mr. Hamilton managed the bar and the grocery shop all by himself too, with the occasional thin-legged child helping to collect the empties, or to pull a pint when told to. I tried my reliable opening gambit about a few changes since I was last in these parts, and there was general agreement among the cluster of locals at the bar that there had indeed been a lot of changes. I asked about the health of Mr. Hamilton, and was told by the barman that he was in good health.

They asked me who I knew in the village, and I told them of Doug Ross, a highly individual Canadian copywriter I had worked with, who used to have a cottage in a boreen further up the inlet. He always began every sentence with "Anyhoo". They looked solemn, and asked me if I knew that he had passed away a while back. I agreed I had heard that Doug had died in Dublin. He had heart problems, and enjoyed a drink too much to take it easy for long.

The last time I saw him was in Hamilton's; I called in on the off-chance while passing through one time. Doug was playing pool. He was back drinking again, and had swollen up to twice his size. He fixed me with his gimlet eye, and told me he had been bitter for a while, but had now found it in his heart to forgive me. I couldn't remember what I had done to need forgiveness, but I felt sufficiently guilty to buy him a drink to celebrate the spirit of amnesty. It didn't occur to me till afterwards that he might have confused me with someone else.

So Doug was dead - but they thought his father might still be alive. Doug's Dad was a pioneering frontiersman from the Canadian backwoods. He was full of exaggerated stories of the wild, like when he killed a bear with his bare hands, and drank the blood to survive, that sort of thing. "It was the B'ar or me!" He was a powerful character, fiercely active in his old age. He dominated his son, even when nearing 80, and was probably the source of most of Doug's problems. It wouldn't surprise me if Doug's Dad had survived his son, but no one was sure where he might be living now. They thought he might have gone back to Canada - where men were men, I thought to myself.

I asked the barman if he was a member of the Hamilton family, and he told me proudly that he was Mr. Hamilton Jr. I looked hard at him. He was perhaps 40, so he would have been a teenager when I was propping up the bar at Hamilton's on a regular basis. I had a vague memory of a skinny youth helping out behind the bar, but I couldn't remember his face. That's not so unusual, because there were many things I couldn't remember about my visits to Leenane.

I forget the name of a mad game Doug had introduced us to, which involved bowling large rocks down the country lane by his cottage. The rules were very vague, and we never managed to finish a game, because we would inevitably lose interest, cut the game short and go to the pub.

"The Field" was a play before it was a film, written by West Coast playwright John B. Keane. The veteran Irish actor Richard Harris fitted the central character Bull McCabe as if it had been written for him. He wore the part like well-worn clothes, and was as much at home as in his youthful role as a Rugby League player (Frank Machin?) in *"A Sporting Life"*, his first important film. In a long career, I remember few parts quite as meaty in between these two.

In *"The Field"* McCabe has a powerful one-take scene where he attacks a returning American Irishman for planning to buy the rented land

McCabe has worked all his life. McCabe believes that all emigrants give up their rights as Irishmen when they emigrate. The true Irishmen are those who stayed on, and suffered poverty and deprivation alongside Mother Ireland. They alone should have the right to inherit the land.

Tourism has brought an unexpected prosperity to Leenane. Killary Harbour is now full of salmon farm cages, the declared enemy of the fishing hotels who have seen a prolific run of sea trout degenerate to a pathetic trickle since the salmon cages arrived.

The way to Delphi Lodge led me along the narrow road which closely follows the contour of the lough shore, past Aasleagh Falls (packed with tourist coaches), and then hairpinning us back into the sparsely inhabited far side of the fjord.

In the middle of nowhere, far from the nearest farmhouse, I met a small group of sheep browsing at the roadside. They were in the charge of a very old man, seated on a stone wall, commanding a fine view across the lough. I nodded as I rode by, and he raised a finger in greeting. I stopped and shared the view with him. It was a fine view, and it was a fine evening, we agreed. Did he live nearby? Just beyond, he replied, waving his arm in the vague direction of the hill behind him. We exchanged goodbyes, and I started up Ernest as quietly as possible, not to frighten the sheep. They seemed untroubled.

Further on, around another bend I came upon a silver-grey Vespa travelling in the opposite direction. This was the first Vespa other than Ernest, which I had seen on this trip. It was ridden by a middle-aged grizzled-bearded traveller, not unlike myself. His luggage included a tent and sleeping bag, and the number plates were British. We both waved excitedly, and Ernest wobbled a greeting. I should have stopped, and exchanged experiences with my fellow scooterist, who was obviously touring Ireland in the approved clockwise direction. But by the time this thought occurred to me, Ernest and his silver-grey counterpart had covered several hundred yards, and we were now lost to each other's view. Had this been a doppelganger experience?

Delphi Lodge is a Georgian mansion, once the seat of the Marquis of Sligo. I found that it was run by a young English couple, Peter and Jane Mantle, who operated it as an old-style fishing hotel. Anglers may book individual stretches of river and lough, known as "beats", on a rotating basis. Local knowledge and assistance is available from traditional ghillies, fishery assistants, booked through the hotel. The very comfortable accommodation includes country-house style dinner around a long table which seats all the guests, with the host at the head of the table. If an angler has caught a salmon that day, he or she is given pride of place at the top of the table. Children are encouraged to take high tea earlier, to leave the evening's proceedings for the grown-ups. This segregation of adults and children smacks of a Victorian attitude to keeping children in their place.

Salmon fishing is expensive, and clients of Delphi Lodge tend to be wealthy or upper class, or ideally both. A timeshare scheme has been brought in, and many of the guests know one another from visits of previous years. The setting is superb, among wooded mountains, tinkling streams and gleaming loughs. Fortunately, they also offer non-fishing accommodation for travellers such as myself. I took delight in carefully parking Ernest under a huge, mature oak tree in the car park, among the Range Rovers, Jaguars, and BMWs.

CHAPTER 31
DELPHI FOLK

Ernest among the Range Rovers (they're the other side of the tree.).

After slipping out of my orange bomb in my room, which was at the bottom end of the tariff, described as being "without a lake-view", I relaxed in the old-world elegance of a large bedroom and an en-suite bathroom, and a walk-in wardrobe. A fellow guest told me on the stairs that dinner was at 7.30, and that one was expected to assemble for cocktails in the sitting room sharp at seven. "Don't be late!" I was instructed.

I wondered idly if I was expected to dress for dinner. My answer was simple: I couldn't. As a special concession, I would change my white trainers for my black shoes. I had time to have a soak in the high-sided bath. Hell, I could even put on tomorrow's clean shirt. But first I would ride back into Leenane to buy some odds and ends, and to see if my fellow scooterist was around. On the road back to Leenane, the very old man was still sitting on his stone wall, watching his sheep; he nodded again, and raised a finger.

In the shop, I bought some postcards, and asked for some stamps: the Post Office had sold out of stamps. How can a Post Office sell out of stamps? Stamps are what Post Offices are for. It's like a pub selling out of beer. Mr. Hamilton Jr. was hovering in the background. He stepped in to explain that there had been a rush of visitors asking for stamps, and they now had none left. I was not convinced. On the way back, the very old man clicked his counter, and raised a finger. Whatever the word against me was in Leenane, it hadn't reached him yet.

Immediately as I walked back into the front hall of Delphi Lodge, I was told there was a phone call for me. It was Tina. She had arrived in Westport safely, and the bicycle shop was already standing by to cure her wobbly spoke. Shortly after I left her, she had been offered a lift by a Canadian couple, who squeezed her sick bike and herself into their back seat. She was so pleased I had taken her luggage on Ernest, because there wouldn't have been enough room for both the bike and her bags in the car. Remembering her manners, she then slipped into conversational mode, and asked me what kind of a day I had had, and what would I be doing tomorrow. Would our paths cross again? she wondered. It wasn't every day she had battled with a wobbly spoke, and entrusted her travel bags to a passing White Knight, and she wanted to share the experience.

I thought I looked rather lovely in my greyish Sligo-washed sweater and my black shoes and socks, as I entered the sitting room. I was greeted by most of the other guests who were already gathered there, dressed, I noticed, rather more formally than I was.

There was one other sweater, however, worn by an early-retired investment adviser from Preston, a regular fisherman. His family was from Galway, and with only mild menace in his measured tones, he announced that he himself had inherited the Republican tradition.

There were two elderly upper middle class couples seated on the sofas. One couple was from Kenya (pronounced the old colonial way - "Keenya"). He complained that he had been more worried than ever lately; he had recently been obliged to introduce razor wire to protect his property. They were thinking of "coming home" soon. They had probably lived in Kenya for 40 or 50 years, but they still considered it somewhere other than "home".

My mind drifted off to think about the lot of ex-pat colonials; there was a book - or was it a play? - about colonials who chose to continue to live in India after Independence in 1947; it was called "Staying On". So all colonials don't necessarily return home to the old country eventually. I wondered at what point the Scottish and English colonials in Ulster had decided to stay on? When did they stop thinking about "going home" and decide that Ulster was their true home? Was this another feeling at the heart of their discomfort, that they saw Ireland as their home, but they also thought of the old country as their home too. I felt my eyes glazing over, so I pulled myself together and got back into the conversation.

The other couple were from Surrey, he a stockbroker. They came here at the same time every year and stayed in the same cottage in the grounds. There were several American couples: one young man said he and his partner were from New York, which puzzled me because his partner had an attractively zany friendliness which struck me as more West Coast than New York. It was she who had warned me not to be late for cocktails. Under my cross-examination, she confessed she was from California, but was now living in what she called the "Big Apple".

Another American couple had travelled across from Dublin, where he was working on an assignment. He was from Albuquerque, she from Los Alamos. She pretended to be surprised that I had heard of it. I couldn't imagine there was anyone in the Western World who had not heard of the town where the atomic bomb was first tested, but she looked surprised. She wanted to know if I believed in Flying Saucers. I said: probably. We discussed the theory that all cases of close contact with extra-terrestrials could be explained as fantasies dreamed up by over-imaginative minds. I said: it's possible. She began to tell me of a Close Encounter she had experienced personally herself, and her partner interrupted to furnish the story with convincing details.

All the while, in amongst the guests threaded our host, Peter Mantle. He has a natural talent for this sort of job, welcoming and charming in turn. He is passionate about the decline of the sea trout, and about the quality of his wine cellar. He remarked on my enterprise in travelling round Ireland on a scooter, and announced his admiration to the other guests. He was leading the battle for the sea trout in the courts: he and four other fisheries had brought a case against the Ministry for Marine for failing to protect the wild fish, and failing to regulate the salmon farming industry. They are suing the salmon farmers for damages arising from an "actionable nuisance".

They claimed that the salmon fishery in Killary Harbour had also exceeded the production limits specified in their license. The West is better known for direct action, such as with the Molly Maguires and the Boycott. Litigation is considered an un-Irish thing, but they claim that they have tried everything else.

In the sitting room, drinks were available from a well-stocked drinks table. The procedure was the old-world one of self-service and self-accountability, by entering one's consumption in a drinks book. I tried an interesting-looking Irish whiskey unknown to me. The atmosphere was jolly, and conversational, but very English. We were led into dinner. As no salmon had been caught, Peter assumed the chair at the head of the table, and invited everyone else to sit where they pleased. Since most guests had been here for at least a few days, they occupied their usual seats.

We were joined by some more abstemious guests who had not been taking cocktails. Among them were two American priests, one very elderly and frail; they were seated close to the top of the table. I sat next to the sweater from Preston, and was introduced to a man from Dublin, by coincidence another investment consultant. Yet a third investment consultant, from Connecticut, joined us with his wife.

He sought to cut a dash, and appeared in narrow plus-twos, tartan socks, and a dark tartan dress jacket. He seemed disappointed that no one else had dressed for dinner, but was presumably used to being overdressed. He was also pompous and boring, talking endlessly about his work, which was clearly very boring. He attributed his success at work to being boring, claiming that caution to the point of lethargy is apparently considered a good thing in investment consultancy. He positively boasted about his lack of action when others around him were advising a change of tack. He confided that he had four children from previous marriages, and paid out large amounts of alimony. His wife agreed with him that they were indeed large amounts, and added that she too had a daughter from a previous marriage.

When he heard of my trip, he mentioned that 29 years earlier he had driven on two wheels around Scotland. He had nothing but problems with his British-bought motorbike, and eventually abandoned it and hired a car. "What make of bike was this?" I asked innocently. He could not remember. This struck me as odd. If I had been severely let down by a motorbike in the way he described, I would have remembered the make of the machine in question until the day I died, probably cursing it with my last breath.

I drew his wife into the conversation. She had recently returned from a first time visit to Portugal, and was very interested in knowing more about the Convention of Cintra which ended the first phase of the Spanish Peninsular War. She had heard of it when she visited Portugal, but didn't know what it was about. I was able to give her a brief rundown, and explained why Wellington thought it was a bad thing, but necessary. Rather like Munich. She looked blank. I think I may have bored her.

The wine list was impressive. Exquisite clarets with exquisite prices, but little to satisfy a punter's curiosity about New World wines. France dominated the list, so I chose a sensibly priced minor red wine, and was well satisfied. It was in nearby Westport that a highly successful London restaurateur taught me a memorable lesson about wine. He ordered a bottle of good, red burgundy to accompany his Dover sole, to impress on me that the tradition of drinking only white wine with fish was hooey. As I ordered red wine with my fish, in his memory, I wondered if the news of the wine revolution had reached Connecticut. The man in plus-twos looked alarmed.

The Republican from Preston took an interest in my choice. He drank only water, I noticed, and I assumed he was another teetotaller, of which there are many in Ireland, where alcoholism is a serious social problem. But this man knew a great deal about wine, and asked if he might sample the bouquet of the wine I had chosen. He swirled the wine in the glass, and looked closely at the colour before taking a deep sniff of the freshly opened wine. He approved.

He explained that he was now reduced to the status of collector of wine rather than a consumer, since he was forbidden to drink it. His greatest passion used to be wine, and fishing came a poor second in his scheme of things. He discovered early on that he was gifted with a good palate, and as soon as he could afford it, he began to buy expensive wines and to take his interest seriously. He went on wine-tasting courses, took wine-tasting holidays, and earned wine-tasting diplomas. When he became confident in his own abilities, he began to collect wines of quality, on the pretence of making an investment. His cellar was now extensive and worth a small fortune. I figured that a man who advised people about their investments for his own living, and could afford to hop on a plane to the West of Ireland when he heard the salmon were running, must know a small fortune when he saw one.

"Then the doc diagnosed diabetes last year, and that was that. No more wine. I can still do tastings, but it's not the same as sitting down with a chum and enjoying a couple of bottles, is it? I wonder sometimes if everyone has the same sensations when they drink wine as I do. For me, it's the subtleties in a glass of wine, the differences between one year and another, one grape and another, one vineyard and another. I can tell a good South American Cabernet Sauvignon from a South African or an Australian. And they are all very different from a French wine, not necessarily better or worse, just different."

His passion for his subject was obvious, and I tried to imagine the mixed emotions of someone whose favourite occupation, and through no fault of his own, had been reduced to just another asset in his business life.

"So will you sell off your wine now?" I asked. "I have to sell some as it comes of a certain age, but I won't be drinking it, so it's no fun anymore. It's very frustrating, but it could be worse." I guiltily sipped my wine, but it didn't taste the same anymore.

The conversation switched to fishing, but that was no better: no fish had been caught. It was generally agreed that more rain was needed to bring the salmon in from the sea, and to bring them running up the short distance from the rivers to the loughs. The prospects were not good, and the long-term weather forecast offered no relief, even to the optimists.

Over coffees in the lounge, the conversation returned to the subject everyone present knew something about: fishing. Many of the guests were on a return visit, and inevitably the talk was about how much better the fishing had been in the good old days. Peter was quick to add that last year's catch of salmon was the biggest on record in numbers of fish, although he admitted the average size was small. The average had gone down over the years so that salmon are now being caught no bigger than the size of a good trout. There are still some of the bigger fish being caught, sometimes as big as they ever were, but the average size is down.

Ever the good host, he brought others into the conversation, to tell of golden days when they had enjoyed dream catches. Would they ever be repeated? Every fisherman thought so; it's what sends them out to the riverbank on a cold wet morning. As different as we all were in that room, we shared that knowledge, we had all known the same delights and the same disappointments in fishing, and would continue to feel as long as we were able to fish.

As the evening went on, and the glasses were refilled, I realised I was in danger of nodding off. The atmosphere was warm and friendly, and I was feeling distinctly warm and dozy. So I pulled myself together and went for a stroll in the darkening grounds. Then I went to my room, to listen to the radio and to enjoy a read. From the sitting room I could still hear the slightly blurred sounds of conversation, as the other guests relived slightly exaggerated versions of earlier successes.

There was a puzzling item of news from the North. A joint statement was issued by the RUC and the British Army concerning the rubber bullets they use to control crowds and protests which allegedly "get out of hand".

This popular name for a nasty piece of military equipment makes it sound quite jolly, all wobbly like a bendy toy. But they are lethal, especially if they strike a delicate part of the anatomy. I'm not sure of the number of deaths caused by rubber bullets in the North since they were introduced, but the friends and relatives of the deceased would agree that it's too many. They are particularly lethal against children and other persons of delicate bone structure.

The announcement, tucked away in a remote corner of the news bulletin, stated that because of an unfortunate oversight, the type of rubber bullet issued in the North was the wrong type. Apparently, the authorities had ordered one sort, and the silly packers in the arms factory had delivered the wrong one: they were too hard. The rubber comes in different grades of hardness to cover use on a range of subjects. With no sense of irony, it was revealed that because of this regrettable mistake, troops and policemen had been shooting at children with bullets meant for tough, muscular terrorists. They were very sorry. The proper bullets would replace the old ones "as soon as possible".

Chapter 32
From Killary to Louisburg

The road from Killary ...much loved by the photographers of car commercials...

I was worried about Ernest's rear tyre pressure. The air pressure in the hardworking wheel had been reduced by bouncing over uneven bog roads with the weight of a heavy top box, and a portly middle-aged man and his luggage. John Wayne as Rooster Cogburn in his Oscar-winning performance in "True Grit" wryly described himself as "a fat old man", but then, although there are certain similarities, I am not John Wayne.

The next morning, I found an air line in the village, and added a few more pounds of air pressure. Ernest showed no other signs of wear and tear, the oil was clean, and the lights all worked. I complimented him on how well he seemed to be bearing up under the strain. I caught up on some more local gossip at the air line.

Prosperity had touched almost every one of the villagers from the old days. There were a few new faces too, doing nicely from the visitors. The former Leenane Hotel had first returned to being a private house, and was now a sort of up-market B & B. They were interested to know where was I staying? I didn't like to own up to my self-indulgence, treating myself to a stay at the Big House, so I waved generally in the direction of Louisburg and grunted.

The locals seemed united in thinking that "the visitors" were a good thing, and who was I to argue? My reasons for preferring the old ways were nostalgic, sentimental even. Ernest has no sentiment, but even he admitted to me he didn't care for the busy cross-town traffic in downtown Leenane, where tourist coaches negotiated their way past drivers of hire cars, more used to having the steering wheel on the other side.

The road from Killary Harbour to Louisburg is one of the most beautiful drives in Ireland, much loved by the photographers of car television commercials. The lakes and river of the Delphi Fishery wind up between steep, grassy mountains, and share the valley floor with a narrow asphalt road. Boats on the lakes snuggle up to the side of the road in scaled-down rock-built harbours, evidence of closed-season work by the gillies. Finally the road rises up and leaves the lakes behind as it crosses Doo Lough Pass.

The view back is quite stunning, and care has to be taken with the coachloads of tourists who stop here to click their cameras. They wander into the road like so many sheep, and seem to resent any passing traffic which does not share the impulse to stop to enjoy the scenery.

In the presence of such natural beauty, it is hard to recall that this area suffered worse than most during the Great Hunger, the famine which followed the outbreaks of potato blight in the mid-19th Century. Inaction by the uncaring Government in London combined with the harshness of most of the landlords, caused the death by starvation of whole communities who used to live in the ruined cottages which haunt the countryside; they drove literally millions into emigration and exile.

A modest plaque at the side of the Doo Lough road commemorates the deaths of an entire group returning to their homes after being turned away from the local workhouse in 1849. Where the tourists gather at the top of the pass, there is a more substantial monument, which records the visit of Bishop Tutu, and unites the suffering poor of South Africa with the starving victims of the Potato Famine. On the shore of Clew Bay, at the foot of Croag Patrick where thousands of pilgrims climb to the top every year, a modern sculpture the "Coffin Ship", has been set up in a memorial park to those who "died, suffered and emigrated due to the Great Famine of 1845-50, and the victims of all famines". It is fitting that a nation as generous as the Irish should remember others, when they consider their own greatest tragedy.

It is said that a smug English historian wrote in an unforgivable observation that: "The Irish fornicated themselves to death in the Potato Famine" This was at the heart of the Laissez-Faire view of the situation: in the opinion of the Establishment, the Irish peasants in large families bore the responsibility for the tragedy because, as good Catholics, they did not practise restraint in birth-control, and failed to trim their numbers to satisfactory reduced subsistence levels. Yet the Church declared such restraint a sin, and the Government believed it could wash its hands of all liability on its own part. It was an important step in the revived Peace Process when the new Labour Government admitted that London had failed to save lives during the Irish Famines of the 19th Century with their resolute inaction.

A road to the right offers the chance to double back to the Erriff River, which is another salmon fishery, once famous for its sea trout. Once through the Pass, all the rivers now flow in the opposite direction, seemingly anxious to empty into Clew Bay as soon as possible.

The Bunowen River does this close to Louisburg, where there used to live a fine man called Joe Philbean. He was responsible for selling day tickets to fish the Bunowen River and loughs. I used to phone him for a ticket, and he would say, "Just one minute now while I look at the water." He lived by the bridge over the Bundowen, so he had only to lean out of the window to look at the condition of the river. If the river was low for want of rain, the fish couldn't enter it from the sea or move out of the holding pools. "I'll not be selling you a ticket today!" was his frequent answer when he came back to the phone. "There'll be no fish in the river till we see some rain."

I turned off at Louisburg to follow the road-signs to Roonah Quay for the ferry to Clare Island. There is a fine new quay, but if the sea is coming in direct from the open Atlantic, there are days when it is not safe to come in here, and operations are switched to another quay further round the bay. Clare Island rises up straight ahead, about three miles offshore. Beyond and to the right is Achill Island, which is joined to the mainland by a causeway. To the left is the smaller island of Inishturk, about 7 miles away.

~☆~

The day was perfect: Clew Bay shone like a saucer of blue paint, and every detail on Clare Island could be clearly seen. There are two different ferry companies operating a service to Clare Island, mainly for summer tourists. Their wooden tool-shed huts face each other on opposite sides of the car park at Roonah Quay as if squaring up for a fight, but the rivalry is more imaginary than real: whoever has the next boat gets the booking.

There used to be only the one boat, but one winter's day in 1992 a rope fouled its propeller and the boat went onto the rocks by the harbour on Clare Island. A second skipper volunteered to maintain the service for the benefit of the islanders with his own boat, and when the first skipper was ready to open up again, the relief boat stayed on. In the summer, there is enough work for two boats, but it was a different story in the winter months.

Another ferry works out of Westport, but it combines the service with a sort of Bay Cruise. I felt a bit unhappy about leaving Ernest alone in the car park for two nights, but the lady in the ferry hut assured me "We don't have any of those problems over here." She was from the Island, a member of the family operating the ferry service. She would be married soon, and go to live in the central Lakelands. She would miss the Island, but she had to admit there wasn't much to do.

There was an hour or so to wait, so I went for a stroll around the harbour wall, and then to the small shop by the waiting room. I wasn't surprised to find it was staffed by the same girl who had sold me my ferry ticket. In the waiting room, I made myself as comfortable as possible on the hard bench and opened my can of lemonade.

After a few minutes there, I was joined by two smartly dressed young men, who greeted me warmly. The suits and the accents were American, and they were on a mission from God. They were very clean, with carefully cut blond hair and perfectly even, bright-white teeth. Most people back away when they meet Evangelists, but in my own way I too am on a mission, and I feel it is my duty to offer my own understanding of the meaning of life to these poor souls. I greeted them back, lustily. I made it clear from the start that they were speaking to the converted.

I told them how I first saw the light when I was in my teens. It was like St. Paul on the road to Damascus, a revelation that Christianity, all organised religion, is wrong, and that the only true religion is Atheism. After my conversion, I became a firm believer in a life independent of any concepts of gods or priests; I feel no need for mumbo-jumbo. For example, I have even overcome my concern about the relationship between, Christianity and Art. All the cathedrals, paintings, sculptures, literature and other works of art which have been inspired by a belief in the Church, can still be enjoyed by others who do not accept the same religious beliefs. I can cross over and appreciate the most esoteric works of art produced in the fullest religious fervour without having to join the artists in their prayers.

It's not very fair to confront the Evangelists with this knowledge, because their own prepared arguments are all based on the same misconceptions. The discussion usually goes around in circles, and ends in my asking them earnestly – sometimes too earnestly – to think again, and to see if they can't think again, and see the wisdom of my way, the true way. Evangelists are trained to work on the doubts of failing believers, and are flummoxed when confronted by someone with equally strong religious convictions which roundly reject their own ideas.

At first they rise to the challenge, and trot out their own well-rehearsed arguments, but this is just grist for the mill, an opportunity for the opponent to counter and dismiss their questionable tenets. Their weapons of attack are thus turned upon themselves, and since they are not prepared to abandon their beliefs, the result is stalemate.

As the two Evangelists rose to leave, suddenly remembering a pressing appointment, they made as if to bless me, but I cut them short, and wished them well, urging them to think seriously about what I had told them. I never try to "convert" anyone unless they try it first on me.

Chapter 33
Ferry to Clare Island

The lighthouse at Clare Island.

It was time to board the ferry for the island. I don't know what I was expecting, but the boat seemed suddenly very small. I have fished from bigger boats than the Clare Island ferry, but the handful of other passengers didn't seem to be worried, and scampered all over the superstructure looking for their favourite, customary perches. The sky was dazzlingly blue, and the sea was spiritedly choppy but not uncomfortably so. We settled down to the short trip, hanging off various bits of woodwork and clinging to makeshift grab handles.

Clare Island was the home of the legendary woman pirate, Grace O'Malley or Granuile in the Irish. The ruin of her 15th Century castle still stands guard at the entrance to the island harbour. It is known that she gave shelter and assistance to the crew of the Armada ships wrecked in Clew Bay, but I didn't have any details of the extent of her involvement.

The *Gran Grin* is said to have been wrecked by Clare Island; of the combined contingent of 329 men, 200 are believed to have drowned, another 60 were put to the sword by the local O'Malley clan, presumably kinsmen of Grace, and the rest were executed in Galway.

It would be nice to think that some of them may have escaped to comparative safety as members of Grace's pirate crew.

In answer to my questions, the skipper of the *Ocean Star* said he believed that the Spanish galleon was sunk in Achill Sound, between Clare Island and Achill Island. No, nothing has ever been found, as far as he knew. There's a powerful, fast current over there, and any wreck would have been torn to pieces many years ago. This particular wreck may have been the second Armada ship known to have sunk in Clew Bay, the *San Nicolas*, originally from Dubrovnik, with 355 souls on board. There were no survivors.

I told him I had been sea fishing in the bay – were there any angling boats working there now? The fish stocks in the bay were no longer enough for commercial fishing, apart from seasonal mackerel, but there were still a few angling boats working, and they came in with good catches from time to time, he believed. Not as good as in the old days though, when giant skate were often caught. Did I know about Granuile's Castle? "That's it over there, the old ruin we're passing just now. You can go inside, and have a look around if you want."

We nuzzled up against the harbour wall, and ropes were swiftly tied into businesslike knots. The passengers disembarked, some more clumsily than others. I was carrying all my gear from the Vespa – the top box, rucksack, helmet and everything – and I struggled along the pier towards the pub overlooking the beach. I had been told to phone the lady at the Lighthouse when I arrived, and she would come and collect me.

There being no rush, I ordered a pint and a sandwich first, and looked out at the view. I could easily get used to the leisurely pace of Island life. There was a boisterous group of youngsters in the bar next door, and I joined them with my pint. Although it was only lunchtime, some of them were obviously very drunk. They were a group of friends from the other side of the bay, and had come to the Island for the weekend bash with a live band in the pub on Saturday night. Some had not been to bed, and were the worse for wear; more pints were seen as the best cure, but money was running out. Three bleary boys pooled their resources to share a pint of Guinness.

There is just the one public call box on the Island, and as usual in the West, my mobile phone wasn't being at all helpful. Wherever the relay station was transmitting from, the signal refused to find its way down to the harbour side. When I eventually got through to my landlady, Monica Timmermans, she didn't show any surprise that I was calling a couple of hours after the boat had arrived. She told me she would drive down to pick me up shortly.

Perhaps half an hour later, she arrived, driving a large Japanese jeep. She wasn't hard to identify, because the only other two cars I had seen on the island were big battered estate cars, both driven by what appeared to be twelve-year-old boys. Monica is Belgian; she and her husband used to run a coarse-fishing centre in County Cavan before taking over the Clare Island Lighthouse.

The lighthouse was decommissioned in the 1950s, and quickly fell into ruin. The Timmermans bought it in 1991, and set to work making it habitable. The group of buildings includes the earlier, squat lighthouse tower, standing next to the later, taller one. In addition to the living quarters, there are walled fields where vegetables used to be grown, and the livestock was kept, to keep the lighthouse crews supplied with fresh food.

The road from the harbour winds up and up to the lighthouse, which is on the north side of the island, passing a few ruins on the way. Occasionally, a slow-moving, laid-back-looking sheep would stroll nonchalantly across our path. It was my impression that they looked at us with positive disdain.

All the island sheep are marked with either a blue blotch or a red one, to identify the owner, I was told. Rearing sheep is not a serious business on the island, the main attraction being the European Union's subsidy rather than the value of the wool or the carcass. The wool of a sheep is now virtually worthless, and there is no butcher on the island. There's an old man who knows how to carry out the occasional slaughtering for home consumption, but that's it.

The achievements of the Timmermans at the remote lighthouse are extraordinary. The rooms they have created are welcoming and comfortable, and it would not be wrong to describe them as luxurious. To put this into perspective, you must realise that everything has to be brought to Clare Island by boat and then lugged up the hill. They only just managed to offload their family furniture in time from the stricken ferry in 1992, before it was wrecked on the rocks.

The water is brought up by a long system of pipes, powered by two separate staged pumps which have to be checked every day. The buildings are perched on solid rock, and the boundary walls are only inches away from 400 ft cliffs dropping straight down to white-water waves below.

Mr. Timmermans has the strength and energy needed for an enterprise of this magnitude, and cultivates a certain bear-like quality in his appearance and his manner. He roars and bustles about his business non-stop, and he would have got on all right with Doug's Dad. When I arrived he was putting the finishing touches to repainting the walls, assisted by a local man who obviously brought painting expertise to the partnership. They made me very nervous as, apparently unconcerned, they wielded brushes and pots of paint on the other side of the boundary wall, with a sheer drop to the rocks below. Safety lines are for wimps was the message, but it made me very uneasy to watch them.

I discovered that Mr. Timmermans was a Land Rover enthusiast, and we immediately took a liking to each other. I have owned two Land Rovers, and Mr. Timmermans had four or five in various stages of disrepair. He even had a 101, which is every Land Rover owner's dream. A short run of these front-wheel driven trucks were built exclusively as army vehicles, but second-hand ones can be bought by the public at government auctions. Mr. Timmermans thrust the latest edition of *Land Rover Owner International* into my hand, and recited the history of his particular 101 acquisition. It was currently on the mainland "awaiting parts". I am sure this rugged vehicle will soon find happiness being driven by Mr. Timmermans around this equally rugged island.

The setting was magnificent, and the weather was superb. The air was piercingly clear in the lowering sun, lighting up the whole of Achill Island and Clew Bay. I could clearly make out the towns of Newport and Westport, and to the right was the mountain known as Croag Patrick.

This is a holy mountain, the scene of many pilgrimages, with the most fervent visitors insisting on climbing the 2500 feet to the top on their knees. It is reported that Saint Patrick fasted for forty days and forty nights on the summit, and then feeling rather faint, rang a bell and banished all snakes from the island of Ireland, for all time - which I suppose is as good an explanation as any other.

This Christian pilgrimage follows the tradition of taking over an earlier pagan feast and converting it to a Christian one. It marks the annual pilgrimage of the priests and followers of the old religion to the summit to celebrate the Feast of Lughnasa, the start of the old Celtic calendar.

I first learned of the existence of Croagh Patrick in strange circumstances. On what was probably my first visit to Leenane, we had justified the weekend trip by pretending we were going to film a sunrise for a TV Commercial. The questionable logic of us travelling to the West Coast to photograph the sun rising in the East over water had not escaped us, so we planned a fishing trip as well.

We explained to the landlady at the St. Anne's Guest House that she was not to worry, but we would be leaving the house at about 4 am, before dawn. She didn't seem surprised to hear this, and took it in her stride. The night before, we got to bed later than we had hoped, after a night spent carousing in Hamilton's, and tumbled out again still the worse for wear after only a couple of hours' sleep.

We set up the camera near the Aasleagh Falls, and then had a very silly argument about which way was East. No one had remembered to bring a compass, or even a torch. To make matters worse, there was a thick mist rising up from Killary Harbour, and we couldn't see much in front of our noses. As the sky began to brighten in one direction, we spun the camera round to face what we supposed was the rising sun. The sky then brightened in the other direction, and we spun the camera round again. This went on for a while, with the mist getting thicker, and confusion greater. Did I mention the mosquitoes? We were their breakfast. They came up with the day.

After about half an hour of us waiting for something to happen, nursing our hangovers, we saw and heard a car driving by on the other side of the fjord, and then another. And then half a dozen, and a dozen. The stream of traffic became unbroken, continuous. In those days, it was unusual to have more than a handful of cars going through Leenane in the course of a day, but here were hundreds of cars going through at about five o'clock in the morning! Was it some kind of motor rally?

The mystery was solved later on when we were told that they were on their way to Croag Patrick, on the once-a-year day when every pilgrim who is anyone has to make it to the top, barefoot, on their knees, walking backwards, intoning endless Hail Marys or just hiking. Oh yes, I should tell you that the sun didn't come at all in the whole day, so we went back to bed to sleep it off.

My first day on Clare Island was quite different. Such bright sunny days with puffball clouds and Mediterranean blue skies and matching blue sea are rare on the West Coast of Ireland, but they do happen. I have seen quite a few bright days, but never as shatteringly clear as that first day on Clare Island.

Before dinner (cooked by Mrs. Timmermans) I was introduced to my fellow guests. He was very clean-cut, and described himself as a "telecommunications executive" from close to Chicago. She was an ex-teacher. Their seven-year-old son had come to them both comparatively late in life, and he was at the centre of their constant attention. The boy had that ill-fitting air of premature adulthood which small children brought up by older parents sometimes acquire. Questions were directed to him as if he were a small adult, and he in turn was conscious that his mother and father were eagerly hanging on his every reply, like proud parents at a school concert.

They were on a punishing schedule, taking a seven-day European holiday before submitting to a worrying-sounding operation on his neck. He explained that the top of his spine was beginning to curve over, causing him to hold his head at a curious angle, and he had to be careful to avoid sudden movements.

Nevertheless, they planned a long, punishing whistle-stop tour involving, if I remember correctly, Chicago to Copenhagen, ongoing to Dublin, a seven-hour drive by hire car to Clare Island (why Clare Island?), a five-hour drive to Clonmel (to visit a dog breeder they had corresponded with), back to Dublin again, on by air to Madrid, then to Austria and back to Chicago. No wonder they went to bed early.

This far west of the Greenwich meridian, it was still daylight at about 11 pm. I read my book in bed with a corner of blue sky showing through a triangle at the top of the curtains, feeling vaguely guilty to be in bed so early.

~☆~

Chapter 34
Cycling in Clare Island

Sunset over Achill Island.

The next day, while the Americans declared their intention to go for a long walk, I hitched a lift down the hill with the Timmermans' twenty-year old son, Ludwig, known locally as Ossy. He came to live in Ireland as a toddler, and now speaks perfect English with a strong West of Ireland accent. He has a small business down by the pier, printing tee shirts for sale to the tourists, very tastefully done, with photographs of sunsets over the Clare Lighthouse and that sort of thing. The profits he makes from his summer activity help pay for his course at Art School.

He was coming to the end of his foundation year at Larne College in County Antrim, before moving to Belfast Art School for the full three-year course. What did they think of his accent in the North? There had been several incidents of town lads beating up students from the South; when he was in mixed company (that is to say, a pub with Protestants and Catholics), he hid behind a strong put-on Belgian accent, and played the dumb foreigner to keep out of trouble.

What painters did he like? He was very fond of the Post-Impressionists, but didn't like modern painting much. But surely he must like David Hockney, who is a truly great draughtsman if nothing else? He had never heard of him. And what about Irish painters, like Jack B. Yeats, from Sligo? Never heard of him either. I said they were delights still to come for him, and asked him where I could hire a bicycle.

In the pub, they sent me round the corner to the Post Office. In a tiny room, a very old lady sold me some stamps and told me her grandson would hire me a bike. She would phone him herself. He had obviously had a late night, and appeared to come straight from his bed when his grandmother summoned him. He gave me a splendid machine, a modern mountain bike, feather-light, with at least about 150 gears.

I wanted to visit the 16th Century Cistercian Abbey along the coast, where I had been told a team of specialists were restoring the medieval painted murals. My mobile phone was still not connecting properly, so I made use of the call box before I set off on my bicycle adventure.

The road headed westwards, parallel to the coast; the land between the road and the sea was a maze of grassed-over disused lanes and stone walls. The evidence of dense previous habitation was everywhere, with bright green moss-covered ruins and collapsed stone jetties. All the inhabited houses seemed to be on the higher side of the road, but it was the green lower side which fascinated me. It was as if the bog was reclaiming the previously intensively cultivated foreshore. Nature could be seen in the very act of dragging the bumps in the landscape made by man back down into the peat bog again.

150 gears means a lot of gears. When I was a boy, my old bike had gears made by Sturmey Archer. A lever on the handlebars adjusted gears located inside the hub of the rear wheel in a way that was a complete mystery to me. The Clare Island monster offered a selection between three different sized chain wheels on the pedal shaft, and at least five more chain wheels on the rear hub. This was more than I could reasonably come to terms with, so I just selected a normal one, another one which made life a bit easier, and a third which allowed me to freewheel downhill.

The coast road was a switchback of small hills, and I soon learned that the secret for a fat old man riding under these conditions is to know precisely when to get off and push. There was no point in puffing and panting as I wrestled with the exact combination of gears needed for climbing a short slope. It was by far much better to take it easy and hop off and walk whenever the going got the slightest bit rough.

By this means, I made good and enjoyable progress along the coast until I came to O'Malleys Shop. This establishment had been discreetly flagged by roadside signs all the way from the pier, and by the time I reached it, I was really looking forward to discovering its delights. But O'Malleys Shop was shut. A little further on was a small church, and beyond that two houses set back from the road up the side of the hill. There were two tiny children playing outside the house, so I called up to them if the church was just a church, or was it the Abbey? "That's the Abbey sure enough" came back the reply.

At the gate to the churchyard, I pulled up short. I have seen many thousands of Commonwealth War Graves Commission gravestones all over the world. They are un-failingly the same distinctive shape, and the arrangement of the lettering is always in the same style. The CWGC is responsible for the maintenance of all British war graves, wherever they may be in the world. Just outside the gate was a lichen-covered CWGC gravestone, but the grave itself was unkempt, and curiously placed just outside the sanctified ground beyond the gate. A rusting child's cycle was carelessly propped against the wall behind it. The inscription below a carved Royal Navy anchor read:
J. J. TWEED
PETTY OFFICER R.N. C/JX.153024
H.M.S. "MASHONA"
28TH MAY 1941 AGE 44
And below a cross it said:
REST, BELOVED,
GOD HATH CALLED YOU
TO SHARE HIS ETERNAL GLORY
THROUGH CHRIST

I concluded that this was the grave of a wartime Royal Navy casualty, probably washed up on the shore, and that he was buried on the outside of the dry-stone wall of the churchyard because he was not a Catholic. Inside the churchyard was a fine, old central cross, and next to it a recent memorial, an attractive large local stone with a metal plate affixed, on which were the names of eleven aircrew from a Sunderland flying boat of 422 Squadron of the Royal Canadian Air Force, which crashed into the sea on 25 May 1945. A small shiny plastic Canadian flag had been placed at the memorial only recently.

The nearest church building was indeed the Abbey, and behind it was the modern church used by the parishioners. I found my way in through the back door of the Abbey, and there, in a tiny vaulted room, perched high on a scaffolding tower, I made the acquaintance of the four women working on the restoration of the medieval painted wall decorations.

The Project Leader is a renowned German academic, but he was not present at the time of my visit. The rest of the team was made up of four restorers from Ireland, England and France, all female, working at different points of the scaffolding. The senior restorer was English, who explained the process to me; she had obviously taken upon herself the responsibility for dealing with inquisitive visitors.

The technique of restoration is to clean the algae and grime from the surface of the paint where it is still integrated with the plaster. Where the plaster has been lost, or is irretrievable, the cavity is cleaned and dried, before being levelled off with the painted surface, using a plain, grey filler. The effect is to create a blank canvas against which the painted sections can then be studied.

I asked if this was to be described as revelation or restoration? Would they be repainting the damaged parts with modern, matched paints? Were they proposing to follow the Italian example of effectively repainting lost murals for the benefit of tourists? My informant almost fell off her scaffold with indignation, and the younger workers exchanged uncomfortable looks, and buried themselves in their work; there may even have been a stifled giggle.

That was not the way bona fide restorers work, I was firmly told. The skill is in revealing what remains of the original work, not in creating a new one. Where had I ever seen evidence of repainting taking place? I answered that I could remember a Giotto fresco which had been damaged by flooding in Florence? I thought I was on safer ground with the palace at Knossos in Crete.

At the beginning of the 20th Century, a British archaeologist of high repute, Sir Arthur Evans, rebuilt the heaps of stones he found in a field, which he maintained were the remains of the Palace of King Minos, having first bought the field from its peasant owner. Because the result looked like little more than a plain stone wall, he employed a Swiss painter, Gilliéron, to decorate the walls with whatever the artist considered to be appropriate frescos. There was little evidence to show how the walls had been painted originally, so Gilliéron used his imagination. Some say he made it all up, but the results have been admired by generations of tourists ever since.

"That sort of thing" my informant assured me "does not go on here. That man was not a real restorer!" She recommended I should visit a church she had worked on in Abingdon in the Home Counties to see an example of her work.

All the while we were talking, she had been working away on a patch above her head on the vaulted ceiling of the room. "Now, is this bird a heron or what?" she asked the room in general. "Does a cormorant have a crest?" The other girls offered no views, just took long draughts from their mugs of tea, and concentrated harder on their work.

There are only three other examples of this type of medieval church painting in all Ireland, and none of them has survived as complete, nor is there one as intriguing as the one on Clare Island. Even in the course of my brief visit, I had been present at the revelation of what was a previously unknown section of the painting, and this project would clearly play an important role in the future careers of the restorers working on it.

So, all those wicked tales I had heard about heavy restoration, involving the extensive use of new paint, were false. Some of this slur against restorers must come from those thoughtless Victorian sloshers, who plastered paint on tired Old Masters with little consideration for the original. It's wrong to assume bright colours are a give-away that modern paint has been carelessly added. Bright colours, it seems, may be revealed in the original purely by careful cleaning, removing centuries of grease and soot to show the original paint in its true colours. According to the Clare Island ladies, modern restorers never add fresh paint to a painting they are restoring - well, hardly ever! I thanked them all for their time, and left them to it.

Outside again, a young girl of about 10 was leading a donkey bearing wicker side panniers which I recognised to be of the type used for carrying peat. She was going up the mountain to the bog to collect a load of turf. The bog was at about an hour's distance on foot, high up in the hills above us. She would take it easy, because the donkey would be very tired coming down again with a full load. She liked my bicycle. Was it new? How many gears had it got? "Oh, about 150 I think". She nodded thoughtfully as she stroked her donkey like any child with a well-loved pet.

On the way back, O'Malley's Shop was now open, and I went inside. It was little more than an unpretentious storeroom, with cartons and sacks piled everywhere, engagingly higgledy-piggledy. The counter was tiny - about the size of a supermarket checkout desk. I bought a blackcurrant drink and engaged young Mr.O'Malley in conversation.

He told me the Canadian memorial was put up last year, when the elderly sister of the pilot came back to visit the site where her brother had died. The wartime flying boat clipped the top of the mountainous Knockmore (1500 feet) in fog, and crashed into the sea just off the shore, with the loss of all lives. He was sorry about Petty Officer Tweed. In those days they had very strict rules about who could be buried in the Island churchyard, and Tweed was not a Roman Catholic. People felt differently now, and a year or so back there had been some talk about moving the churchyard wall so Petty Officer Tweed could effectively be brought into the Churchyard. He had never heard of the Commonwealth War Graves Commission, and didn't know if they still looked after the grave or not.

As I was leaving, I received a call on my mobile phone, which created a minor sensation in O'Malley's Shop. It must be the only spot on the island where there is a signal. I enjoyed my blackcurrant drink outside, looking at the view, all the while closely observed by a child in a pram. There was a string of brightly dressed walkers now making their way up the road from the pier. They didn't stop at the turn-off for the Shop and the Abbey, but pressed on purposefully, ever westwards. I thought it was time for me to return eastwards: the pub was probably open.

Beyond the pub, further round the beach-fringed bay, was a sports field with tall rugby-like posts and a seating mound. There must have been 100 kids of all ages milling around on the grass, while a cluster of teachers gossiped among themselves and watched the kids. There seemed to be no organisation or order to the activity. How could there be so many children on the Island? I had only seen about 20 inhabited houses at most. One of the teachers explained the children had gathered here from the mainland and all the islands around for a sports day.

There were not enough boys to form a Gaelic Football team on Clare Island, so the girls played too, to make up numbers. The other teams had the same problem, and they gathered together like this so they could play against one other. Would I like to play for the Clare Island team? She clarified that she meant the senior team, of course, not the junior one. I declined on the grounds of poor fitness, and an insufficient knowledge of the rules. She told me gravely that no one worried too much about the rules.

I cycled on past a row of cottages where an old man in a straw hat was sitting out in the sunshine, looking at the sea, in conversation with a young woman. His battered straw hat made him look like the painting of Cézanne's gardener.

Further along was the hotel, an unprepossessing building with tables and benches arranged outside like a Swiss Chalet. The chef was sitting at a bench, looking at the view. He was in his early 20s, and I learnt he was from Lyon, which many say is the heartland of French cuisine. He had come to Ireland to learn English. He was surprised to discover so many people in the West spoke Irish. His English was weak, so he hoped I didn't mind him speaking to me in French. He seemed very lost, and suffering from an acute case of culture shock. He agreed the view was beautiful, but his baleful manner suggested that wasn't enough. He was missing the gourmet ambience of Lyon. What sort of cuisine did he produce here on the island? I wanted to know. He returned to English: "I have the tarte tatin," he said with some pride.

The bar was deserted, but I was drawn to a fascinating collection lining the walls of sepia-toned photographs of Islanders between the wars. The very last framed exhibit I looked at while I supped my pint was an incongruous memento of a visit to the island by the members of the Rolling Stones and their families.

As I was enjoying my sandwich, the doors opened and a string of exhausted, rosy-cheeked hikers staggered in. They were Americans, under the leadership of a local guide, all very sensibly dressed, and there was a great variety of ages represented. They had walked the island from end to end, and were looking forward to their reward of hot soup and smoked salmon sandwiches at the bar. The braver ones gingerly tried a glass of Guinness.

I am impressed by the fact that walkers come in all shapes and sizes. Walking is a very natural exercise, and you don't have to be an athlete to enjoy it. It doesn't have to be taxing, and it gives an opportunity to relate to a landscape at the right scale of speed of travel. Walking tours are an excellent way of meeting people, and the attraction is as much social as it is physical. I didn't fit in with this group, who had obviously been together for some time, and I made a discreet withdrawal to check out the view.

Outside again, I met a red-bearded man; he was wearing a sailing cap. A Sligo man of strong opinions, by profession a psychoanalyst, he had worked in Guy's Hospital in London, but moved to a job in an Essex hospital because of the opportunities for sailing. He was a keen sailor, he explained. "Thames sailing barges" he murmured with a faraway look, remembering the Essex days.

When he was offered a new job back in Sligo, he became a fan of the traditional heavy sailboats known as Achill Luggers, and that's what he sails now. I said I knew the traditional sailboats known as Galway Hookers, which used to work the Connemara coast and islands as general purpose boats. He confirmed they had similar sail rigs to the luggers – open wooden clinker-built hulls with big, dark sails, with rocks for ballast in a round-bottomed hull, instead of keels.

He gloried in the decline of Protestant influence in Sligo since his youth. He referred to the pre-war Irish Government Land Act which had broken up the large estates and sold them off to small farmers. This undermined the Protestant landlords who hitherto had monopolised trade and industry in the northern provinces of the Republic. His own father now lived in the house of his former employer, who had been obliged to sell up and move on. Revenge comes in all shapes and sizes, as does the new prosperity in Ireland.

He cautioned me not to believe everything I heard about the salmon farms being harmful. According to him, the stories about the decline in game-fishing were dreamed up by a couple of Englishmen, Johnny-come-latelies who had come into the area not long ago, bought up fishing hotels for a song, and were now whingeing about the decline in their trade. They were bellyaching about the salmon farms, but that was just a convenient scapegoat for their sorrows.

He was proud to be an Irishman, and proud to be a Sligo man. The future was bright, now they'd put the Protestants in their place, driven many of them back to the Six Counties and beyond. He welcomed recent foreign investment from America, Japan and the Germans, and the Celtic Tiger was on the rise. But what excited him most was this, and he produced a rock chip from a pocket in his sailing smock. He showed it to me as if it were a gold nugget.

"Can you see where it's burnt?" he asked, his eyes growing narrower, and he spoke with awe in his voice as he continued: "Five thousand or so years ago, my ancestors dug a hole in the bog, filled it with water and tipped in all manner of roots and chunks of raw meat and shellfish. They heated some rocks in the fire, and when they were glowing hot, they pushed the rocks into the pit. This boiled up the liquid and cooked the meat – the first Irish Stew. When the tribe of nomads moved on, they left behind them the rocks, which had cooled and shattered into chips: they're called "fulachte fia" in Irish.

"The campsite became buried under the bog, and then thousands of years later when Man stripped away the bog for fuel, they found the rock chips, still burned on the outside from the Stone Age fire. That's what this is. My ancestors held this rock in their hands 5000 years ago, and I picked it up on the bog at the back of Sligo Town. Sometimes they find a complete circle of standing stones buried under the bog." I wondered to myself if he truly was descended from the Stone Age fire-makers. Wasn't it true that most redheaded people like him in Ireland were descended from the offspring of Viking invaders? Donegal means "Fort of the Foreigner" and was a Viking settlement. So was Dublin. I left him smiling absent-mindedly and stroking his chip of rock in his pocket. He was a happy Sligo man.

I wobbled back down the hill on my pushbike, and saw that the old man in the straw hat was now alone, but still staring out to sea. I parked my bike carefully, so as to avoid any obstruction of the highway, although I needn't have bothered, because no vehicle came past all the time I was there, and I climbed up the short slope that led to the row of cottages.

This was a very West-of-Ireland scene, as might be described by John Millington Synge. An elderly returned emigrant sits by the open door of his rough dwelling, staring empty-mindedly into the distance, waiting for a few words with passersby, and waiting for death, which he knows will not be long in coming.

I asked him if he was from the Island, and he said that he was from England. He said this in a broad West-of-Ireland accent. "But where were you born?" I pressed. "I was born across the bay there, in Westport. And then I went to England to work. I lived in Reading – do you know it? – and then in North London, by Kentish Town – have you been there yourself? I had a lot of friends thereabouts. But they sent me to Birmingham, and I lived there for 12 years. I've been back living here for 4 years now. I've no family in these parts, because they're all died, or they're gone to America." And he added as an afterthought, "And I think some went to Australia, or perhaps New Zealand."

These words didn't come out in a rush, as if he'd given the same reply many times before, but were drawn out by him, as if he was recalling the story of his life from a dimly remembered past. "What did you do there, what was the work that took you away from here for so long?" I asked.

"There was a lot of building work in those days after the war. I was a carpenter, and could have as much work as I wanted. I sent money home to help my own mother when my father died. I believe my brothers and sisters that went to America – and some to Australia – they did the same. Just a few pounds or a few dollars went a long way back here. I didn't have much in the way of savings, though, so when I gave up working, I came back. Yes, it is a fine day, and a fine view. I can't complain! There's many have a worse life."

There was a reluctant acceptance of his fate in his manner, not quite apologetic, but quietly sad. How many times have I met similar returned emigrants, belonging neither to one country nor to another? They live out their days in a tragic limbo, waiting for the end. As I gathered up my fallen bike, he gave a last wave and disappeared indoors.

In the distance, the ferry was coming into the harbour as I free-wheeled down the hill, past a party of council workers who were laying cement over a small round space just above the beach; I recognised the painter from the lighthouse among them. The schoolchildren had now moved down in force from the playing field to the beach, and they were calling out to one another and opening their packed lunches.

As I see-sawed towards the pub, I met with the group of ferry passengers coming up from the harbour. There was a family group of tourists, and I spotted Robert Timmermans, returning from the mainland. He offered me a lift up to the lighthouse "in an hour or so", and I joined him in the bar. Michael the Painter was already there on his lunch break.

I said I was made very nervous just watching him paint the outside of the wall at the lighthouse, and he confessed he was a bit worried himself. He had a fright when he stepped on a loose piece of rock and almost fell. He was a man of many jobs; and there was a lot of work of all sorts for him on the Island. Today he was working for the Council. They were building a helicopter pad down by the beach, thanks to the EEC, so the Island wouldn't be cut off in the winter gales.

I told him that the air service to the Aran Islands had made a great difference to the residents. They no longer lived in fear of needing medical attention at a time when the boat couldn't get through to the mainland. Michael said they had the Nurse, but sometimes the island was cut off for days. There was a move for a regular island air service too, like they had in other places. He wasn't specific.

No, they didn't have any police anymore; they only came to the Island when they were needed. The barmaid chipped in that there was the occasional family feud for them to deal with, but Michael didn't know anything about that. "Is it my impression, or are some of the car-drivers around here extremely young?" I asked. "You're right there. Some of the boys are very young, and they shouldn't be driving, but that's not a matter for the Gards."

He asked Robert Timmermans if he knew the story about their friend, John Eddie, and the Tourist? It seems a certain tourist asked John Eddie how it was they could manage without law and order on the island, and John Eddie told him about a particular case. A man and his dog were accused of rustling a sheep, about ten years ago it was. The Island Court was made up of the oldest man living on the Island who acted as the judge, and the jury was formed from whoever among the islanders wanted to volunteer for duty. They found the man and the dog guilty, and they sentenced them both to death. They were to be tied to a heavy stone and thrown off a cliff into the sea to drown together. And that was an end to it. There was no appeal. The sentence was carried out, and the man and the dog paid the price with their lives.

The tourist was appalled by what he heard. By the time he got back to the hotel he was raging with anger, and wanted to denounce the "Judge" and the "Jury" to the authorities. He would take it to the EC he said, he would take it to the Court of Human Rights, he would have the law changed. But as the evening wore on he was eventually talked out of it, and he left the next morning as soon as his hangover allowed. No one knew if the tourist ever found out it was just one of John Eddie's stories.

I asked Michael if he knew anything about the grave outside the Abbey churchyard. "Tweed, do you mean? We'd like to do something about that now, but it's the way people were back then." "I'm sure the Commonwealth War Graves Commission people would help move the grave, if necessary," I said. "And who are they?" he wanted to know. I explained their role, and he became very interested. Would I tell it to the Island Manager, Donal O'Shea? It could be just the answer they're looking for. I promised I would write to the Commission and to Mr. O'Shea. "They're good people" I assured him.

Had I seen the Canadian Memorial? Michael wanted to know. What did I think of the rock that was used? He had chosen that rock himself, and when the sister of the pilot saw it she had a cry, and said it was beautiful. Then she spoilt it by wanting to pay him some money for his work. She didn't understand it was not a thing you do for the money.

It was thirsty work building a helicopter pad, but Michael wouldn't accept a drink from me until we had completed Robert's outstanding round. Michael had come to the Island from Belfast more years ago than he cared to remember. He had no strong political feelings himself, and he couldn't take the violence. Had I read about that Protestant terrorist a short while back? "He was known as "The Butcher". Over the years he killed about 15 people and was finally caught and sentenced to life. He was a nutter. They had them on both sides.

"He only did about 12 years in jail, and then he was out on the streets, again a free man. Within a week of being let out he was quietly "taken out", liquidated, put down. It could have been his own side did it, for all anyone knew. He was a psycho, you see. The last murder he did, he went out drinking and he went looking for a "Teig", a Catholic. They drove along and picked up a young Catholic lad walking down the street. They knew nothing about him. They took him somewhere and beat him up and then hanged him, just for the fun of it. While he was hanging there they stabbed him about 50 times till he was dead. And there were two women involved as well, stabbing that poor lad. It doesn't bear thinking about."

We finished our drinks and Michael went back to work. While Robert was driving me back up the hill to the lighthouse, he told me there were some Swiss guests expected to stay the night. We talked Land Rovers like a couple of nerds, and arrived home in a state of high excitement.

I met the Swiss guests before dinner. Two immaculately dressed middle-aged men in well-cut tweed jackets, and a very smart but younger, and rather attractive woman. They all spoke perfect English, and they laughed a lot. I have met quite a few Swiss, but I don't remember many of them laughing very much. The men introduced themselves as a lawyer and a publisher, from Zürich. When they spoke among themselves they did not speak with a Swiss German accent, which has a distinctive burr. Were they from the city of Zürich itself? They confessed they were Germans, one from Hamburg and one from Cologne. And they laughed some more.

The publisher had a very impressive list of writers, high quality international best sellers, whom he published in translation. Tomorrow they would be staying in the deluxe St. Ernan's Hotel, just this side of Donegal. They drank a lot of wine with dinner, and later they took photographs of one another in different corners of the lighthouse buildings by the golden light of the setting sun. Their laughter could be heard from a long way off.

Lying on my bed, I listened to the radio news, and heard how two RUC policeman had been murdered in Lurgan. It was a particularly horrible

IRA-style execution. In very bright sunshine, the two policemen were shot in the back of the head in a busy High Street, while housewives and young children were going about their shopping. There was no apparent motive, other than a clear political message about the way the Peace Talks in Stormont were dragging on with no sign of progress. The radio report was a sickening account of a depressingly pointless and unfeeling act. As I took off my Walkman headphones, I heard the German-Swiss party asking for another bottle of wine.

CHAPTER 35

CONNEMARA TO CORRIB

Lough Corrib.

I was reunited with Ernest the next morning on Roonagh Pier. He was obviously pleased to see me, and roared into life with the first swing of the kick-start. We rode happily together in the sunshine, back through Louisburg, the Doo Lough Pass, Leenane, then past Kylemore Abbey and on towards Clifden.

Kylemore Abbey is on the itinerary of every Connemara tourist coach, and I didn't stop as I passed the packed car park. The narrow country lane doesn't really go anywhere, and the growth in tourism seems to have taken the road-planners by surprise. There is a constant parade of charabancs hogging most of the available roadway, and the heavy traffic has made its imprint on the road surface. This was one of the worst sections of tarmac I met on my travels, with some sections reduced to short ridge-like bumps. When this road was made, probably by the Relief Works gangs of the turn of the century, the foundations were laid in the bog in anticipation of the occasional pony and cart.

Ernest and his Piaggio suspension did their best, but there were boneshaking moments when my teeth chattered as I dodged the leviathan coaches bearing down upon me around the bends. Why were they always head-on and never behind me? Because I was doing the anti-clockwise circuit, surely. The mountain range known as the Twelve Pins of Connemara could be glimpsed between the trees on my left. These distinctive bumps appear in almost every picture of Connemara, and for me it was a sign that I was entering familiar territory.

The role of Tourist Centre of Connemara was taken on many years ago by the town of Clifden, and I was fearing the worst. In fact, Clifden has kept much of its atmosphere of a bustling country town, and has absorbed the tourist traffic into a one-way system of wide streets. I parked Ernest centrally, and strolled around in the sunshine, doing boring things like collecting cash from the bank machine, buying a newspaper, and window-shopping for a new non-greyish sweater (I didn't buy one).

I eventually selected a well-positioned pub for my lunch. I realised my mistake at once. This pub had been modernised to handle family tourists, with kiddies' rooms and child meals. It was still a pub though, and there was a free table by the window, with the sun streaming in. I deposited the orange bag, and asked for a beer and a sandwich.

The barmaid-waitress was from New York. Not been-to-New-York Irish; she was a native New Yorker, come to Ireland to work and to enjoy the crack. It was surprising to see that the traffic of young people seeking employment now flowed in both directions. She had even picked up the local speech. Instead of saying "Can I get you anything?" over here they say, "Are you all right there?"

Leaving Clifden, I must have missed the turning, because after a while I found myself entering the port of Roundstone from the wrong direction, with the sea on the wrong side of the road. The cosy little pub I remembered overlooking the harbour was now mainly a quick snack restaurant. There used to be a factory here for processing the kelp seaweed gathered by the boatmen of Connemara. Iodine was the main by-product, and kelp was an important cash crop for an area where agriculture and fishing were at survival levels. Tourism is now the principal industry, and walkers, cyclists and noisy families of motorists packed the outdoor tables outside a wide variety of eating and drinking establishments.

There was a signpost showing the way to a musical instrument workshop and museum, where the best selling items are bodhráns, those large hand drums like a Salvation Army tambourine without the jingly bits. The bodhrán is an essential element in Irish folk music, almost as important as the fiddle itself. Jigs and reels are first and foremost dance music, and while the fiddle contributes the lyrical element, it is the bodhrán which marks the rhythm.

I passed by a fly-fishing class receiving instruction on a very pretty stretch of river. There are several game-fishing hotels along this stretch, and they must be suffering badly from the recent decline in migrant sea trout stocks. It was encouraging to see a good number of anglers on the riverbank and standing in the water, practising the gentle art of casting an artificial fly.

We took a good road over the bog, around a deserted peninsular and down to Carna, Kilkieran and Kinvara. A signpost shows the way to the country cottage of the patriot Padraig Pearse, who was executed after the Easter Rising in 1916.

There is a perverse pleasure to be had in avoiding looking at maps, and finding the way by signposts and the seat of one's pants instead, but I had already got it wrong once today – fortunately without consequences. I believed I could remember a minor road across the mountains northwards from the coast of Galway Bay, a cross-country road which came out to the inland lake of Lough Corrib by the village of Oughterrard, which was my next destination. We pootled along uncertainly for a while, and I was relieved when I saw a sign offering "Teas" at a remote private house. A building at the end of a modern bungalow had been converted to serve as a small tea-room, and I studied the selection of homemade cakes on display. The tea-room was the enterprise of the Woman of the House, who served me with a warming mug of strong tea and a fresh scone, while I sat outside and looked at the view. The Man of the House was collecting a box of groceries from his car, parked nearby, so I asked him if there was still a road across the mountains to Oughterrard. He told me it was no more than three or four miles further on.

He had just come back from a holiday in America. He found pubs in Boston where they spoke in Irish, just like here, and Connemara was the very centre of the Irish-speaking districts. Did I know that just down the road was the Irish language radio and television station? He had lived hereabouts all his life, and was born within a mile of where we were talking.

When he heard that I had been touring in the North, he told me that he had been up there on a holiday a couple of years ago, and he didn't like it at all: he was sorry to say that he felt uncomfortable the whole time. "They don't seem to be very well organised for the tourist trade over there, do they? There were hardly any B and B's, and they were weren't properly signposted." I told him that things had changed a lot for the better over there in a very short time.

I asked what the sticker "MV" meant on his car? Was it Malvinas? Malagasy? He shuffled his feet. "It's more of a joke really. It stands for Martha's Vineyard, you know, in Massachusetts. Teddy Kennedy and all that. My niece bought it for me when we were over there as a - what you call it? a conversation piece."

Another customer came in, and was warmly greeted by the man of the house. How was he keeping? What did he think of the weather? Had he got time for a cup of tea? The new arrival had a shyness I have seen before in these parts. He kept his eyes down, and answered the questions only with an embarrassed-sounding breathing-out hissing. If I had to write the sound, it would appear as something like "Pshah!" Then the man of the house spoke to him in Irish, and this time the newcomer answered in Irish that he would take a cup of tea, thank you.

He was about fifty, with a stubbly beard of a few days' growth. He wore a rough tweed jacket, tight-buttoned across his narrow chest. "It must be wonderful to have the Irish," I said to him, and he looked up and said that it was. I was relieved to hear he could speak English too.

He noticed my crash-helmet, and looked around for my motorbike. "Will it rain, d'you think?" I asked, taking the lead from the proprietor's questioning. "Oh, it might" was the only reply I got.

The man of the house re-appeared at this point with a mug of tea for each of us. "Now you leave that young man alone, Sean Willie" he said, indicating me, "You musn't be boring him with your idle chat." He winked at me to show he was only joking, and the newcomer buried himself in his mug of tea, to hide an embarrassed smile. "Have you told him about yourself at all? Sean Willie drives the local school bus" he explained to me, "although he's been a fisherman most of his life. Isn't that right, Sean Willie?"

Sean Willie was gaining confidence: "Fishin's no good no more" he confided between sips. "Where are you from?" I asked, and he looked at me thoughtfully before answering. "Do you know the islands here by? Lettermore, Lettermullen and such?" I told him that I did. "Well I was born on Gorumna, d'you know it?" In my mind I ran through the names of the islands in the group, linked together now by causeways, and only about 4 or 5 miles from where we were sitting. I remember it as a wild and very beautiful place, with water at every turn; with lakes and inlets everywhere, it is as if water has been sprinkled liberally from a great height, and is gathered in droplets and rivulets, waiting for something to happen.

"It's many years since I was there, but I remember it well. The first time, I went out to the very end of the tarred road, where it stopped by an old churchyard. A track led down to the crossing place to the island of Dinish, but there was no sign of a ferry to cross over." "That's it all right," said Sean Willie. "My father built boats there, the old way, with just hand tools. I helped out, and later I did a bit of fishin' as well. But I'll tell you, I was never as happy as I am now, taking the kiddies to school, and fetchin' them back home again.

I did some travelling for the work too, mind – I've been to Boston, and Liverpool, and Birkenhead, and I lived in Camden Town for a long while – do you know it? Never married though. And when I came home again I was nearly an old man. My parents were gone, and there was nothing for me to stay on for. I hardly knew anyone anymore, my brothers had moved away, and my sisters had married. So I sold up and moved to the mainland here. I drew the benefit for a while, and then I got this job. It's a fine job."

He looked up at the sky, and finished his tea. "It'll be time to go now. Can't keep the customers waiting. Be sure to take care on your bike now; there'll be rain later." And all shyness forgotten, he was off, with a broad smile to his friend and a wave of thanks for his tea.

The road across the mountains was grim. It was little used, and had fallen into disrepair with potholes and a poor road-surface forcing me to slow down to negotiate the worst bits. When I eventually passed the highest point though, I was rewarded with a view of almost the whole of Lough Corrib, spread out before me as far as I could see. I rode down and joined the trunk road again just above Oughterrard.

I knew that my destination was to the south of Oughterrard, close to Aughnanure Castle, the ancient seat of the O'Flaherty clan who once ruled this part of the West. The Castle was clearly signposted for the visiting coach tours, so still riding by instinct rather than by the map, I followed my nose in the direction of where I thought my B & B should be, and by chance saw a sign directing me to "Lakeside". This was the house of Mrs. Mary O'Halloran, with lawns running down to the lakeshore of Corrib itself. I was instantly made very welcome, and I set about unloading my luggage.

~☆~

CHAPTER 36
ON THE BANKS OF THE CORRIB

The view from Mrs. O'Halloran's dining room.

I was very conscious of the need to stay reasonably fit while riding on two wheels on such a long trip. If I were incapacitated in any way, it would be both difficult and dangerous to have to ride back without complete control of Ernest. Although a committed enemy of physical exercise, I even briefly thought about doing a gym programme to get my body into shape before setting out, but fortunately, it must have slipped my mind. All the while, I was being very careful to avoid over-exertion, and to lift the top box and backpack as carefully as possible.

When I arrived at Mrs. O'Halloran's I was still wearing wet weather gear because occasional showers had been forecast. I carefully removed my pack and the top box, then leaned against the wall of the house to pull off my over-trousers. While I was easing the ends of the trousers over my trainers, Mr. O'Halloran drew up and parked alongside. As I struggled to remove the over-trousers and wave a greeting at the same time, I heard a click and felt a sharp pain in my back.

My first thought was that I had broken a rib, well if not broken, certainly fractured one rib, perhaps two. Perhaps it was only a hairline fracture, but a fracture nonetheless, or a muscular strain, a severe muscular strain. Of all the possibilities, I concluded it was probably the last, and I hobbled into my appointed room and gloomily considered the situation. I immediately took a hot shower to ease the pain, but there was only a slight relief.

The most important thing was to discover if I could still ride, so I took a short ride to the village. I suffered the occasional twinge, but the riding position was quite comfortable. Encouraged, I set off along the maze of lakeside country lanes to seek out a pub which I vaguely remembered was in these parts, from a previous visit. But nothing looked familiar, and I couldn't find it.

The road makers had been busy in the district, and had scattered vast quantities of loose gravel on the surface of these country lanes. At times I had to slow right down to avoid losing control. This liking for loose gravel must be a local characteristic, because the driveway of "Lakeview" was deep in loose gravel too, and Ernest's stubby wheels slewed in the gravel pudding of the drive.

Lough Corrib is probably the most famous lough in Ireland for fishermen. There is a natural head of very large brown trout, seen at their best during the time of the Mayfly, when fishermen from all over the world are drawn to the lakeside to try their luck. Oughterrard is the angling centre, but boats manned by gnarled old gillies are available all over the lough, which is immense, measuring 30 miles from Galway City in the south to Teernakill Bridge in the north. There is a run of salmon into the lough, and there are regular catches of legendary monster pike, most of which have been stuffed, and have now found a place in a local bar or hotel to entertain the visiting fishermen.

The first time I fished Lough Corrib is a time I would rather forget. I had arranged to fish the Mayfly on Corrib with a friend. At that time, perversely, the Mayfly didn't hatch in Corrib until mid-June, and it was essential to hire a boatman who knew the water, and could provide the live insects, which are traditionally caught by small boys.

When we met up at the appointed hour, we quickly realised that we had been let down. The boat wasn't where it should have been, and the boatman was no longer available. There weren't even any live insects for us, and we tried for a while to catch our own. It was very frustrating, because all around us excited fishermen were setting off to fish, and fish were rising and being caught far and wide across the lake.

There were no other boats or boatmen available; but it was suggested we should adjourn to a local pub used by the boatmen, in case there were any last minute cancellations. We each had a pint, and a glass of whiskey to keep out the cold (this was when I learnt that a "glass" of whiskey is actually a double whiskey). We discussed what to do next. Then we had another pint-and-a-glass, and we checked if anyone had heard of any cancellations. There were none, so we had a farewell pint-and-a-glass, and made our way to another lake further along the road to spin for pike instead.

We arrived, and went directly to the pub overlooking the new lake, to ask for advice. We had a pint-and-a-glass, or maybe it was a glass-and-a-pint, but no one seemed to know anything about the fishing in the lake. So we had a farewell glass-of-pint and made our way down to the shore.

The shore lay behind a network of tiny fields enclosed by dry-stone walls. I am told that I walked in a straight line to the lakeshore, going over walls like hurdles, rather than around them. I assembled my rod, and cast my spinner as far as I could into the lake, and started to wind back with a slow retrieve. I did this about two or three times without any sign of a fish, and feeling rather tired, I sat down. I made myself comfortable, and found I could still cast out from a sitting position, so I carried on casting my spinner, and winding back. When my friend found me half an hour later, I was fast asleep, lying on the shore with my fishing rod still in my hands. He had a bit of trouble getting me back home.

I have had more successful visits to Lough Corrib since that disappointing day, and the water holds a great fascination for me. It is very dangerous, because rocks lie concealed just under the surface. The deep, safe channels are marked by white painted sticks and piles of rocks, and during the season a pleasure steamer threads its way along the channels.

A storm on Corrib is a dreadful thing, whipping up huge waves which a modest outboard motor cannot compete with. It seems that every year there is a tragic accident, and anglers meet their deaths by drowning after being caught on the lough in an unexpected storm. The situation is aggravated by inexperienced anglers going out in rented boats without a proper knowledge of the lough. On one occasion I almost became a statistic myself, when the antiquated outboard motor of a rented boat failed in bad weather, and we were driven across the lough with nothing but oar-power. We were shipwrecked on the far shore. It was a very frightening experience, especially for my companion who I learnt later was a non-swimmer.

It seemed a very different place from the tranquil lough I saw at the bottom of Mrs. O'Halloran's garden, the mirror surface was broken only by the occasional dimple as a distant trout took a fly "on the top".

I was advised to have dinner in the local golf club. The food was fine, but the atmosphere of all-boys-together was not to my liking. The car park was filled with empty spaces marked "President", "Club Secretary" and "Captain", but I parked Ernest between a BMW and a Jaguar. It is curious that abroad these cars have a reputation for quality, whereas in England the BMW is associated with flashy estate agents, and the Jaguar is the chosen vehicle of a second-hand car dealer.

Chapter 37
Galway City

I spent an uncomfortable night because of my painful cracked rib (I had gone back to the theory of a clean break). Once astride Ernest, it wasn't too bad, and in the morning we rode into Galway City to have a look at whatever new traffic controls and one-way mazes they had introduced since I was last there. The spider's web of new bypasses seemed to be working well, and most of the through traffic was kept away from the city centre.

The very best bookshop in the whole of Ireland is Kenny's in Galway, but now, sadly, it has become mail-order only, and has moved out to a warehouse in a trading estate. But at that time it was still in a central street, open to the public, and it wasn't long before I was happily running my eyes over the well-stacked shelves. I was almost sure I would run to ground that out-of-print title about the Peninsular War I had been looking for, but the second-hand department was uncharacteristically light on the subject. Generations of Irish writers looked kindly down from framed prints on the walls, and very young people tottered on spindly ladders as they stocked the higher shelves in room after room. Expansion and modernisation has taken place since I was last here, but I was pleased to recognise from an earlier visit one of the more senior ladies at the counter. We exchanged knowing smiles, and she offered to put me on her mailing list.

I chose a modest bar for an early lunch, across the narrow street. Murphy's was the name over the door, and Murphy's the name of my glass of stout. The collection of customers could have been assembled by a film casting director. A very elderly, eccentrically dressed gentleman teetered on his bar stool, threatening to fall off at any moment; all his movements were in slow-motion. A young impressionable female student listened open-mouthed to a literary-looking forty-year-old, who could have been her university tutor, or a working writer – or both.

There was a small group of professional-looking people, accountants perhaps, or legal clerks from a firm of solicitors around the corner. On the wall was a poster showing all the World Champion

Heavyweight Boxers since the 19th Century. I toyed with my pint, munched my cheese sandwich at a corner table, and watched the scene before me. I could have stayed there quite happily with the sunshine coming in at the window, and the noises from the street reduced to a background murmur, but I had an appointment at 2 o'clock.

I can't remember when I first heard of the Connaught Rangers; I might have read it on a gravestone in a military cemetery. The Connaught Rangers was one of the oldest regiments in the British Army, with a string of battle honours going back to its founding as the 88th Foot in 1793, before the Act of Union, and only a few years after the establishment of the first Bushmills distillery.

The Regimental Headquarters was in the City of Galway, in the ancient Irish province of Connaught, and recruitment was by tradition limited to that most westerly province of the British Isles. The regiment was posted to the Iberian Peninsular shortly after it was formed, and fought with distinction under Wellington in every major battle of the Peninsular War, bringing about the eventual defeat of Napoleon and his Grande Armée.

The Crimea, India and the Boer War were added to the battle colours, and the First World War brought Mons, Ypres, Loos, the Somme, Gallipoli, Palestine and Mesopotamia. When the regiment was disbanded in June 1922, following the birth of the independent Irish Free State, King George V received the regimental colours into his personal care.

The story of the Connaught Rangers Mutiny in July 1920 is too complex to go into in great detail here, but suffice it to say that it is believed to have arisen from a typically Irish stubborn reaction to injustice. A full account is well documented in Anthony Babington's *The Devil To Pay* (published by Leo Cooper 1991). Men serving in the British Army with "C" Company of the 1st Battalion Connaught Rangers in Jullundur, India, are believed to have received news of the atrocities being carried out by the infamous Black and Tans against their loved ones back home in Ireland.

A small group of Rangers presented themselves to the Guard Room and asked to be locked up. They said they felt they could no longer serve His Majesty while he permitted their families to be mistreated and "tyrannised" in this way. The effect of this action – technically an act of mutiny – spread through the whole camp, and was carried to others in nearby Solon.

In the noisy but non-violent demonstration which followed in Solon, an inexperienced young officer opposing the mob, fired off a loose shot from his pistol, which accidentally killed a private soldier, innocently watching the rumpus from the sidelines. The fact of his death meant that murder was added to the charges in the court-martial which followed. On appeal, thirteen of the death sentences handed down were subsequently commuted to life imprisonment, but nevertheless the one remaining prisoner, James Daly, was not pardoned, as an example, and the sentence of execution by firing squad was carried out in the courtyard of Dagshai prison.

Barely a year earlier, there was a Court Martial following the Amritsar Massacre, in which 400 Indian civilians, men, women and children, were murdered by British troops. It found the officer responsible guilty and his punishment was to be "sent home"; against serving rank and file defendants, the British Army behaved somewhat differently. No proper defence facilities were provided for the trial, and the prisoners were inevitably found guilty, and sent back to jails in England by sea, chained in irons like galley slaves.

A year later, after suffering miserably in the British Prison system in the UK, the mutineers were reluctantly repatriated to what was now an independent Ireland by a grudging British Government under the terms of the Treaty. Despite frequent requests, the remains of James Daly were not returned from India for burial in his homeland until almost fifty years later, in October 1970.

The Headquarters of the Connaught Rangers were at Renmore Barracks by Galway City, now renamed Tun Melissa Barracks, after an Irish Volunteer patriot who took over the barracks when the British

Army withdrew in 1922. He was something of a local hero, but was later executed by the new Irish Government during the Troubles.

The modern Barracks is now home to the 1st Infantry Battalion of the Irish Army. I had heard that a small Regimental Museum is still maintained in the barracks, and I obtained permission to make a visit at 2 o'clock. A very proud sergeant received me and personally conducted me around the exhibition.

It is extraordinary how a collection of dusty objects and photographs can convey so much, but I suppose it helps if you are already in possession of an enthusiastic knowledge of the subject. Exhibits fill in the gaps, and faces can be put to the names you have only read about in books.

I found nothing incongruous about an Irish Army soldier speaking with pride about the history and achievements of a regiment in the British Army, because he was talking about the Irishmen who had gone before him. His account illustrated an almost seamless transition from the British Army through the Volunteers (IRA) to the Irish Army.

Throughout history, Irish soldiers have been adventurous mercenaries, often finding themselves on both sides in a foreign conflict. There were Irishmen in the armies of Napoleon as well as with Wellington; more recently during the Spanish Civil War there were Irishmen in the International Brigade of the Spanish Republic, and also in the army of Franco's rebels.

The modern, fully professional Irish Army has achieved a formidable reputation, serving in the United Nations armed forces. In the Regimental Museum stories of their achievements in Third World hotspots can be seen alongside illustrations of the 88th Foot storming the castle walls during the Siege of Badajoz in 1812. It may sound dull to others not familiar with the history of the regiment, but in many ways my visit to the museum was one of the highlights of my trip, because it filled so many gaps in my knowledge of the Rangers.

~☆~

Chapter 38
Return to the Islands

A traditional thatched cottage in the islands.

The rhythmic massage from bumping gently along winding country roads on Ernest's accommodating suspension was doing my ribs a lot of good. As long as I avoided any sudden turns, I was in no pain; occasional discomfort, maybe. I made my way out of town and along the coast road around the Galway Bay made famous in a favourite song of music-hall tenors. The rain started again as I arrived on the north side of the bay.

A few miles from here was the mountain road I had taken to Oughterrard the day before; I had come around in a circle almost to cross my earlier route. One Easter holiday, I stayed hereabouts with my family in the straggly hamlet of Inveran, in a rented holiday cottage overlooking the bay, which belonged to the District Nurse, Mary. It rained for a week, but on the last day the clouds lifted, and for the first time we saw the glistening, rocky Aran Islands not far offshore in the bay.

The landscape here is divided up into hundreds of tiny fields marked by dry-stone walls. These fields were created by the ancient system requiring the equal division of small farms between all the children upon the death of a patriarch. Most of the fields are too small to support agriculture, but are perfect for fattening up a single calf on the rich grass concentrated in such a small sheltered space. Every morning we used to watch an elderly cloth-capped farmer drive a single calf up the lane and into a handkerchief-sized field close to the house. There was no gate, so he first removed some of the stones from the wall, and then replaced them when the calf was safely inside.

It is hard to explain why I keep finding myself constantly attracted back to this part of the world. It is certainly true that I find the soft, natural landscape to my liking, and clichés like "pace of life" come readily to mind as an explanation. The real reason must be: the people. There is something in the nature of the people who live in or come from this remote corner which I have met only occasionally elsewhere. It is an open frankness, often combined with a friendly disposition. John Millington Synge described it well, when he wrote, *"the complete absence of shyness or self-consciousness in most of these people gives them a peculiar charm."*

When I visited the Aran Islands fifteen years earlier, I flew by Aer Arann, which then operated a small fleet of Britten-Norman Islander planes, a diminutive propeller-driven island-hopping plane, dating from the mid-1960s, with a short take-off and a capacity for about 10 passengers. The fleet linked each of the three islands to a small grass airfield South of Galway City, flying in all weathers. I was now puzzled to see new Airport signs here, near Inveran, and discovered that a new mini-airport has been created on the seashore right in front of the house where we stayed.

The Aer Arann service now operated from this new airfield. There is also a boat ferry working from the nearby harbour of Rossaveal in Cashla Bay. The short trip across Galway Bay in the teeth of an Atlantic gale was once described to me by a friend as the worst journey he has ever made – anywhere! – but the modern ships are quite a different story.

On a minor road which forks off towards the islands along here, there is a thatched pub which is almost too picturesque to be true. It used to be run by a very elderly man who always wore a tweed jacket and a cloth cap, but I knew he must now be long dead. The pub was still there though, and seemed in good shape. I was surprised to discover it wasn't open yet. I rode on down the curling road, remembering how it looked at the start of the 80s.

There were new houses now, where once there were classic old cottages and roofless ruins. In these parts an old house is rarely demolished to make room for the faceless modern bungalows which are so popular. Central heating and double-glazing are a strong attraction if you have been brought up in the full force of the Atlantic gales, and aesthetic considerations are a very long way down the list of priorities. The original cottages can often be found hiding behind a brand new roadside bungalow. The idea of a spirit which lives in the hearth is present in most ancient civilisations, and a Connemara farmer is not about to risk offending the house-spirits by knocking down an old house.

As I came to a group of cottages on a corner around a farmyard, I struggled to remember how they had looked before. The red painted doors were familiar, because I had asked the farmer permission for us to film these very buildings; he had asked us to wait while he tidied up for us, and he removed an unsightly rusting tractor from the yard "for the photo". As I paused there now, a light drizzle was falling, a "soft day" as the saying goes. Down the lane I could see a tall figure striding out towards me carrying a scythe over his shoulder. It was the same farmer returning from a day working in the fields. He couldn't have remembered me, but he was happy to pretend that he did.

He told me he was now 79 years old, but was thinking that he would be retiring soon. "I just have the three cows and three calves to keep me occupied, something to look after." We stood chatting in the lane as if I had last seen him only yesterday, with the drizzle gathering in beads on the downy hair on his cheeks, and running off his chin. He grasped my elbow as he spoke with concern showing in his pale blue eyes. He was very worried about the young people. "What good is it when they're being paid £60 a week to do nothing? They just sit on their backsides and drink Guinness, and watch the violence and the shooting on the television. What can the future hold for them?"

I asked about the thatched pub and the old man in the tweed cap - and why was it closed at this time of day? He told me the old man I knew had died about 10 years back. "There's new people have it now, and they keep their own hours. I'm hoping it'll be open by the time I go up there for a pint later, because I've a thirst on me after a day working in the fields." He thought Mary the Nurse had moved on to another district. He was wearing only a check shirt and a cloth cap, and I was worried about how wet he was getting, but he didn't seem to mind. There's no sense in worrying about things you can't do anything about. It's only townies like me who dress up in waterproof clothing, and dodge from doorway to doorway beneath an umbrella to keep out of the rain.

I thanked him for his time, and hoped I would see him again in another 15 years. He laughed and said he didn't expect so. I was very warmed by meeting this man. He was typical of the open, friendly, placid and level headed characters I have met in these parts, where they have learned to come to terms with a hard life at an early age. I share his worry for a generation brought up on idleness, alcohol and "NYPD Blue". They will not be as well prepared for the rigours of life as he and his generation were.

Encouraged by meeting this farmer I had known before, I decided to make a quick visit to the first of the islands. The causeway was much longer than I remembered it, but the familiar landscape unfolded before my eyes like a map I had studied many times. Across the water, I could already see the group of trees which sheltered the cottages where we had stayed. I remembered a photograph I had taken by this telegraph pole on the other side. A flock of starlings had settled on the wires one evening, silhouetted against the setting sun. Click!

The pub next door to the cottages seemed unchanged, and I parked Ernest and went inside. I vaguely recognized Lucy, the landlady, who greeted me as she poured me a Guinness. She said she remembered me, but she was unconvincing, and on the defensive, as if she thought I was trying to wheedle my way into her confidence. I vaguely remembered this characteristic in her from my previous visits, a remoteness which might at first be mistaken for unfriendliness, but is closer to shyness.

The pub occupies the gateway to the islands, and anyone entering or leaving the islands passes by her door. Perhaps she sees herself as some sort of guardian of the other islanders. There was a younger man working in the bar, and he stirred the fire and tossed some more turf strategically into the flames.

But where was the man of the house? I remembered him as a quiet-mannered man, but always friendly and with never a bad word to say of anyone. I took a breath, and asked the landlady about her husband. I was saddened to learn he was dead, carried off some years ago by cancer at an early age. There was bitterness in her voice as she said he was never the same since the fire. "What fire?" I asked.

The couple were very proud of their holiday cottages, laboriously restored keeping the original thatch and walls and all. They were very pretty, and something indeed to be proud of in days when such cottages were frequently allowed to fall into disrepair. And although they didn't have a penny's support from the Tourist Board, they won an award for their work. And one day, one of them was maliciously set on fire. There were no arrests, but she knew who it was all right, though the police couldn't touch him. "He was an Englishman," she added, eyeing me accusingly.

"And the insurance took their own time in paying up. We lost three years' rental on the house, while the insurers argued the toss, and dragged out the day before they paid up a cheque. And there was no compensation for the loss of rent either, just the bare bones of the work for repairs to make good the harm done by the fire. It was all a strain on my poor husband, God rest his soul. He was a good man, but a worrier. He was found to have the cancer, and carried off soon after. I was up at his grave just this morning."

I listened in silence, making the occasional sympathetic noise, and slowly sipping my Guinness. I think she was more interested in talking than in hearing. "We have a new priest up at the church now, a good man, likes to preach outdoors in the open air, as was our custom out here in the islands in the old days. Sometimes he says mass out there in the churchyard, out amongst the graves where my husband is. I find that a great comfort."

She paused and I saw a chance to say something: "I remember him as a very kind man, and I'm sorry to hear of your loss." When she heard these words, her expression changed. She visibly relaxed. "Yes he was that indeed. You stayed in the cottages, did you say? And when was that? It'll have been a long time ago now." And without waiting for my answer, she disappeared through the doorway behind the bar. I sat by the fire for a while, looking into the curling flames and trying to remember the face of the man who was only ever referred to as the landlady's husband. But nothing came, so I finished my drink, and called out goodbye to the Lady of the House as I left. She answered, but she didn't come back into the bar, and I couldn't really hear what she said from behind the door.

Chapter 39
Spiddal and Oughterrard

Starlings.

It was growing late, and once again I planned to cross to Oughterrard by a lonely mountain road which came in to the coast road at the town of Spiddal. The road into Spiddal was a new bad experience, rippling in ruts just the size of Ernest's wheels, so I was jerked around like a bouncing cork. They were so regular; it was almost as if it had been purpose-made, like a fairground ride. John Millington Synge also commented on the bad condition of the road beyond Spiddal, and that was almost a century earlier.

Just outside Spiddal lies a remote pub called the "Poteen Still". It is one of the few places in Connemara where I remember seeing graffiti "Up the IRA" on the outside wall; (the thought occurred to me that it might have been painted there by a film production company, as dressing for a period film.) The pub was well known as a music venue, and I went to a wild wedding reception there many years ago. I couldn't just pass by now, so I parked Ernest outside and went in. I looked around at the other customers, and I dripped noiselessly onto the bare stone-flagged floor.

All eyes turned to me, and the atmosphere was definitely hostile. I went up to the bar, and a reluctant barman detached himself from his conversation and came up to ask me what I would have. As he served me, the atmosphere relaxed and softened slightly, and the other customers returned to their drinks, so I decided to open a conversation.

They were all locals, all male, all in their 20s. By the time of day, they could be enjoying an after-work drink, or they could have been there all day. "There've been some changes since I was last in this pub" I ventured to the barman and his companion. "There used to be a big music room out the back there, as I remember. I was last here at a big wedding reception; that would be about 1982". The barman's companion looked up. "We're re-building" explained the barman. "It was a Hell of a wedding" I went on, "A friend who used to live up the road a bit was getting married to the daughter of the French family that had just taken over the fish factory down at Rossaveel."

The barman's companion put down his glass. "I was at that wedding," he said, suspiciously. "You may remember me then. I was wearing a white suit," I said. "Well now, I think I do. And I've got some photographs of that wedding somewhere." "I was there too," said the barman, "But to tell youse the truth, I don't remember much about it. It went on for a couple of days, you know." "Are you staying hereabouts?" asked his companion "I could bring in the photos tomorrow." "I'm afraid not. Just passing though" I admitted. The atmosphere had changed completely. I was now accepted, and the others picked up the conversations they were having before I intruded, to drip on their floor, and to recall wilder days.

As I turned into the mountain road at Spiddal, the evening sun came out and shone warm on the side of my face, and there was a slight wind at my back. I sped happily over the little-used road which was surprisingly good in some stretches, showing signs of recent repair. My back was feeling better with every mile I covered. The theory of cracked ribs was vanishing in favour of the more likely diagnosis of a slight muscular strain.

~☆~

Back at base, I talked a little with the man of the house about the season's fishing. It had been an excellent start to the year; the Mayfly had arrived earlier than usual - in May, rather than June - and the weather had been generally kind. Of the many good catches he had brought to his boat, one day was the best he had ever had in all the years he has spent fishing there.

The land where the house stands had been in his father's family for generations; the opportunity came up to buy it from an elderly uncle. He and his wife couldn't really afford it at the time, because they had only just built their own house further down the road, and were still paying it off, but they got their heads together and agreed they should not let the opportunity pass them by. It was a struggle financially, and for a while they were running two houses and two mortgages, but they were able to built the new house exactly as they wanted it. The rooms for the B & B guests were all on the ground floor, all with en suite bathrooms included. The first floor was just for the family. "The position couldn't be better," I said, indicating the lawns down to the landing stage on the lough, where his fishing dinghy was bobbing gently at its mooring. The field next to the house and alongside the road held a strange collection of sheep, goats, rabbits, geese and chickens, for the entertainment of the houseguests.

Mr O'Halloran told me he didn't hire angling boats to guests, it was too dangerous, too great a responsibility. Anyone who asked, he would refer to a professional boatman across the bay. Many visitors had no respect for the water, and no idea of how dangerous it could become, suddenly and without any warning.

He minded a young man one night only two years ago who had been driven ashore onto his water frontage by a sudden storm which sprang up out of a blue sky. He was in a bad way, shivering and soaking wet, wearing only a tee shirt and jeans. He was shaking with fright. He had taken refuge on one of the islands, waiting for the storm to pass by. When he realised it wasn't going to clear up, and that night was approaching, he set off again for the shore, but the winds and the waves were too powerful for the boat's small outboard, and he was driven for miles down the lough. He eventually made landfall on the promontory of Mr. O'Halloran's waterfront, completely exhausted. Mr. O'Halloran remembered the fear in the shipwrecked angler's eyes, as if he had stared death in the face. He was that close to becoming just another annual statistic of the tragedies on the lough.

Mr. O'Halloran was very shaken up himself; he phoned the young man's B&B, and spoke to his father. The poor man was distraught, convinced that his son was already drowned. He drove round immediately and the two fell into each other's arms in tears. Mr. O'Halloran was very affected too, and swore he would never be responsible for such suffering.

On my way into Oughterrard for dinner, I stopped to fill up with petrol and two-stroke oil. I was served by a very young lad, a schoolboy, who didn't seem at all sure about what he was doing, and so I decided to pour the two-stroke oil myself, rather than risk him spilling it all over the tank. The oil was in an old-fashioned, steel oil-jug measure, with a properly shaped spout, so the task was carried out without spilling a drop. I had to let him put the petrol, but he managed to do it without incident.

In the restaurant, a middle-aged English couple at the next table were trying to explain to the waitress that they wanted to reserve exactly the same table for the next six nights. They had spent their holidays here last year, and they used to eat here every night. They wanted to make a reservation for every night now because they knew that the restaurant sometimes got busy. The waitress was very young, a local girl, probably at a sixth form college in Galway City. She understandably found it difficult to get her head around a request from people who wanted to do exactly the same thing every day of their holiday. Nevertheless, she said she would try to keep a table for them for the whole week, but her furrowed brow showed she clearly didn't really understand the importance of why it should be the same table every night.

When I returned to Ernest, a sportily dressed American was standing over him, studying Sr. D'Ascanio's elegant lines closely, and pointing them out to his Irish wife. Had I come far? He was impressed by my answer. He hoped the weather would stay fine for me tomorrow. He had a BMW motorcycle back home in the States, and he knew what it can mean to have to ride in wet weather. He hoped I had some good waterproofs, and waved me on my way with a kindly smile. I fancy there was a little envy in his regard.

~☆~

Chapter 40
Galway to Dublin

The next morning, I made my goodbyes to Mrs O'Halloran, while Ernest waited patiently on the gravel drive in front of the house. As I loaded him up with my bits of luggage, I was puzzled by the sight of small muddy footprints all over the saddle and handlebars. There was no doubt about it, and I asked Mrs. O'Halloran what could be the cause. Maybe birds? It may sound silly, but from their position, it looked as if something very small had stood on the seat and reached forward to the handlebars, "Vroom vroom!" as a child might say. "Could it be the Little People?" I asked jokingly, but Mrs. O'Halloran looked uncomfortable and didn't answer.

At that moment it began to rain suddenly, in what we could see was going to be just a short summer shower, so we took refuge in the extensive kitchen. "Funny, that" I added, meaning the footprints and the sudden shower, but Mrs. O'Halloran said nothing, and bustled about providing me with another cup of tea. In the West of Ireland, it is considered poor etiquette to speculate about the Little People.

She changed the subject: "How did you find out about our place here, do you have a B & B guide?" I told her I found her in the Tourist Board Guide, and said what a useful publication it was, how it provides an excellent service to travellers such as myself, and is very good value. Presumably there was some government scheme to encourage people such as herself to offer accommodation to travellers; were there improvement grants? Did they give tax concessions or something? "Not at all!" she replied, "the very opposite is true. I have to declare the earnings in our tax return, and we pay tax on it. And we have to pay £400 a year to appear in the Tourist Board Guide as well. And that's a lot of guests we must have, just to cover the cost."

I was astonished. Ireland is a country which long ago realised the value of foreign tourism to the economy, and provides grants for all sorts of large-scale tourist facilities such as hotels and Heritage Centres. Why should they be so hard on ordinary people who open their doors to travellers, providing a much-appreciated service which often gives better value, and welcoming comfort often better than the average hotel? By charging such high fees to appear in the Guide, the Tourist Board must be guilty of discouraging many landladies, to the detriment of the traveller and the taxpayer alike. I would look at my copy of the B & B Guide with different eyes after hearing that.

I have no reason to believe or disbelieve in the Little People, and I certainly had no idea what other rational explanation was available to interpret the footprints. It might be that local sprites were trying to make contact for some reason. I felt guilty as I wiped off the footmarks on the saddle, although I left them on the handlebars. Ernest started without hesitation, and seemed anxious to be on his way. As I tried to move off, I realised something was wrong. The rear wheel slurred in the deep gravel. I couldn't see the wheel properly, so I got down on my hands and knees to have a good look. I had a flat tyre, the first problem of any kind Ernest had given me in all Ireland.

Thanks to Sr. D'Ascanio, changing a wheel on a Vespa is a piece of cake. I noticed the surface of the flat tyre I removed had been severely worn down by the over-inflated pressures I had been using, and the tread was worn almost smooth, and probably a bit unsafe in wet weather. Perhaps the Little People were looking after me by warning of a possible danger? In no time at all the spare wheel was in place and we were on our way again.

I was reminded of these thoughts when I took the tyre to be repaired at a garage at my next stop, and the mechanic removed a bright silver pin from the tyre. Was this a fairy rapier?

I would now be turning inland to cross from Galway City to Dublin, so I would be leaving the coastline I had been following since my arrival in Belfast. I had already accounted for a dozen or so ships from the Spanish Armada fleet, and I knew a similar number had just disappeared at sea, never to be seen again, lost with all hands. In their desperate attempts to find a route home, some ships had come to grief further south from Galway Bay, as they followed the coast down past County Clare and County Kerry. *San Juan de Oporto* came closest to a happy ending, by making repairs in the Shannon estuary, before taking on board the survivors from the *San Marcos*, scuttled in the Shannon, and from the *San Juan Bautista Ferrandome*, scuttled off the Blasket Islands. They made it safely home to Corunna in north Spain.

The crew of the *Trinidad* were less fortunate. After being shipwrecked in Tralee Bay, 100 survivors delivered themselves up to William Bourke of Ardnerrie, who promptly rewarded their trust by handing them over to his axe-man bodyguard, McLaughlan McCabe; he was reputedly personally responsible for killing and chopping up 80 of them.

However ruthless and brutal was the institutional killing of survivors of the Armada whenever they fell into the hands of the English, or the Irish who served them, the killers did not account for all of them. The rich ones were ransomed, a profitable business with roots in medieval times. Others, like Captain Francisco Cuellar, were helped by dissident Irish, and escaped through friendly Scotland and France back to Spain. Others just melted into the Irish landscape.

There is a strong mythology of Spanish survivors settling down in West Coast communities, and some typical regional names are said to be of Spanish origin. Did Fernández become Flaherty? Some of the faces in the West look very Spanish; among the Viking redheads and the Nordic blondes, there are some very dark-skinned raven-haired Irish to be found supping their Guinness alongside the rest. I like to think that at least some of the Armada survivors may have been responsible for the founding of a minor Latin dynasty in the cosmopolitan West.

I rode off down the road to Galway City, and waved as I passed Ross Lake, where stood Ross House, the home of Somerville and Ross, who wrote "An Irish R.M." at the turn of the century; this eccentric pair of aristocratic women created one of the funniest books in the English language. The road beyond Galway was the main Dublin road, a major trunk road of the type I had been avoiding so successfully.

As the rain came down, the trucks thundered by, and I went slower and slower. The weather worsened even more, and conscious of the need for caution, I tucked myself into the narrow hard shoulder of the carriageway. Unfortunately, I had to concentrate hard on the road ahead, because potholes would suddenly appear, and every few miles, the hard shoulder would end suddenly, obliging me to swerve into the main carriageway, and into the paths of fast-moving lorries.

The weather continued to grow worse, and I tucked in my chin, and drove on through the spray of passing traffic. I have a favourite New York recording from the 1920s of a popular song called "From Galway to Dublin" by Dan Sullivan's Shamrock Band. The singer ticks off the towns on the sightseeing train tour from Galway to Dublin, and I know all the names by heart. They were now unfolding on the road signs in front of me. I had just passed Ballinasloe, where according to the song "they hold the finest fairs in all of Ireland."

In recent years, many of these old recordings of traditional Irish music have been dusted off and re-packaged in digital CDs. Rare 78s in the private collections of a fortunate few are now available to the public of this generation, sounding better than they ever did before. For many years, there was very little available in the way of recording facilities in Ireland, and the best recordings were made by Irish musicians abroad, in London or America.

I remembered that it was around here that I met an old man in a hardware shop on one of my first visits to the West. He must have been in his 80s, and was very frail. In the shop, his produce was just piled up on the floor, tapering from floor level up the walls, with no shelves or a counter. A winding path threaded its way around the various items of hardware that you would expect to find in a country district. I couldn't recognise some of the more strange-looking artefacts, and when I asked him what they were for, he was happy to give me an explanation.

As we spoke, he looked at me strangely, and eventually he said "Are you English?" Fearing the worst, I apologetically admitted that I was. "The English killed my brother, you know" he announced. I was even more apologetic, and began checking out my exit to the door in case I needed to leave in a hurry. "We were both in the War, d'you see, 1914-

1918 in the British Army. And my brother was gassed, gassed by his own side mind, the English. They killed him." I said I was very sorry he had lost his brother in such tragic circumstances, in an accident of war, and that I too had lost members of my family in the same conflict, but the old man wasn't really listening. "He didn't die straight away, but it got to his chest, and he was never the same again. It killed him in the end. He died seven years ago, and he was younger than me." A rough calculation suggested his brother had died in his 70s, perhaps 50 years after his time in the trenches.

Just beyond Ballinasloe I found a huge modern pub advertising lunches. The packed car park suggested it was the most popular place for miles around, so I parked and peeled off layers of waterproof clothing before going into the dining room. Inside, the place was heaving, and a pinafored waitress was bustling from table to table. She spotted me looking for a seat, and gently but firmly shepherded me towards a place on a high stool by the bar. My waterproofs had kept me very dry, but the rain was cold, and I was dressed for a summer's day underneath it all. So I had a steaming bowl of hot vegetable soup, a double-thick cheese sandwich, and a huge mug of tea, all for a handful of coins. It seemed so little, I told the waitress she must have made a mistake, but she insisted the price was right. She got a good tip.

I went back onto the road much refreshed and warm again, and soon passed by Athlone, "the home of John McCormick, the sweetest singer that ever came out of Ireland" according to the record. Just outside my destination, Tyrrellspass, I overtook a line of traffic waiting at a temporary red light at road-works. I drew alongside a small saloon with a young couple inside. Noticing that the driver's door was not properly closed, I risked startling them by knocking on the driver's window.

The driver wound down his window and asked "Wass?" Recognising foreign tourists, I called upon the richness of my Sixth Form German to explain to them that the driver's door was open. "Offen! Nicht geschlossen!" I cried through the aperture in my helmet, pointing at the offending door. "Wass?" he begged. The girl leant over to the driver's window. I pointed again at the door with a gloved finger. "Tür nicht geschlossen!" I pleaded with a growing sense of urgency.

The urgency was communicated to the two Nordic faces before me, but their anxious expressions made it clear they could still not understand me. The girl struggled to carefully enunciate in a remarkably clear English for my benefit, "I'm sorry we don't understand Irish. We are Italian!" "La porta!" I exclaimed, and made a gesture of pulling the door to.

This violent action initially terrified them. A crazy scooterist in a red waterproof yachting suit, a full-face crash helmet, and an orange backpack, was clearly upset by some unforgivable traffic violation they had committed further down the road. He had begun shouting at them in a foreign language, and now he was physically attacking their car. Suddenly inspired, the driver got the message, and he smiled and triumphantly closed his door with an exaggerated flourish. "Thank you very much!" The girl smiled. The driver smiled. We all smiled. I patted Ernest and shrugged conspiratorially: "Is from Italy too!" I offered brightly. Fortunately at that moment the lights changed and we drove off, saving me from further embarrassment.

Chapter 41
Jim Daly's town

Tyrellspass

I wanted to stop over in Tyrrellspass on my way to Dublin, because it was the home town of James Daly of the Connaught Rangers. I wanted to visit the grave of the only prisoner executed by the British Army in India over the Connaught Rangers Mutiny. An example was made of him, and he became something of a martyr, a symbol of Republican resistance for the new Irish nation.

Tyrrellspass is roughly halfway between Galway and Dublin, between the East Coast and the West. The houses of the village straddle the main road, which skirts one side of a neat village green. When I rode into town, it looked familiar; then I remembered I had stopped here for 'refreshments' on several occasions in the past - it is the natural place to break the journey from East to West. I noticed posters advertising the 400th Anniversary celebrations for the Battle of Tyrrellspass, and I was almost immediately given a publicity leaflet. It was signed by the Chairperson of the Organising Committee, one Peter Daly. A relative of the great James perhaps?

The hotel proprietor was very interested in Ernest, and insisted on coming out into the rain to have a good look at him. He had been a Vespa scooterist as a young man in the 60s, and the look in his eye suggested a longing for something more than lost youth. He was a big man, and he made Ernest look very small, as he grasped the handlebars, half-closed his eyes, and dreamt a little. He asked me questions about Ernest's performance, rapt in thought as the light rain steadily darkened his shirtsleeves. Perhaps he was envious, and thinking: "If he can do it, why shouldn't I?"

The hotel sits on a pretty village green. The cluster of houses around the green wouldn't look out of place in an English village; small Georgian houses with crisply trimmed hedges, and neatly painted woodwork. The village church was next to a handsome building which, according to the engraved frieze, was donated by the Lady of the Manor for the benefit of "deserving orphans". It didn't actually say "provided they are not Catholics", but this was implied in its stony assertiveness. The Church is Protestant, and the graveyard is Protestant, and so James Daly had to be buried in the other cemetery on the outskirts of town.

On the green itself, a discreet but doubtless provocative memorial was erected in 1970 by the local branch of the IRA, shortly before the return of the remains of James Daly from India. It shows a larger-than-life group of three school children, and an engraved paving stone flush with the grass shows it is dedicated to those who died in the Famine in the surrounding area.

James Daly's grave in the Catholic cemetery was not so easy to find: I found three other James Dalys, but not the one I sought. Two lads were talking quietly together by a recent grave, and I hesitated to intrude upon them. Yes, they had heard of Jim Daly, and yes, his grave was somewhere close by, but they couldn't just remember exactly where it was. They insisted on helping me, but eventually, I stumbled upon it myself. The headstone was erected by Sinn Féin and the inscription is written in Irish. James Daly's name appears as Sheamuis Ui Dalaigh.

As I stood there at the graveside, two elderly ladies were driven up to the cemetery gates in a saloon car, and they came inside to pay their respects at another grave. The driver may have been a relative, or he may have been a taxi driver, but he stood apart from them as they approached their chosen grave.

On impulse, I took the opportunity to ask him if he spoke Irish, could he translate the Irish engraving on James Daly's grave for me? Yes, he knew of Jim Daly. When he was at school, the teacher brought the whole class out to visit the grave. He struggled a little with the translation, explaining that when he learnt Irish, there wasn't any letter 'h' in it. He apologised that he wasn't familiar with what he described as "this modern anglicised version" of Irish. He did very well: the engraving tells the story of Jim's death, in suitably anti-English phrasing, for which the translator apologised again.

As if to make up for it, he told me that Jim's sister used to live in the same lane as the cemetery. She died only about eight or ten years ago. Her children have all grown up and moved away long ago. Some were now living in Manchester, and there were others in Canada, and he thought perhaps in Australia.

I felt it was fitting that immediately after leaving the cemetery, I should make a bee-line for the nearest pub to pour a libation – or better still, to drink one – in James Daly's memory. I asked the guidance of the barman: what would a twenty-year-old Irishman from these parts choose to drink on a special occasion? He recommended the local-brewed Irish whiskey, and on this occasion I remembered not to ask for a glass, but for just a single measure. This was especially appropriate, because according to some accounts, James Daly was a teetotaller.

Another customer said that he too had heard that of James. His own father told him he almost joined up with James Daly. On the day Jim went to Galway to sign up, his father was supposed to go with him, but he changed his mind at the last minute, because he was offered a job on a local farm. If he had gone, it's unlikely his son would have been here now to tell the story, he said. With all this talk of temperance, as he ordered another pint he felt obliged to explain himself.

He didn't normally drink much, but he had been out in the fields all day, putting up electric fencing, and that had given him a powerful thirst. He was running electric fencing all the way round a big estate for a private contractor. He had turned his hand to all sorts of jobs in his time. Farm work of every description, of course, when there was any about. He liked to work in the open air if he could. The other long-term interest he had was breeding dogs for hunting.

You could never tell if a dog was going to turn out to be a good gun dog. It helped if the bitch and the sire were proven in the field, but you could never be sure until the day came when you fired a gun over the dog's head. Even he had a few failures, but not many. The rejects were fine looking gun dogs that were worthless except as house pets, he said disdainfully. It was best to destroy them, rather than let them breed and weaken the strain, but it was hard to turn down the money if someone wanted to buy one of the dogs. Some people would pay a good price for a good pet. His expression made it clear he couldn't really understand why they should pay good money for a bad dog.

No one referred to James Daly as "James", it was always a more friendly "Jim", as if he would be back in a minute – he's just popped down the road for a paper and a packet of cigarettes. Certainly no one I spoke to called him Seamus or Sheamuis. A big quiet man in the next pub told me Jim used to live in a house two doors away from where we were sitting. His sister had lived on the cemetery road, and she used to keep his memory alive with fresh flowers on the grave. The people of the village were very proud of Jim, one of the Republic's first heroes.

He said that he had been away in England at the time when they held the momentous funeral when Jim was brought home. The barman interrupted to say that he had seen it all right: a long procession all around the village. They even stopped the through traffic on the main road to Dublin while the funeral cortege went by. There was a band, and a lot of new faces he'd never seen before – they were from Dublin, he imagined. The big man asked me where I came from, as if he already knew the answer. When I told him I was from North London, his face spread into a wide grin. "Thirty years I was in East London, are you familiar with Manor Park?" It was a forgivable exaggeration on my part to reply that I knew it "quite well".

He told me he was one of "Murphy's Boys", and by that he meant that he had worked for Murphy's, the biggest building contractor on almost every important construction site in post-war London. There is a saying that Hitler may have made most of the car parks in London, but it was Murphy's who rebuilt the city after the Blitz.

My new friend was stockily built. He told me he used to play football, but Gaelic Football, you understand, at Eltham in Southeast London. He played in different teams in the local leagues there for 25 years, and came back to his hometown when he retired. He was always with Murphy's; they were one of the best, and generally had a good reputation as an employer. Perhaps they did look after their workers even in those far off days, and my friend retired with a comfortable pension. He didn't have a bad word to say against them after 30 years, but that may be because he never had a bad word to say about anyone.

The door opened and a teenage girl came into the bar. "My mam says, when will you be coming for your tea?" she asked, and the gentle grandfather giant smiled and reached out a hand towards her. "Tell your mam, I'll be along directly." It was clearly time for me to start thinking about my own dinner too.

~☆~

In the hotel bar before dinner, I was able to guide a French tourist couple around the intricacies of Irish whiskeys. I recommended they try the obscure but local Irish whiskey called Tyrconnell Whiskey.

When I finally went into the dining room, I was seated at a cosy table surrounded by walls full of amateur oil paintings, which I was not at all surprised to discover were for sale. But although the display sounds dire, somehow it worked! A dark room was livened up with these splashes of bright colour, and the food was surprisingly good too, so I ordered a half bottle of white wine to accompany my grilled salmon.

My friend the ex-mod manager came to my table himself, full of apologies. He showed me an open bottle of wine, the level lowered by perhaps the measure of one glass. He was desolate. He didn't have any half-bottles left, so what he normally did was to leave a whole bottle on the table, so the customer could pour as much as he or she wanted. He had only this last remaining bottle, which he had opened at lunchtime, but the customer had only drunk one glass, and my friend was sorry to have to tell me that unfortunately my half-bottle was on the bottom; he hoped I didn't mind. "Laurel and Hardy!" I cried, identifying the film reference.

The Laurel and Hardy sketch about Stan drinking Ollie's share of the bottle of lemonade to get to his half, which was "on the bottom" is well known to me. The high point of my school career happened when I was an obnoxious, spotty fourteen-year-old. I was behaving particularly badly one lunchtime in the school dining hall, and the schoolmaster supervising the meal made me stand in the corner while everyone else was allowed to finish their meal in peace. I wasn't fussed, because I had eaten as much of my mashed potatoes, greens and gravy as I wanted (the reason for my loss of concentration).

When it came to the time for the serving of pudding, I livened up, but the schoolmaster refused to let me collect my suet pudding and custard with the rest of the boys. "But Sir!" I protested "You can't do that. I've paid for my school dinner!"

The schoolmaster fancied himself as a bit of a wag, and he positioned himself where the audience of schoolboys could see him clearly as he delivered his riposte: "School dinners are subsidised, and half is paid by the taxpayer" he smirked. "I am a taxpayer, and I am telling you that you cannot have the pudding, because I have paid for it." He half-turned to the audience to deliver the last part of the sentence. "No Sir!" I challenged: "I have already eaten the half you paid for, and now I would like the half I have paid for, which is the pudding."

While I was still wondering if I had said it right, the schoolmaster exploded with anger. He made me stand outside the staff room for the rest of the lunch break (a severe punishment), and accused me of being a "barrack-room lawyer". It was the first time I had heard the phrase, and I quite liked it.

All through the meal which followed, I kept glancing at the painting by my table. It was a copy of an early Van Gogh called something like "My Room at Arles". Vincent was struggling with his craft at the time, and the original picture is delightfully naive. The perspective of every piece of furniture has a different vanishing point, and the whole has an over-the-top wonky wide angle lens look, executed in thickly applied bright colours. I think the copyist had even added a few false perspectives of their own.

When my dear old Mum took up painting in her sixties, she couldn't handle painting from live subjects, so she just made copies from prints she liked. Van Gogh is one of her favourites, so one of the first copies she made was of Van Gogh's "Sunflowers"; it hangs on my wall at home.

I could understand perfectly why the Tyrrellspass artist had chosen to make a copy of "My Room at Arles", and when I asked for my bill at the end of the meal, I asked the waitress if I could buy the painting? Could she add it to the bill? I would worry later about how I was to transport it all the way back to London through wind and rain, strapped to an over-laden Ernest. But at that price it was such a bargain.

Chapter 42
Running repairs

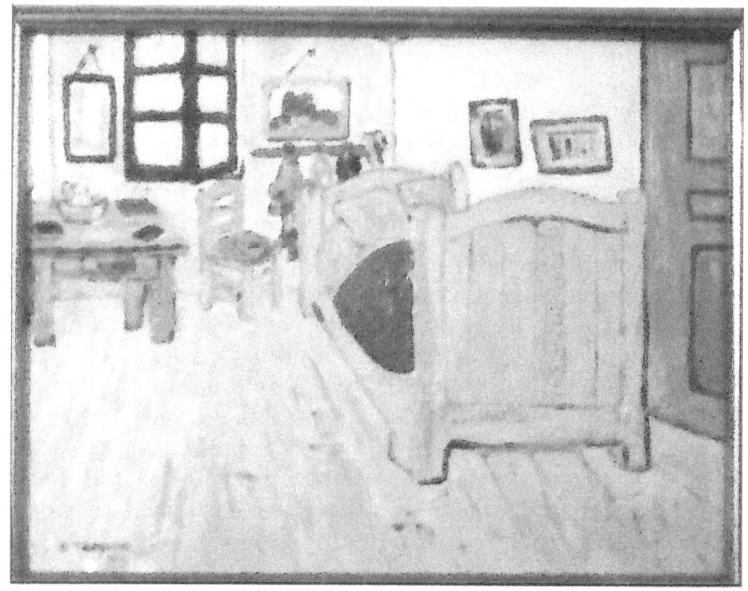

Van Gogh's room in Tyrellspass

Before retiring, I went for another walk around Jim Daly's town, and called in on another pub, which I had not yet visited. There I met a very interesting man. He told me that when he was made redundant, it came as such a shock to him that he stayed in bed for two whole weeks, refusing to get up. Eventually he recovered, and determined never again to allow himself to be at the mercy of an uncaring employer: he would set up his own business.

Tyrrellspass is in the middle of the Bog of Allen, the biggest peat bog in Ireland. He had an idea for a machine to cut peat without stripping it like loose earth, as do the mechanical monsters which are ripping the heart out of the Irish bogs in other parts of the country. His special machine cuts square-shaped turfs for the hearth, like the ones which have been cut by hand for centuries, but it does it in an efficient, eco-friendly way. He has made a small fortune from his machine, and has now passed over the running of the business to his son, while he enjoys a comfortable retirement. He has joined the ranks of Ireland's Happy Men.

In the morning, I took my punctured spare wheel to the garage next door to the hotel. As one would expect in the middle of the Bog of Allen, the main repair business is for tractors, and Ernest's tiny wheel held no problems for such a garage. The boss himself took it upon himself to make the repair, and I followed him into the workshop to help.

At first, he could find nothing wrong except a puncture in the inner tube, but I ran my fingers around the inside of the tyre, and felt a tiny pricking sensation. I showed it to him, and he took his pliers to it, grasped a minute piece of metal in his pliers, withdrew it carefully and dropped it into my palm. This was undoubtedly the cause of the puncture. It was a tiny, bright silver pin – like a fairy rapier – which had been driven hard into the middle of the outer casing of the tyre. I have it still; let me be clear about this: I am not saying one of the Little People thrust his rapier into my tyre to warn me it was unsafe to ride on because of its worn condition, but I don't have another explanation to offer.

The shed was filled with rusting tractors and bits of tractors, and bits of bits. By acting as his assistant, I was able to find the cause of the puncture, and discovered the fairy rapier which had been driven through the tyre. While he fitted a new inner tube, I looked around at my surroundings. The ceiling of the workshop was unusually high, and the tall, narrow window had a pointed, vaguely ecclesiastical shape. There were some faded letters painted over a niche on the end wall, and when I deciphered them, I realised that it was a religious text, and I suddenly realised I was standing in what used to be a Methodist Chapel.

The boss was in his late 60s, and the woman at the spares counter where I paid the bill looked like his sister. They would be retiring soon, and when they were gone, the agricultural garage would probably be rebuilt as a supermarket. And where will you be able to get a scooter puncture repaired in Tyrrellspass then?

The rain was still raining, in the way that tells you it will be at least two or three weeks before the sun comes out again. When I asked for the painting that I had bought the night before, I think the receptionist had assumed I wasn't serious, that it was just the wine talking.

My friend the manager was delighted when he learnt I was in earnest – he knew the artist, and she would be delighted to have made a sale. It was a lovely painting. He would wrap it up especially for me against the rain. Although I didn't ask for it, he even gave me a discount on the modest asking price. What would I do with it? He wanted to know: take it back to London? I told him I would be giving it to my Mum, and he thought that was very nice. Buying a painting as a present for someone gives as much pleasure as buying it for yourself.

Ernest seemed to appreciate the care and attention that had been paid to him over the puncture; whatever the reason, he sang more happily than usual as we took to the road, following the signs to Dublin. As the engine warmed up, I opened the throttle and we were soon speeding along, although I was careful not to go flat out.

Just as well, as it happened: coming round one of the few bends on that stretch of road, and facing a gentle slope at an exhilarating speed, Ernest's back wheel suddenly locked, and I was hard put to keep it all in more or less a straight line. The effect was frightening, and I only managed to keep upright by instinctively pulling in the clutch. Fortunately, there was no other traffic near, and I was able to pull into the side of the road, to take stock of the situation.

The engine had stalled, of course, and my first thought was to restart, but the kick-start was solid: the engine refused to turn over. This was obviously something serious, something I had never faced before, and I would need help. But where would I find help in the Bog of Allen? Instead of immediately calling the AA for assistance, I first tried to work out my approximate position. I could see a river, and what looked like a pub, then I remembered the bend I had just come through, and of course I knew which side of Tyrrellspass I was, and approximately how far.

I thought of the friendly garage that had repaired the puncture, but it was unlikely they would be familiar with the problems of a high compression, aluminium two-stroke engine (with five ports). My local scooter garage in London didn't have a branch in the middle of Ireland, as far as I was aware, but one of the mechanics was Irish, I recalled, and there was a chance he might be able to give good advice.

"Fergus? Is that you, mate? Yea, I'm still in Ireland, about ten or twenty miles east of Tyrellspass. Do you know where that is? The Galway to Dublin road. It's grey, and it looks like more rain. Listen, I've got a problem: the engine has seized up, and I'm stuck at the side of the road here, middle of nowhere. I don't know, but it's locked solid, the kick-start doesn't move either. Fuel? No it's got fuel, about half a tank. Do you know anyone over here who could have a look at it? I haven't called the AA yet. OK, call me back then; this is my mobile."

It's amazing how rubbish accumulates at the side of a busy highway. I pulled and dragged Ernest away from the tarmac for safety, and examined the debris around me. Plastic bottles, supermarket packaging, cigarette packs, and numerous bits of wire and unrecognizable metal pressings, plus other odd, mud-covered shapes which I had no idea what they were. My phone rang, and I pulled out a biro to make a note.

"Yes mate; you have? That's great. And you're confident they can sort me out? A friend of yours, is he? That's great. OK. I'll just read that back; thanks mate, I'll come and see you when I get back. I owe you!"

I called the RAC and told them I wanted to be taken to the address just outside Dublin that Fergus had given me, and they sent a local man within a couple of hours; I was lucky - they weren't very busy that day. I had managed to push Ernest as far as the pub I had seen, and was comfortably installed by the peat fire when help arrived. It didn't take much to convince the mechanic that Ernest was a delicate creature, and that I had located a nearby specialist, who was expecting us. He seemed relieved that his services were only to be called upon to provide transport to the rendezvous.

Ernest was safely loaded up, and I joined Michael in his cab. We located Fergus's friend with a little help from Michael's satnav. Confusingly, Fergus's friend was also called Fergus, but he wasn't my Fergus's friend, but a friend of Fergus's friend. All this didn't matter much; what really mattered was that he seemed familiar with Ernest's symptoms, and once we had got Ernest into his workshop, and I completed the niceties of signing off Michael, Fergus looked me in the eye and said: "Now what have you done to this nice machine?"

He pulled on a pair of latex gloves, like a skilled surgeon, and had the side blister off in a flash: after a cursory look and a few prods and pokes, he informed me that the piston was locked in the cylinder. "You haven't done the miles to suggest parts failure, so it must be down to the fuel. What petrol have you been using?" Satisfied that there must be another cause, he turned to the two-stroke oil, and took some from the reservoir after disconnecting a plastic pipe. He put some on his finger and smelt it, rubbed it between his fingers, and held it up to the light. He did everything but taste it. "What's this?" asked Fergus, accusingly. "Where did you get this shit from? You didn't bring this all the way from England now, did you?"

My mind went back to the half-daft boy in the petrol station in Oughterrard, and the battered oil can, and I told Fergus that this would have been the last time I put two-stroke oil. "Oughterrard was it? Now that would be by Lough Corrib, wouldn't it? Lots of boats, and not many high-compression scooters, I'll bet. He's given you the wrong kind of oil, and it wasn't very clever of you to let him, now was it? Some outboards use two-stroke, you know; perhaps you didn't know that? Did he sneak it into your tank while you were looking at the scenery, perhaps? Lots of pretty lasses up that way, I'm told." He seemed satisfied with my sheepish silence, and got on with the work.

I looked around; the work area was spotless, with a good selection of tools carefully located, and all to hand. There were only two other scooters in the room, an automatic Piaggio, and an old Lambretta, probably "waiting for parts". Apart from some neatly stacked wheels, the obligatory posters, and a small rack of tyres, and some odd cans, that was it; so where was all the usual junk that one associated with a workshop – half-started projects, broken bits of bike that might come in useful some day? "We've a store shed round the back where we keep that sort of thing," said Fergus. "This is my workspace, and I like to keep it shipshape. Five years in the navy taught me that." I thought to myself: Would this be the famous Irish Navy that I had heard about? the one which consists of two fishery protection vessels? I just nodded.

While he was talking, he had already started to strip the engine, and in a few minutes, he had the cylinder head removed and using a mirror, peered inside. "Not pretty. You'll need a new top end, and with labour that'll set you back about three hundred quid. Is that all right with you? I can take a card." He grinned.

I would guess that Fergus was in his mid-thirties, with thinning, sandy hair, below average height, the beginnings of a beer belly. And I had no doubt that he knew his onions as a mechanic. Someone appeared with two grubby mugs of tea, and I was introduced to Fergus's assistant, Joseph. While Fergus sat down to phone around for the spare parts, Joseph proceeded to continue to strip Ernest's engine, while I took off as much of the excess luggage, including the Van Gogh I had purchased the day before, and stacked it in the corner of the workshop which they referred to as "the office". I was fixed up with a nearby B & B – well, actually it was a lady who "took in visitors". I checked it out, and it was fine, and if all went well, it would only be for one night, two at the most.

When I went back to Fergus's workshop, he said that he had been lucky; he had located a genuine, Piaggio-made part in Belfast, and it would be delivered to him overnight, so he could start work first thing in the morning. Were the digs all right? The lady was his mother's cousin, sort of. Had I found the pub? They did a nice bit of dinner in there too, not much choice, but good grub. And so it proved to be. As I contemplated my pint of Guinness, I thought about the three hundred quid. Well, it couldn't be helped, and if the pre-trip prep, the tyre repair, and the (gulp) new piston were all that the maintenance on the trip would cost me; that was fair enough.

I was just finishing my early fish and chip supper in the pub when Fergus and Joseph came in, changed from their working overalls, so I didn't recognize them at first. They accepted my invitation to a drink, but said they couldn't stay long, as they wanted to make an early start in the morning. "We have to fix some careless bugger's bike", offered Fergus, by way of explanation.

Sometimes he smiled when he made a joke, and sometimes he didn't; this time he did. Joseph left first, and as the door closed behind him, Fergus nodded after him and said in a stage whisper: "Police". It seemed that Joseph had learned his trade "on the mainland", meaning, in England, working in the maintenance depot of the motorcycle police In the West Midlands. "Once I get the BMW out of him, he'll be all right," said Fergus, and ordered up another couple of pints. The conversation got around to scooters, and I told him that I had once owned a Vespa GS 150, and forever regretted not having held onto it, for nowadays it would be worth a fortune. "What year? Do you know which model?" I hazarded a guess. "Then you'll be interested in seeing mine; I'll show you tomorrow morning when you come round. It's kept round the back, away from prying eyes."

Fergus's personal GS was every Vespa owner's dream, and I was no exception. It was the same model as mine, the last 150 before the GS 160 was introduced. Dark silver, beautiful lines, immaculate, but with an attractive patina of signs of wear, a slight rubbing of the handgrip here, a rounding of a pedal rubber there. There is something inherently wrong about a machine that has been restored to look like brand new. Fergus's scooter looked as if the speedo reading was true, and I wanted it desperately. "So, I'll trade in my T5 Classic for yours; how much do you want on top of that for this quite nice GS then?" Had I got the right tone - interested but not too interested? Fergus seemed to understand, and his answer was to the point: "Fock off" he smiled.

Chapter 43
Dublin

...intensified drizzle...

As it happened, the boys had Ernest finished just after lunch. And that included flushing out the offending outboard motor two-stroke oil. They even threw in a can of the new, modern synthetic stuff, with a word of advice not to cane the engine for the first 100 miles or so, until the new piston was safely run in. "And I was told you can run these things on olive oil, if needs be," I said. "Well maybe you can, but I wouldn't try it" said Fergus. The payment went through, and I pointed Ernest in the direction of the Dublin road.

The early morning drizzle had intensified a bit, and I wasn't looking forward to an afternoon in the rain. But I was behind schedule, and could wait no longer. Fond farewells to Fergus and Joseph, a last joke about the GS, and I was gone, cautiously at first, remembering that I was to be on my best behaviour for at least the first 100 miles.

The road into Dublin was long and wet, so I just got my head down and watched the miles go by. I sang the Galway to Dublin song to myself as loud as I dared within the confines of my crash helmet. Thinking about a comfort break, I recalled a pub I knew on the route, called the Salmon Leap Inn at Leixlip, on the main road just outside Dublin, and I stopped there for a teatime sandwich. The pub has now been bypassed by a motorway that carries all the passing-through traffic to the outside of the village.

I apologised for the puddles I made on the floor, but the barman couldn't have been more welcoming. I thawed out gradually with a mug of bitter-tasting filter coffee.

In the next bar, a handful of customers huddled round the afternoon television news. Two more villagers had been arrested, and charged in connection with the killing of PC Gregory in Antrim; a bomb had been found under the car of a Sinn Féin Councillor in Belfast. But the big news was that Patrick Kane has been released from jail. It seems he was wrongly convicted and imprisoned in connection with the murder in 1987 of the two undercover British Army soldiers at the funeral of the IRA agents murdered by the SAS in Gibraltar. It is quite usual for the television news in the Republic to be dominated by reports of events in the North, and even I was getting used to the idea.

By now, I was warm again, so I plunged out into the rain, and slotted in alongside all the lorries making their way into Dublin town. The centre was easy to find, although the one-way system seemed determined to keep me from finding my guesthouse. Ernest was parked out in what the receptionist referred to as "secure parking" round the back, but I brought everything inside with me anyway. I checked in and carried all my kit up to the top floor, guiltily dripping on the carpet as I went. I took a hot shower to restore my circulation, and went straight out into the rain again and immediately bought an umbrella.

The next call was to the Shelbourne Hotel, more specifically to the Horseshoe Bar. When I first came to Ireland on business, I used to stay at the Shelbourne, which at the time was one of the best hotels in Europe, proud of its ratio of one member of staff for every guest. This was before the price of business hotels was driven up through the roof - I wouldn't dream of staying there now, and anyway it's part of an international French hotel chain.

The Horseshoe Bar was famous as a meeting place of celebrities and politicos. There is a special buzz to be found in this unusually shaped windowless room, and the central bar really is horseshoe-shaped.

I was in the Horseshoe Bar in the 70s when there was a bombing campaign against Dublin, and excited individuals were dashing in to report on the latest discovery of a car-bomb round the corner in Grafton Street. No one knew if it was the Republicans or the Nationalists, trying to stir things up, and there was no shortage of rumours.

The Shelbourne has been bought and sold many times in the shifting sands of leisure group deals since I used to stay there, but the staff are as friendly as ever, and the atmosphere in the Horseshoe Bar was fantastic. My first impression was that I was severely underdressed in my Australian stockman's trench-coat. The other customers were all seriously well dressed. But I slowly worked out that I had stepped into a crowd composed of two separate wedding groups. Mums and aunts, cousins and grandfathers were all dressed up in their Sunday best. Bow ties and tails were everywhere, and the wearers posed awkwardly alongside outrageous I'll-wear-this-but-just-the-once hats.

Mixed up with these happy groups, from which exploded the occasional raucous squeal of delight, there were tight groups of international jet-set business men, taking themselves far too seriously, as they fawned to their clients, and laughed exaggeratedly loudly at their wit and repartee. A huge but delicately mannered American gent in a suit swapped jokes with his Irish hosts. I enjoyed one of the most expensive half-pints of Guinness to be had anywhere in Ireland, and tottered out into the rain again.

The attitude of the Irish to rain is very different from other nationalities, and this difference was particularly evident on the streets of Dublin. Some took the battle with the elements to extremes, setting forth in the most expensively labelled yachting gear, designed to keep the wearer dry through the worst weather that the Atlantic Ocean could throw at them. If Dublin should be hit by a monsoon, these folk were ready for it. Others did the metropolitan thing of wearing a smart raincoat, sporting a large umbrella, and stepping niftily around pavement puddles.

And then there were those who were not prepared to make any concession to the weather whatsoever. I saw a group of youths in tee shirts and shorts, walking along as unconcerned as if they were taking a stroll in the park. One held a book over his head, as if that would achieve anything other than make the book wet.

A wall-plaque on a fine Georgian building reminded me that the poet Gerard Manley Hopkins was Professor of Greek at University College, and that ten years later, James Augustin Joyce was a student there.

I was feeling very relaxed now that my circuit of the North of Ireland was almost complete. When I set out, I wasn't even sure if I would finish it: I half-feared I might suffer unbearable back-pains after the first day; but at last it looked as if I would make it. The next day all I had to do was cross on the ferry, and make my way leisurely to London. I would even be home in time for my wife's birthday. I had planned to visit the Connaught Rangers memorial in Glasnevin Cemetery in Dublin, the national cemetery where many of Ireland's heroes are buried. But in view of the weather, I reasoned, I would leave that visit for my next trip. The combination of a glass of Guinness and unrelenting rain has a powerful effect in persuading a soul to put things off for another day.

Chapter 44
In the Footsteps of Mr. Bloom

After the relatively uncrowded byways of the West, the streets of Dublin seemed as packed with people as Brighton on a bank holiday. Boutiques bustled, and old-Ireland quaintness was tucked away from sight down narrow side streets. Much of the street atmosphere came from students of all shapes and sizes, for I was in the University district. I soon found the shipping office and bought my one-way ferry ticket for the next morning, on the fastest crossing – by hydrofoil. My guesthouse was more like a super B & B, housed in an elegant Georgian terraced house just off St. Stephen's Green.

The hotel on the opposite side of the road was jumping. That is to say the bar was jumping, and the restaurant was just doing average business. The large bar was packed with mainly young people in a hurry. They were in a hurry to get the next drink in; they were in a hurry to decide where they would be going for a night out; they were in a hurry to score, and were surreptitiously looking round to see what talent was available. And was it time for another drink yet?

I made a booking for dinner later in case they were expecting a rush, and stood for a while in the middle of a crowd of heaving youth in the bar, as I supped a glass of Guinness. I was easily the oldest person in the room. Indeed, I calculated it would have been hard to find two people whose combined ages would have made up the venerable total of my years. Maybe three people... Despite the enormous changes in Dublin since I was last there, I was pleased to see that I still liked it as a city. I liked it very much.

The receptionist at the guesthouse greeted me unusually warmly on my return - well, she wasn't really a receptionist, so much as the person who had met me on my arrival. She was about the age of the young people in the bar, and I took her for a student, helping out and earning some money at the same time. She had that frank, friendly air common in many Irish girls, almost cheeky, and she called out to me as I came back in through her front door. If I'd been there a few days earlier, she told me scoldingly, I could have joined in on Bloomsday. Did I know about that?

Well, it so happened that I did; I read *Ulysses* by James Joyce when I was about her age, and I retained an interest in anything associated with that extraordinary book. So I knew - but had temporarily forgotten - that some years back, Dublin had revived a recreation of the day in the life of the leading characters, Stephen Dedalus and Leopold Bloom, and events were held at sites which feature in their ramshackle walk around the city in one day on 16 June 1904. I suppose that to call it "Dedalusday" might have seemed a bit awkward, so the authorities settled on "Bloomsday", and I had missed it by a few days.

"You've a good bit of daylight left yet," my informant urged; "You could zip round the tour on your scooter thingy in no time at all. Have you got one of these?" She produced a small paperback, whose title *The Ulysses Guide* made the contents very clear. It traces the routes taken by Dedalus and Bloom on 16 June, with maps, photos, points of interest, all cross-referenced to episodes in the book. It immediately had me hooked. "I must have one; where can I get it?" "You can have that one there if you like; it's my own copy, but just pay me the price and I can get another one in the morning. Why don't you go out to the Martello Tower now, and do that tour for yourself? Go on with you." So having no other plans, that's what I did.

The Martello Tower is an old watchtower built in the Napoleonic Wars, but in the book it is inhabited by the friends of Stephen, and it is where the story opens. Much has been written about the difficulties presented by the symbolism and multi-layers in *Ulysses*, but when I read it as an eighteen-year-old, I enjoyed it for what it was: a story told in great language, with great writing that shook the world.

The road to the coast was easy to find, and from the ferry port of Dun Laoghaire, Ernest took me down to Sandycove, and there was the Martello Tower, right in front of us. It was still drizzly, so I pulled over under the awning of a greengrocer's shop to read the tour instructions.

The tower itself is now the James Joyce Museum, but its opening hours are strictly daytime, so there was no chance of me going inside. My memory was once exceptional, and I used to be able to seize long passages of prose or poetry and store them away. As I looked up towards the top of the Tower, I could not see the flat roof, but I could remember the opening lines of the book, and so I could picture what it was like:
"*Stately, plump Buck Mulligan came from the stairhead, bearing a bowl of lather on which a mirror and a razor lay crossed.*"
Now if that's not great writing, I don't know what is: it just bounces along.

I was pleased to read in my guidebook that the Tower was opened as a museum on 16 June 1962 by none other than the farsighted, first publisher of *Ulysses*, Sylvia Beach, of Shakespeare & Company, Paris.

A short step away, I followed the trail to the Forty Foot bathing place, which features in the first chapter, and although it is now, according to the guidebook, famous for nude bathing, I would not personally take a chance in the murky waters. I went back to the comparative safety of Ernest, and together, Bloomsday guidebook in hand, we followed the instructions to follow Stephen's tracks along Sandycove Avenue, Breffni Road, and Ulverton Road ("noting Bullock Castle on the left"), to what was once the village of Dalkey, before Dublin reached out to swallow it up within its boundaries. Many of the Victorian houses would have been there in Joyce's day, and following the trail was fun.

When Joyce wrote *Ulysses*, he was living in exile, so although he had walked these streets many times before, while he was writing he had to use a guidebook of the time to help him remember what he was describing – a bit like we were doing now.

Ernest and I somehow missed the school which features in Stephen's walk – maybe it is now a residential house – but eventually found ourselves at Dalkey Station, where Stephen would have taken the train into Dublin, to Lansdowne Road Station.

The name of Lansdowne Road nowadays has stronger associations with the home of Irish rugby, but as far as Ernest and I were concerned, we had done enough; we had finished the first part of the tour, it was still drizzling, and the street lights were lit. Besides, I had a booking at the restaurant, and wanted an early night to prepare us for what promised to be a long day tomorrow.

Ernest seemed quite happy with his new cylinder, and I have always suspected that engines are generally happier in the rain anyhow.

As I left the hotel the next morning in what had now become persistent rain again, I walked straight into a traffic accident involving a motorbike, right outside the front door. The motorcyclist was ok, although he looked from the position in which he was lying as if he had broken a leg. The police and ambulance arrived in a matter of minutes, and the atmosphere was relaxed but very businesslike, as the woman motorist apologised to the policeman for her moment of silly carelessness, and the motorcyclist cheerfully excused himself to the paramedics for being a trouble to them.

It's easy to get carried away with the thought that accidents will never happen to you, but the difference lies in the fact that on two wheels any kind of accident, however slight, is potentially very serious. The car and the bike seemed undamaged, but the unfortunate rider was probably facing several months of discomfort or worse. I was extra careful as I picked my way through the rain back to the port of Dun Laorhaire.

~☆~

Chapter 45
Home in two stages

The luxurious super-fast ferry made the ferry to Belfast look like something from the Third World, and at least one hundred years older. The parking for motorbikes in the vehicle hold was modern and efficient. I parked alongside two massive Japanese super-bikes with Italian registration plates. "Bologna?" I asked, pointing to the number plates. The overdressed bikers replied with an avalanche of speech far too fast for my restaurant pidgin Italian, but because they were smiling, I smiled back and patted Ernest. "Pontedera" I indicated, and there were more smiles, and admiring and congratulatory noises.

As I tucked into a late, large breakfast on board, I was joined by another biker, on his way to a weekend rally in Anglesea. He had trained as a ship's engineer, before getting a shore job as a garage mechanic. I have often wondered what happened when engines started to go wrong at sea, so I fired a number of questions at him, as I watched the minutes ticking away on the short high-speed crossing.

It seems that there is enormous variety in the types of marine engines, which are designed to produce high power over long periods at low engine speeds. I asked the question which must have troubled most of us who have ever been at the mercy of a ship's engine as it chugs away, carrying us across an expanse of landless ocean. How is it possible to carry out work on an engine which develops a fault while at sea?

Well, the good news is (and you may find this hard to believe, as I did) that a marine engineer can isolate a cylinder without actually stopping the engine. The design of the engine is such that he can remove the whole cylinder, change a few parts, put it back again and carry on as if nothing had happened. Apparently they do this all the time, as part of regular maintenance, just to keep themselves busy and on top of the job. I must say I find that a very comforting thought.

Before I negotiated the ramp and took to the road, I had no idea that Holyhead, at the top left-hand corner of Wales, was so far from

London. Even so, in good weather, I might have completed the ride in a day, but the unrelenting rain and cold wind wore away at my determination, until I was forced to admit defeat near Birmingham as darkness drew in. I felt the cold and the wet was getting to me more than just physically.

My concentration was drifting, I was feeling low, depressed, and could no longer trust myself on two wheels. Fortunately, I recognized the symptoms, and so I pulled off the main arterial road and drove down the High Street of a typically depressing middle-England town.

The local inn was awful, the harassed, overworked manager was both rude and incompetent, there was no food available, and the streets were miserable. I thought for a moment that I might be in luck after all, when I discovered that there was a decent, listed restaurant next to the church; I knocked on the door, and I was told rather grumpily that it was closed for a private function. I bought a plastic-packed sandwich at the nearby petrol station; everywhere else was closed.

The best that can be said of the inn is that it was cheap. It was old, and unsympathetically modernised a few decades ago, when formica and rexine were the fashion. There was no sign of another hotel, so this had probably been an important centre of events in the past, but now it was just an unprofitable white elephant in a backwater town, with no passing trade.

It is normal to suffer withdrawal symptoms after any adventure, but these depressing surroundings were just too much.

I gave up on the idea of a walk around the town in the cold, drizzling rain, and after a nightcap, because, oh yes, the bar was still open, I went to an early bed, feeling rather sorry for myself. There was the noise of drunken revellers elsewhere in the hotel, and I slept fitfully, but awoke early to a morning that I was pleased to see was an improvement on the previous day; it had stopped raining, and a weak, watery sun was struggling to make its presence felt through a light cloud covering.

I decided to take the walk around town that I had shunned the night before, so I dressed quickly, and stepped out into the early-morning streets, which still showed signs of the previous day's deluge. Picking my way around the puddles, I was delighted to find a small green of sorts, not unattractive, with a modest country church in one corner, and one of the new-style coffee shops that can be found all over the country now – did I say the country? – all over the world is closer to the truth. There are several brand names for these establishments, but they are all much of a muchness. A simple marketing approach means that overnight they have almost trebled the prices, but at least you can be assured of a decent cup of coffee, which is more than can be said of the miserable place where I had spent the night.

Starbucks-Costa-Nero or whatever it was called was an early opener, so I paid my money for a comforting, takeaway ("take-out"?) cappuccino, and retired to a conveniently placed park bench on the green, from where I looked at the day with an improved disposition.

It was still comparatively early, and although there were sounds of traffic in the distance, this quiet corner was deserted, except for myself and the occasional coffee shop customer passing by. A dog-walker entered stage left, and I observed the mini-drama as the retriever pooed, as it was expected to do, and without warning the dog-owner produced a small, black, crow-black, plastic bag, and duly scooped the poo into it. Now some readers may not be surprised by this observation, but I am just old enough to remember when such an exhibition of social responsibility among dog-walkers was the exception, rather than the rule.

Then a young mum, complete with pushchair and occupant, entered the green and crossed towards the coffee shop. The child, who I judged to be less than 2 years old, protested, and demanded to be given the opportunity to walk the last few steps. This is a unique spectacle, funny, yet essential in the scheme of things. I resisted with difficulty the temptation to applaud the efforts of this child as it reached the coffee shop – obviously a familiar stopping point – and staggered unsteadily inside.

So when I noticed the figure of an elderly, shabbily dressed individual moving towards me, my first reaction was to resent his invasion of my space: it seemed to me that I was about to be panhandled by an old tramp, who probably included this green in his beat to prey on the unfortunate clients of the coffee shop - "Spare a pound for a cup of coffee, Guvnor?" - and I prepared to fend him off.

But Tom, as he introduced himself, was nothing of the sort: he was just pleased to see another soul, and only wanted a bit of company and conversation. He asked if he could sit down, and I took the chance to take a good look at him. His clothes weren't shabby: just old. He was freshly shaven and clean-looking; and he was polite, without being obsequious or forelock tugging. I liked the way he spoke to me: straight and honest. He appeared to be well into his 80s, but seemed fit enough for a younger man. He was well built, and strong-looking, but with a gentle manner.

Why was I here? he asked, and listened politely for the answer. I told him that I had driven here with Ernest, and had been forced to stop over because of yesterday's cold and rain. "A scooter?" he said, and went on to tell me that when he first got a bicycle, it was the making of him, because it allowed him to get away from the village. His father never left the village, except to go to the war in France, and he never came back: killed in action. He never knew his father, because when Tom was born, his father was already dead. They told him that his dad's name was on a big memorial for the "missing", in France.

His Uncle Jack, his Mum's brother, took his place and brought up him and his brothers, and looked after his Mum too. As soon as Tom could ride a bike, he was off, discovering the world, riding all over the place, to the seaside - everywhere. When he left school at fourteen, he went to work on the land, like his brothers had done, and his Dad and Uncle Jack before him: they were all farm labourers. They all did the same job, and it was hard physical work, before tractors or combine harvesters. In those days it was all horses, wagons, pitchforks and hard graft. In the summer months, the days were very long indeed.

Then the second war came, and he saw that as his chance to escape, to get away; he went to join up in the Army, the local Yeomanry, like his Dad before him, "but they wouldn't be having it." He said bitterly; "they said I was in a "reserved profession" - what a load of old...

horse manure! - pardon my French."

I wanted to know if he ever had managed to get abroad later on, but Tom said that he stuck out the whole of the second war right here. Two of his brothers went though; the Army wasn't so fussy later in the war, and if you went down South, they didn't ask too many questions about "reserved professions". It didn't do them any good though. One got as far as North Africa, and was wounded; the other one was killed in Italy. "I did think of riding down there on my bike to see Harry's grave after the war, and to see Dad's name up there in France on the way, but it didn't work out."

Then he had a bit of luck; good men were hard to find after the war, and there was a job going, helping out the gamekeeper on the estate. Tom grabbed it with both hands. They had all done a bit of what he called "hunting", to put something on the table when they were growing up, and Tom was good at it: rabbits and pheasants were plentiful in the woods around there at that time. "My boss said I had a natural feel for it, and I think he knew where I got it from. It turned out well for both of us for a good few years, working together.

Anyway, when he retired, I took over - they couldn't afford any help for me though, no assistant gamekeeper, none of that, as times was hard then. Even the gentry were feeling the pinch, so they said. My old keeper friend lost his estate house, and they sold it off to townies." When Tom retired, they didn't replace him but brought in a company to look after their birds.

"Did you have any kids of your own, to carry on?" I asked, and Tom said that he had never married. He had girlfriends, but he never got round to settling down. He went for long bike-rides on his days off, even after he retired. "I'll always be grateful to that Mr. Attlee and his Labour Government: they brought in a decent pension, free hospitals, council houses, all that. When I retired, I lived a life of Riley."

Tom got a bigger allotment, and managed to sell off a few spare vegetables, for a bit of cash on the side. But he added that before that, when his Uncle Jack gave up working, he and Tom's Mum had next to nothing, and the rest of the family had to chip in with what they could spare, to help out with food, and the rent. They couldn't afford any luxuries, but they never complained. And Tom didn't complain, either. "I've got a bit of money saved up for a rainy day, I'm in good health, I have a pint every day, sometimes more; and I've always got a bit of baccy for a smoke." He produced from his pocket a crumpled packet of Boar's Head roll-up tobacco, to which was fixed a packet of Rizla papers, with what looked like a rubber band.

I asked him what happened when he needed extra cash for something unexpected, a new coat, a pair of shoes? I told him that I could see that he did all right in that department. He beamed and told me proudly that he found whatever he needed in charity shops. "God bless the charity shops! We've got three right here in town. When someone dies, or they have a clearout, they send most of the stuff to the charity shop – suits them, and it suits the likes of me too.

See this coat?" and he struggled to open the front of his overcoat to show me the inside label "*Marks and Spencer, 100% real wool.*" Now where would the likes of me be able to afford that if it wasn't for the charity shops?" He had a three-piece worsted suit at home with two pairs of trousers. People just give their unwanted clothes away, rather than have them taking up space in the wardrobe, he told me. "And it makes no difference to me if they're a dead man's clothes; they can still do me a favour all right on a cold morning."

"I heard a joke yesterday," said Tom, "do you like jokes? I say to you: 'What did the ten foot canary say?' and you say 'I don't know. What did the ten foot canary say?' and I say: 'I wants my seed, and I wants it *now!*' at which point Tom started shaking uncontrollably with laughter. "D'you get it? I wants it NOW!" and there really were tears in his eyes. I'm not sure if I began laughing at the joke, or just contagiously, at this spectacle of a gentle giant of a man enjoying his own joke.

We must have made a funny sight: two strangers sharing a joke, roaring with laughter, sitting on a bench somewhere in the middle of England. Order was gradually restored, and we lapsed into just the occasional stifled giggle, and then silence again. So I told him my favourite joke, and we went through the same performance again.

Raucous laughter - we did everything except hug each other: that would have been too much. I don't know if I made his day, but he certainly made mine. I hadn't had such a good laugh in weeks, and we forged a bond, there and then, which I will not forget for a long time, a very long time.

Tom sighed, and looked around, and then he took a breath, and indicated the churchyard behind him. "They're over there now, the two of them, me Mum and me Uncle Jack; I keep an eye on them; take them some flowers out of the garden on birthdays, that sort of thing. Well, they looked after me all right, didn't they, brought me up, and all?" He then said that he would be going over there now, and would I like to join him?

Country churchyards are always worth more than a passing look; English Heritage says that they represent a sort of living archaeology of a region. Here there were a handful of vaulted tombs of the local gentry from Victorian times, when such things were thought of as important status symbols. Names straight from Dickens were in abundance; some neglected gravestones had subsided, and were leaning at a funny angle, or had been laid down flat on the ground. Granite or marble lasts longer than local stone, where erosion can make the names and the dates and other details hard to read.

Not so in the headstones of what Tom told me were the graves of his mother and his Uncle Jack, side by side. The graves were well kept, and the engraving was perfectly legible. I noticed that they died within a few months of each other, on a date which must have been around the time that Tom was getting used to the delights of retirement under a Labour Government - Labour for a farm labourer, resting after a life of hard toil.

"You keep it nice, don't you" I offered by way of encouragement. "Well, you've got to, don't you?" he said, and set about carefully teasing out the few weeds that had dared to show themselves since his last visit.

He leaned back, reaching into an inside pocket and pulled out from an envelope a striking photograph of six smartly dressed country lads.

"There he is; that's my Uncle Jack on the left," he said, "on his way to join up, with my Dad and some of his pals." When I asked why they were all wearing their Sunday Best, Tom said that according to Uncle Jack, it was because they wanted to look smart for the recruiting sergeant. They certainly looked smart, and I wondered how many of them, like Tom's dad, never came back.

The church clock struck the hour, and I jumped and looked at my watch. Probably three quarters of an hour had gone by in conversation, and I had to get back on the road, so I made my goodbyes to Tom, and turned back to the hotel to get my things together, and to tell Ernest about the nice old chap I had met.

Back at the hotel, the duty receptionist was a bit brighter than the manager of the night before. She hoped that the noise hadn't kept me awake? She explained that it was a leaving party for a member of staff. (Well that made it all right then, I thought.) She told me to have a nice day. No thank you, I wouldn't be having the breakfast. Yes, I know it's included.

The road home was uneventful, with no more than the now customary time-stops for fuel, and to stretch my legs. The landscape was more open than that of recent weeks, more built-up between open fields, and with road-signs gradually became more familiar as I travelled south. I was home again in London by lunchtime. It had started to rain again in a half-hearted way, just enough to be annoying, and to cause a mild discomfort, reviving memories of a cold dampness from the day before.

I had the empty house to myself, so I soaked in a hot bath and waited for my wife and daughters to come home from a Sunday morning screening of a film that someone's friend had worked on.

No sooner had my body temperature returned to normal, than I already began thinking about going back to do a circuit of maybe the south of Ireland, next time. My memories of the physical discomfort of the cold and wet conditions I had ridden through with Ernest towards the end of the trip were slipping away in the bath. If this was summer, even winter couldn't be much worse, could it? And there were all sorts of things I hadn't done, places I hadn't visited, and had vowed to return to. I would start in Dublin, so I could visit the Glasnevin cemetery at long last, maybe take in some more of the Bloomsday trail, and then work things out from there. We could track along the frontier with the North, and then down the coast, and perhaps back through the Midlands? That sounded promising. I would have a look at the map, and start to make plans.

That has always been the story of my relationship with Ireland – forever thinking about going back the next time, like going home.

And what was my favourite joke that I shared with Tom? I can take no credit for it, because it comes from a book of jokes by the king of one-liners, the Jewish American stand-up comic, Henny Youngman. "What do you get when you cross a parrot with a tiger? I don't know, but when it speaks, you'd better make sure you're listening!"

"That's my Uncle Jack on the left, with my Dad, on his way to join up."

www.ingramcontent.com/pod-product-compliance
Lightning Source LLC
Chambersburg PA
CBHW022334300426
44109CB00040B/313